Negotiating Software Contracts

Negotiating Software Contracts

Sixth edition

Susan Singleton LLB

Solicitor, Singletons
www.singlelaw.com

Bloomsbury Professional

LONDON · DUBLIN · EDINBURGH · NEW YORK · NEW DELHI · SYDNEY

BLOOMSBURY PROFESSIONAL

Bloomsbury Publishing Plc
50 Bedford Square, London, WC1B 3DP, UK
1385 Broadway, New York, NY 10018, USA
29 Earlsfort Terrace, Dublin 2, Ireland

BLOOMSBURY and the Diana logo are trademarks of Bloomsbury Publishing Plc

British Library Cataloguing-in-Publication Data

A catalogue record for this book is available from the British Library.

ISBN:	HB:	978-1-52652-563-5
	ePDF:	978-1-52652-565-9
	ePub:	978-1-52652-564-2

Typeset by Evolution Design & Digital Ltd (Kent)
Printed and bound by CPI Group (UK) Ltd, Croydon, CRO 4YY

To find out more about our authors and books visit www.bloomsburyprofessional.com. Here you will find extracts, author information, details of forthcoming events and the option to sign up for our newsletters

Preface

This book provides an overview of the issues relating to negotiating and drafting software licences in the digital age. The book also provides an overview of the UK law relating to other computer contracts.

Although mass market software is usually capable of being delivered from the web, many software products are still delivered or installed by the software vendor or bundled with hardware or developed as one-off solutions. This book, therefore, discusses many of the issues relating to the traditional software licences and support and maintenance agreements and many of the precedents relate to the traditional delivery of software solutions.

However, as the business of software licensing moves from traditional paper licences through to click-wrap contracts and software as a service (SaaS) agreements and as the new licensing methods of the application service providers come to the fore, so these issues are also be addressed in this book.

There are already many excellent books covering in detail the subject matter of computer law and information technology law. This book is intended to complement such academic works by providing a general explanation of the law whilst covering in more detail the practical and commercial aspects of computer contract negotiations.

The text is divided into five Parts and Part I is divided into two chapters, with chapter 1 looking at the nature of software licensing and chapter 2 examining different types of software licence agreements.

Part II looks at the laws and regulations affecting software contracts, with chapter 3 addressing the different types of intellectual property laws and chapter 4 providing an overview of European Union law which, despite the UK having left the EU, is still relevant to many who operate in the EU.

Part III deals with the issues of preparing for negotiations. Chapter 5 looks at negotiating principles, with chapter 6 looking at the preparations for negotiations carried out by both suppliers and buyers.

Part IV addresses the issues involved in preparing for drafting software licences agreements. Chapter 7 looks at the use of heads of agreement and memorandum of understanding and chapter 8 contains a check list of the contents of a typical software licence agreement.

Part V looks at some of the tactics and techniques of contract negotiation.

In the first edition of this book, the precedents covered a variety of software licensing scenarios from shrink-wrap and click-wrap, through standard licence and service to distribution, escrow and software development. In the second edition, a number of new precedents were added to cover software evaluation, IT services outsourcing, loan of hardware and software, data processing and trans border data flow, as well as a computer games development and licence. In later editions, updates have been made to many chapters and additional precedents have been added.

In addition, a glossary of software and web definitions are included in the book.

Robert Bond wrote the 1st to 5th editions of this book so this sixth edition, the first by the current editor, Susan Singleton, very much relies on his work on all earlier editions.

In the ten years since the fifth edition was written there has been a huge increase in UK and EU laws relating to e-commerce and data protection law as the internet, artificial intelligence and 'Big Data' becomes more and more a part of every day life, accelerated by the 2020/21 global Covid 19 (coronavirus) pandemic with so many more people working from home, court hearings heard via Teams/Zooms calls and the like.

Robert Bond and the current editor have each practised as solicitors for over 40 years, indeed both, at separate times, at solicitors Bristows in London and similarly both at different times on the board of the Data & Marketing Commission. In that time the Data Protection Act 1984 came into force and the stock exchange became computerised at Big Bang in the 1980s (when the current editor worked at Slaughter and May, inter alia, on the computer contracts relating to that change) and then the Copyright, Designs and Patents Act 1988 came out. Since then the rate of change in this field has never slowed both in a technological and legal sense. Indeed it was the fact the internet and email were taking off that meant the current editor could set up her commercial and IT/IP firm of solicitors, Singletons, in 1994 from home on leaving Bristows from which firm (Singletons) she has continued to practise ever since.

IT Law shows no signs of slowing down and remains one of the most interesting and biggest growth areas, not least now in the field of artificial intelligence. It is hoped the negotiation tactics and the precedents in this book will continue to prove a useful resource to readers.

The law to which reference is made in this book is correct as at 1 June 2023.

E. Susan Singleton
www.singlelaw.com
1 June 2023

Acknowledgments

Robert Bond, who wrote the 1st edition to the 5th edition of this book, is owed most acknowledgment as without his hard work the book would not exist.

Many thanks are due to all the staff at Bloomsbury Professional for their assistance and attention to detail on this sixth edition of the book.

Thanks are due to my family for their support:

- to my five children, two of whom are solicitors – my daughters at Macfarlanes and 3 Mobile respectively and my twin sons, who are trainee solicitors and qualify in early 2024, for all our family discussions about law which are always interesting and to my non-lawyer oldest son who works for Ocado;

- to my three grandchildren, Rose and Frederick and their toddler cousin Tabitha Mary for making it all worthwhile.

Finally, my clients should be thanked since I began as a newly qualified solicitor at Slaughter and May in 1985 and over the years since at my own firm Singletons. Without them I would not have practised IT law which began for me in 1985 handling IT contracts relating to the computerisation of the stock exchange in the lead up to Big Bang, when the Data Protection Act 1984 was new. Then continued through to the legal issues of Y2K in Year 2000 (the so-called 'Millennium Time Bomb') after I had set up my own firm of solicitors, Singletons, in 1994, to legal issues relating to the UK leaving the EU on 31st January 2020 and on through to 2023 when the growth, not just of the internet but all aspects of computer software, and resulting new laws, has continued at a fast pace, accelerated by the Covid 19 (coronavirus) pandemic lock downs of 2020 and 2021 which moved so much of life and work on-line for some people.

Contents

Contents

Table of Statutes

GERMANY

UNITED STATES

Table of Statutory Instruments

Table of European Legislation

Table of European Legislation

TABLE OF TREATIES AND CONVENTIONS

Table of Cases

Table of Cases

Glossary

3G /4G/ 5G
Third, fourth and fifth generation. methods of sending Internet information to mobile telephones at increasingly faster speeds, significantly faster than traditional GPRS. 3G, the slowest, as being phased out as at early 2023 and 5G introduced.

Access Provider or Internet Service Provider (ISP)
An organisation that sells connectivity to the Internet such as BT in the UK. It provides a gateway into which users via modem access various speeds of usually continuously "on" broadband services.

Acrobat
A programme from Adobe that allows the creation or reading of PDF files. PDF is a format that enables a reader to see the exact layout, graphics and typestyle of the document that the producer intended, without having to have the correct fonts installed on his machine. Users only need to have an Acrobat reader which is freely available from Adobe's web site. The format is useful for creating brochures to download.

ActiveX
Microsoft's answer to the Java technology from Sun Microsystems, allowed the creation of a self-sufficient program that can be run anywhere in an ActiveX network (whether Windows or Apple). It is now deprecated software and Javabeans is more commonly used.

Address or IP Address
An 'address' can mean the unique location of either an Internet server, a specific file or an email user. The server or IP address is the unique string of numbers of a particular server linked to the Internet (eg 194.72.83.225). This equates to a domain name such as singlelaw.com. Individual files such as web pages have an address based on the domain name (eg www.singlelaw.com/home). This is known as the uniform resource locator (URL). Finally, individuals can have a mailbox linked to that domain name, providing them with their own email address (eg, the editor's – susan@singlelaw.com.

ADSL
Asymmetric Digital Subscriber Line. This provided fast access to the Internet in its day. It is a standard which provided high bandwidth for data and voice connection. A problem many home users of the Internet had encountered has been the low bandwidth (effectively the slowness of access and download). ADSL, a technology for transmitting digital information at high bandwidths on existing phone lines, changed that. BT and others through Openreach is now commonly able to provide fast broadband services 'always on' services. In 2023 for example BT provided the following types of packagers for home users with the following average speeds:
Standard, ADSL broadband – 10Mbps
Fibre Essentials – 36Mbps
Fibre 1 – 50Mbps
Fibre 2 – 67Mbps
Fibre 100 – 145Mbps
Fibre 500 – 500Mbps
Fibre 900 – 900Mbps

Glossary

Agent or bot

A program that collects information or performs some service in the background. It can be used, for instance, to create personalised search or news services. Also known as Intelligent Agents.

AI

Artificial Intelligence. The simulation of the human intelligence processes by computers. An important business area as firms look to develop AI or expert systems to provide initial legal advice, build first drafts etc., eg. ChatGPT.

Analogue technology

This technology conveys data in the form of electronic signals of varying frequency together with carrier waves of a fixed frequency. Analogue technology is being replaced by digital technology.

Ananova and Alexa

A virtual assistant. Ananova was an original such creation who 'retired' in 2004 and by 2023 readers will be more familiar with Amazon's Alexa to whom they can speak when ordering goods (if the user has bought the Alexa device). Most smart phones now have various voice activated functions by 2023.

Anonymous FTP

Many hosts provide information free, which can be downloaded to your machine, using FTP. Where the information is free, an 'anonymous' facility is provided, as the system has no need to know who you are and is widely used for archive sites.

App

Any software programme which can be downloaded for all kinds of functions and typically might be downloaded free or on a paid for basis to a personal computer/laptop or smartphone often from an 'app store'.

Application Service Provider (ASP)

An authorised provider of its own as well as third-party software products to customers on an on-line rental/licence basis which is increasingly the way software is provided (hired and used from the cloud) with regular fees paid rather than the traditional one off perpetual licence of software downloaded to a personal computer. ASP is an application service provider.

Architecture

The increasingly complex art (or science) of thinking out and specifying the interrelationships of computers, operating systems and networks.

ASCII

American Standard Code for Information Interchange. The ASCII code table consists of 128 characters and is a way of representing ordinary text as a stream of binary numbers. The first 32 characters in the ASCII table are control codes and the last 96 characters are upper and lower case letters, numbers and special symbols. The most common format for text files in computers and on the Internet. Documents in ASCII (or plain) text are readable on almost any device.

Avatar

A computer-generated character or persona adopted by a user of an on-line environment. Another example of the attempt to create a more human feel to the online experience. In Hinduism, an avatar is an incarnation of a deity, hence an embodiment or manifestation of an idea or greater reality.

AVI file

Audio Visual Interleaves file. Microsoft's standard for sound and motion picture file first introduced in 1992. Apple has developed the Quicktime format that also plays on PCs and to which MOV (the most common film files) are stored. Users need a special player that may be included with a web browser to play the video and must download the complete file before playing, unlike streaming media formats that begin to play almost immediately.

Backbone	A central section of a network to which other networks connect. In the context of the Internet, it refers to the high-speed links between the main access providers.
Bandwidth	The capacity of a communications link between two nodes – the rate at which information can be transferred. A given message may travel through many nodes to reach its destination. However, the speed with which this is achieved is constrained by the slowest link, ie the one with the narrowest bandwidth. It is often referred to on internet discussions such as Reddit where the writers of long and verbose messages may be accused of wasting bandwidth, ie the time taken to pass unnecessary information around the network.
Baud rate	The speed at which data is transferred between pieces of electronic equipment.
Blink	An activity performed by an off-line reader. A blink is the act of connecting to a host, downloading any new mail and posting messages or mail. The line is then disconnected. New mail and messages can then be read 'off-line' and responses composed for the next 'blink'. This approach minimised connect time and hence telephone charges although in the days of always online broadband this is not usually an issue.
Blog or Vlog	A blog or web log is an internet diary made publicly available and was the precursor to the modern social media feeds users follow which may be photographs or video (Vlogs) such as on Instagram or Youtube or more text based. Initially blogs were run by individuals without any commercial purpose but more recently businesses have set up marketing blogs and other similar blogs for commercial purposes too.
Bluetooth	A short range wireless connection standard. Its aim is to link a wide range of computer, electronics and telecoms devices. The technology uses a low power two-way radio link which is built into a microchip.
Boot up	As you switch on your PC, it goes through the boot up sequence, which includes checking hardware for errors and loading DOS system files.
BPS	*Bits per second.* The unit used to measure baud rate.
Broadband	Where used as a term relating to the internet it means internet access which is always on (to be contrasted with having to dial up each time) and is faster than traditional dial-up access.
Browser	A program which will allow your computer to download and display documents or pages from the World Wide Web. Examples include Firefox, Microsoft Edge and Google Chrome.
Buffer	A small area of memory used to hold frequently accessed information, or data that will be needed at any moment.
Bulletin board	Using a modem, you can hook up to an electronic bulletin board. From here you can chat to other people or download useful files (such as the latest software drivers for your video card). The term bulletin board is much less used these days.
CA	*Certification Authority.* A body which is set up to authenticate electronic signatures.
CcTLD	*Country Code Top Level Domain.* The part of the TLD which indicates the country of location, eg uk, .au, .ca,.fr.

Glossary

Click-wrap
The description for and method of providing on-line or on-screen Licensing terms, for mass market software products and services, whereby a software licensing contract is intended to be entered into without necessarily being negotiated or signed by hand written signature, but may be signed by electronic signature or where the terms may be accepted by the doing of some action such as the 'clicking' of a particular icon or button. Services such as DocuSign (used extensively for entering to business contracts) are better alternative as both parties sign the document but not so feasible for terms which are not individually negotiated and which a website wishes to impose on users.

Client-Server Applications
Applications which run in two parts. Client applications, usually concerned with taking input and displaying information communicating with Server applications running on host machines.

Cloud
Term used where data, software and the like is stored other than on the computer of the user being instead stored online hosted by a third party.

Cookie
A small piece of computer code which transmits data about the user across the Internet. It might include data concerning the type of computer software and hardware being used, and other web sites visited by the user. Its value in market research terms is significant. Cookies are regulated in the UK and EU.

Copyright
An intellectual property right, giving the copyright holder ownership of and an economic right to control or prevent the unauthorised copying or reproduction of copyright material during the life of copyright, a term varying from jurisdiction to jurisdiction, and applying to the expression of an idea. Copyright protects computer software, photographs, slide presentations, letters, books, plays, even mundane written information such as business plans and also protects music and films.

Cyberspace
A term used to refer to the place where the Internet resides. First use was by William Gibson in his book *Neuromancer* in 1984.

Database
A program used to store and access large amounts of information. The Data may be stored in different forms such as text, sound and graphics. In the UK and EU databases which may not have enough creativity to have copyright protection may have protection by way of the lesser shorter right known as database right. All databases protected by copyright also have database right protection.

DEFCONS
A series of standard contract terms and conditions issued by the UK Ministry of Defence in the acquisition of a variety of goods and Services, including software. These are intended to override the provider's standard licensing terms and are heavily balanced in favour of the customer.

Dialup
A term used to describe traditional on-demand access to the Internet. In other words, you dial up when you want access and 'hang-up' when you have finished. These days most areas of the UK instead have broadband and Wi-Fi.

Digital certificate The equivalent of an Internet passport in that the certificate provides assurance of identity to an individual's digital signature. A digital certificate is a message which at least: (a) identifies the issuing certification authority; (b) names or identifies the individual; (c) contains the individual's public key; (d) identifies the terms of use of the certificate and (e) bears the digital signature of the certification authority itself.

Digital signature A transformation of a message using an asymmetric encryption system and a hash function such that a person, having the initial message and the digital signers own public key can accurately determine: (a) whether the transformation was created using the private key that corresponds to the signers public key; and (b) whether the initial message has been altered since the transformation was made. Frequently this is used in electronic contracting simply to mean the signature an individual uses either choosing one from the service provider or drawing it on the screen such as can be done when using contract creation software such as DocuSign.

Digital technology Digital technology represents signals in the form of a series of binary numbers rather than as analogue electronic signals.

Disintermediation The commercial process whereby intermediaries in a supply chain are bypassed or circumvented. In the travel industry, it applies to the process whereby Principals are seeking an increasing proportion of direct bookings from their ultimate clients, via various media, including the Internet.

Disk compression Software that processes the files on the hard disk so they take up less disk space. Disk compression software can effectively double the size of most hard disks. Most files can be compressed, as they contain portions of identical data repeated throughout the file.

Dongles Also known as keys, security devices and locks, these are made up of software and hardware and are intended to be a security device between the hardware equipment and the software program licensed by the provider. An authorised licensee only would have access to the dongle for attaching to the hardware input/output ports, without which the hardware would not allow the software to run. Usually a dongle is provided for every machine the software is to be run upon where these are used. These are much less common these days and instead confidential passwords and login detail are provided and much software is hosted online on the cloud.

DOS *Disk Operating System.* The software you need before you can get your computer to do anything. All other programs need the operating system to be loaded before they can work. The operating system is a bit like having a slave permanently at your disposal. If, say, you want a letter filed away, ask the operating system to put it somewhere and let it worry about how the hard disk stores the data.

Download A method of copying a file from one computer to another, but most frequently used when referring to getting a file from the Internet.

Driver A small program sitting between the operating system and hardware, which relays messages. For instance, the operating system tells the sound driver to play a note and the driver tells the soundcard to do it.

Glossary

DTP	*Desktop Publishing.* Software used to create documents or publications.
E-Commerce	The facilitation of business relationships by electronic means.
E-mail address	A unique address which can be used to send e-mail directly. For example: susan@singlelaw.com is an e-mail address for Susan Singleton within the domain singlelaw.com
Emoticons or Emojis	A picture embedded in text and used in electronic messages and web pages. See Smilies.
Emulation	Emulation makes a peripheral appear to an application as if it is another type of that peripheral. Take printer emulation as an example. Software publishers produce applications to work with a few popular printers, like the HP LaserJet, rather than making sure their product will work with every printer on the market. If other printer manufacturers make sure that their printer can mimic or 'emulate' a LaserJet, they know it will work with software compatible with the LaserJet.
Encryption technology	The means by which information is encrypted and decrypted using ciphers or codes in order to keep data confidential as well as to authenticate the identity of message senders and receivers.
EPOC	The original operating system for wireless devices, such as the handheld organiser developed by Psion for some of the first such devices in the 1990s.
Escrow	The holding on deposit by a third party of confidential material on certain terms as to its release or control and use. In software terms it is often source code which is placed in escrow and frequently using the NCC Escrow service
Extranet	A semi-private network of computers using a combination of fixed connections through both cables and the telephone system, via modems. The essential feature of an Extranet, which distinguishes it from an Intranet, is its more open nature. An Extranet is like an Intranet which has been opened up, to one degree or another, to one or more outsiders. For example, a law firm in the past would set up an Extranet with a particular client, so that the lawyers and the clients can exchange information and documents freely and with more security than via the Internet. These days on a sale of a business various forms of online hosted "data rooms" are used with strong security to ensure confidentiality during the due diligence process.
FAQ	*Frequently Asked Questions.* Usually found in Newsgroups which contain collated answers to questions most commonly asked by new users. An invaluable source of information for 'newbies' – the Internet name for new users.
Fibre	Either fibre optic cable to bring fast internet speeds to homes and businesses or a service partly using overhead copper telephone wires used as a brand name by some providers (see also **ADSL** above for a list of BT 'Fibre' services and speeds as at 2023.
Firewall	A security system, which sits between computers on a local area network (LAN) and the point of connection to the Internet, designed to restrict access to the LAN from the Internet.

Flame	An abusive or personal attack against the poster of a message in a newsgroup. The Internet equivalent of losing your temper and the nearest you can get to thumping someone. Occasionally a flame might start a flame war with insults being hurled to and fro until common sense prevails.
Frames	The use of the structure of a particular web site to surround material derived from mother site, and make the entire page appear to be the creation of the host.
FTP	*File Transfer Protocol.* The basic way of transferring files across the Internet. An FTP 'client' program is required to run on your own computer. Products such as Netscape include this facility.
GIF	A standard way of storing graphics images, used extensively across the Internet. See also **JPEG**.
Gopher	As in Go-for. A menu-driven application that runs on your own computer to read documents and download files stored on hosts. The host computer must also be capable of running a Gopher server application.
GPRS	*General Packet Radio Service.* A method of sending Internet information to mobile telephones at high speed. GPRS will be capable of delivering information at a speed of up to 100,000 bits per second, compared to the 9600 bits which is currently the norm.
GSM	*Global System for Mobile Communications.* Common European standard for mobile telephones.
gTLD	*generic Top Level Domain.* A TLD which indicates the type of organisation, eg .net, .com, .gov, .edu.
Hard drive cache	A small area of memory dedicated as a buffer.
Hard drive	A chip responsible for operating the hard drive when given **controller** instructions by the PC's processor. The controller can have almost as much effect on PC speed as the hard drive itself.
Host	The computer you dial into at your service provider to get access to the Internet. It will have a unique Internet address.
HTML	*HyperText Mark-up Language.* The language used to create documents for the World Wide Web, and which enables them to link to one another.
HTTP	*HyperText Transfer Protocol.* The standard way of transferring HTML documents between Web Servers and Clients (browsers).
ICANN IDE	*International Corporation for Assigned Names and Numbers. Integrated Drive Electronics.* IDE hard disks are what you will find in most PCs today. They have smart features such as built-in controllers and the ability to match the drive type specified in your PC's set-up. The latest IDE standard is known as Enhanced-IDE (E-IDE). E-IDE drives have a higher data throughput than conventional IDE drives. They also support more drives (two rather than four) and boast speeds that approach those of SCSL drives.
Intellectual Property Rights (IPR)	Also abbreviated to IPR, these are the bundle of legal rights or protections which include patents, copyright, trademarks and design rights.

Glossary

Internet	The network of constantly changing connections between otherwise unconnected computers using modems and telephone lines.
Internet of Things	Generic term used to mean access to the internet and control of devices other than the traditional personal computer. It includes smart kettles, smart fridges, security devices, control of elements of motor cars and much else.
Intranet	A private network of computers using fixed connections normally using cables, usually all within the same building. The same effect can be achieved through the telephone system, via modems. The essential feature of an Intranet which distinguishes it from the Internet is its closed nature. An Intranet is a private network, most commonly confined within a particular organisation.
IP (and IPR)	*Internet Protocol.* A layer of the set of protocols which devices on the Internet use to communicate with each other. It defines how packets of data get to their intended destination – often used with 'Transmission Control Protocol in the form TCP/IP. Also is often used to stand for *Intellectual Property* and **IPR** for *Intellectual Property Rights.*
IP address	The internal Internet address for a domain, expressed as a group of four numbers eg 158.152.34.2.
ISDN	*Integrated Services Digital Network. A* traditional digital communications infrastructure, which superseded lower performance traditional analogue lines of the early days of the internet. Those with an ISDN line can send digital information at speeds of up to 128Kb per second. Broadband speeds are now much faster although not all areas of the UK are able to obtain broadband.
ISP	Internet Service Provider. See **Access Provider**.
JANET	*Joint Academic NETwork.* Links educational establishments in the UK.
JPEG	A widely used way of compressing still images and video. See also **GIF**.
LAN	*Local Area Network.* See also **Intranet**.
LDAP	Lightweight Direct Access Protocol.
LINK	A connection between one page on a web site and another page, either on the same site or on an entirely separate site, possibly hosted by a completely unrelated third party in a different part of the world. Links are most easily created by the use of HyperText Mark-up Language (HTML).
LISTSERV	An automated mailing list distribution system, used to distribute electronic newsletters.
LRA	Local Registration Authority.
Lurker	Someone who joins areas where people gather to chat and post online such as Reddit but does not contribute – the equivalent of a voyeur. However, it is usually best to lurk for a while to gauge the feeling of the group and accepted dialogue before making your own contributions.
Mail Gateway	A system which translates e-mail between different systems, for example, between Internet mail and your own Microsoft office mail.

M-Commerce	The facilitation of business relationships by the means of mobile communication devices.
Meta-tags	The embedding of key words or identifiers into the HTML script of a site, in order to generate as many visitors or 'hits' on a site, is called key meta-tagging. The result is that any user of a browser or search engine inputting a key word or phrase that is the same or similar to the key word or phrase in the HTML script on your site, will be led to your site.
MIME	*Multipurpose Internet Mail Extensions.* A method of encoding or decoding programs so that they can be sent as normal text e-mail messages.
Mirror sites	Heavily used sites, particularly FTP ones, are often replicated at other locations to relieve the load. These are mirror sites.
Modem	*Modulator/DEModulator.* The device that takes signals from your computer and translates them into a suitable form for the telephone system. The reverse procedure takes place at a modem on the host computer. The faster the speed of a modem, the better the response when transferring large amounts of information.
Moderator	The person who runs a discussion group, newsgroup, conference or message area.
Mosaic	The first browser which increased the popularity of the World Wide Web.
Motherboard	The main circuit board in the PC. It accommodates the process, memory and expansion cards.
MP3	Software using sound compression technology which facilitates the transmission of sound signals via the web. See also **Real Player**.
MPEG	A type of video compression which makes it possible to have full screen, full-motion video on your PC.
MUG	Multi-User Game.
Multi-tasking	The ability of modern computers to carry out several functions at once.
Net Police	A (derogatory) term for those users who find it necessary to tell others how they should behave in Cyberspace.
Net Surfer	Someone who 'surfs' the Internet looking for interesting files, places to visit and people to talk to.
Netiquette	The supposed etiquette of the Internet community – for example avoiding the use of quoting, spamming and SHOUTING – use of capitals is taken as being the equivalent of shouting in real life.
Newbie	A new user – can also be used as a term of abuse.
Newsgroups	Internet Bulletin Boards or other places online where people gather to chat and post comments. There are around many thousands of such groups covering just about every subject imaginable including on Reddit and many other places. The collective name for these newsgroup servers is the Usenet although these days the term is not so often used and instead people find the area of the internet of most interest to them whether in a specialist field or more generally such as on Reddit's various sections. Users may start conversations with new messages or comment on current messages.

NNTP	*Network News Transfer Protocol.* The internal protocol used between news servers to exchange articles.
Node	Any device connected to the Internet, with an IP address, is a node.
Nominet	The UK 'not for profit' organisation – which oversees domain names ending with the following TLDs:
	– co.uk
	– org.uk
	– ltd.uk
Nominet– *contd*	– plc.uk
	– net.uk
Object code	Computer code, derived by a computer or assembler program, from source code, into a form understandable by machine rather than human forms – also called executable and/or machine code.
OLR	*Off-Line Reader.* Enables information to be downloaded and read offline without maintaining a connection to the Internet. Material may also be prepared for mailing and then sent in a Blink. See **Blink**.
On-line	This term is actually used in association with using the Internet, referring to a service or information accessed through the telephone network via a modem.
Packet	A bundle of data that travels over the network. A message may comprise many packages. It contains information about its source, destination and an identifier for the recipient to understand how it relates to other packets.
Patent	An intellectual property right, granted by legislation, to the inventor of a novel idea which is an invention capable of industrial exploitation, and giving the inventor a monopoly for a limited period of time to control the exploitations of the patented idea or invention. Patents are available only for industrial inventions which are new. They usually last for 20 years.
PC	*Personal Computer.* A computer substantially capable of operating in isolation from others, although it might be part of a network.
PDA	*Personal Digital Assistant.* Small, hand-held devices which typically integrated with computers in the early days of the internet. The Psion and Palm product ranges were early examples. These days people use smartphones instead.
PING	*Package Internet Groper.* A program used to test if Internet destinations exist and are operational.
PKI	A public key infrastructure comprising a set of technology components combined with practices, policies and a supporting legal framework which provide a highly trusted infrastructure. At its core is the application of asymmetric encryption techniques that ensure trust in the confidentiality and authentication of data and entities within electronic systems.
PoP	*Point of Presence.* A local access point provided by an Access Provider to give Internet access for the cost of a local call.
POP3	An e-mail transfer protocol.

Port	A term used for different points of entry into a single computer. For example, FTP, e-mail and WEB browsing may use different ports. However, the technicalities of ports are usually handled transparently as far as the user is concerned.
Post	To put content online such as under an online newspaper article, below someone's comment or photograph on their social media feeds or on an online discussion group.
Postmaster	The person responsible for e-mail handling at a domain.
PPP	*Point to Point Protocol*. Allows, amongst other things, IP connections between a computer and access provider. Any dial-up service used with an access provider will use PPP or SLIP, its predecessor.
Principal	The party which takes direct responsibility for the provision of an activity, eg, travel arrangements to the client or the person appointing a commercial agent. Note that the term focuses on the activity in question, rather than a description of the type of business. Thus, some businesses operate as the principal in the appointment of an agent or sub-agent, but themselves may also be agents or retailers.
Protocol	Industry jargon for a standard rule or set of rules.
RA	Registration Authority.
RAM	*Random Access Memory*. Physical memory on your PC used to store and edit data which is cleared when the power is switched off.
Real Player	Software using sound compression technology which facilitates the transmission of sound signals via the web. See also **MP3**.
Reboot	When you restart your PC, by switching off and on, pressing the reset button (if you have one) or pressing Ctrl, Alt and Del simultaneously on the keyboard, the PC goes through a reboot process, wiping items from short-term memory and reading all your system files again.
Reformat	When you format a floppy or hard disk, the PC subdivides the whole magnetic disk into sectors for storing data. If a drive has been formatted once, it can be reformatted, which wipes the disk clean, and sets these sectors up again.
Refresh rate	The speed at which information on screen is updated. This takes place many times a second so the eye detects no screen flicker.
RFI	The abbreviation for Request for Information – a particular request issued by the customer in advance of negotiations for the acquisition of software, or hardware or both. The customer requests as much, or particular information as is required from the provider.
RFP	The abbreviation for Request for Proposals – a particular request from the customer often issued after receipt of an RFI, for the provider to complete answering specific enquiries of the customer for software, hardware or both
Root directory	The starting point on a hard disk, the root directory, (eg c:\) displayed within DOS and Windows, contains all the files and directories that exist on your hard disk.

Glossary

SaaS (and Software as a Service)	The most common method for provision of software which is hosted on the cloud and for which the user, whether an individual or a business, pays regular fees (see also ASP above) (to be contrasted with the more traditional perpetual licence for which a one off fee is paid and software hosted on the individual's own computer/laptop.
SCSI	*Small Computer Systems Interface.* A fast system that can be used to control many types of peripheral devices, such a hard disks, tape streamers and CD-ROM drives. All of these peripherals can be connected in a daisy chain to one SCSI controller card.
Server	A computer system on a network which provides services to Client applications. For example: a Gopher application requires both Client and Server applications which communicate with each other.
Shareware	A method of distributing software. Programs are provided free of charge or for a small handling fee, for the user to test for suitability. If, after 30 days, the product continues to be used, it should be registered with the author and paid for.
Shrink-wrap	The description for, and method of providing, printed software licensing terms, for mass-market software products, where a software licensing contract is intended to be entered into without necessarily being negotiated or signed.
Signature or sig	The personal tag used at the end of an e-mail message or posting. May include name, tel, e-mail, business, etc. Anything from one to seven lines. Users with excessively large signatures, especially in relation to the text of their message, are often accused of having a low signal to noise ratio. In other words, the useful content is small, the noise, their sig, is large.
SIM	*Subscriber Identification Module.* Plastic card (sim card) which is placed in the back of a mobile phone and allows you to store information on your phone.
SLIP	*Serial Line Internet Protocol.* Allows devices to use IP over communications links being superseded by PPP.
Smilies or Emoticons or Emojies	Punctuation used to impart emotions within e-mail messages. Particularly in Whatsapp texts and other social media. When viewed at ninety degrees, they represent the human face. For example: :-) = happy, :-(= sad, :-o = amazement.
SMS	*Short Messaging Service.* Technology which allows text messages to be received and sent on mobile phones.
SMTP	*Simple Mail Transfer Protocol.* The Internet protocol for transferring mail.
Software	computer programs which provide instructions to computer hardware, or other software, and which comprise data or information which may be stored in or upon a variety of media, and may be transmitted or disseminated by a variety of means.
Source Code	Instructions or statements written in eye-readable form in programmers' language (high level or assembly language) and capable of being compiled into object code.
Spam	Internet slang for posting the same message to several Newsgroups (also cross-posting) – an activity which is frowned upon.

Swapfile	Complex programs that handle many data, such as Windows, often require more memory than is available, so they use swap files. Data that is not needed immediately is transferred or 'swapped' into a temporary file on your hard disk.
System disk	A floppy disk that contains all the essential files needed to run DOS. If anything happens to your hard disk, you can start your PC using a system disk, helping you to fix the problem without losing any data. By 2023 very little software was supplied on disk however and most downloaded or stored in the cloud.
System files	Special description files, which control how your PC starts up.
TCP	*Transmission Control Protocol.* A higher level of protocol than IP. IP is concerned with packets of data. TCP is concerned with messages which may comprise numerous packets. Almost universally used together and referred to as TCP/P.
Telnet	A protocol which allows you to connect over the Internet to another computer in such a way as to appear as a local user of that computer. Requires the use of a terminal emulator simulating your view of the remote computer. This is steadily being superseded by the WWW.
Title	Legal ownership of hardware or intellectual property rights in software. When title passes from seller to buyer it is usual for possession and risk for insurance purposes, also to pass.
TLA	Three Letter Acronym.
TLD	*Top Level Domain.* The most general part of a web site or e-mail address, often indicating the type of organisation, country of location or both, eg org.uk
Trademark	A mark, image or identity applied to goods or services, registered or unregistered, which are unique to the business of their owner, but not necessarily descriptive of such business. These can be registered as registered trademarks. Trademarks are available for logos, words, sounds, colours and even smells.
Trade secret	Confidential information which may or may not be protectable by copyright or patent, but which is valuable to its owner. There is no property right in such confidential information, but through common law, contract, data protection and other rights there may be ways to control its use.
Trolls	Trolling occurs when someone posts a message on the Internet and makes it appear as if the message came from someone else.
Trumpet	A Winsock-compatible Windows program that provides a dial-up connection to the Internet using the SLIP protocol first released in 1994.
TTP	The abbreviation for a Trusted Third Party; an independent individual, firm or company set up or licensed by the state to provide, amongst other things, escrow services and certification or verification services for public and private key algorithms or codes used in cryptographic software, and providing authentication services in respect of digital signatures used in e-commerce.
UNIX	A host operating system which supports multiple users sharing resources. Many host computers use UNIX Servers to provide their email, FTP and Web services.

Glossary

URL
Uniform Resource Locator. An attempt to standardise address details of Internet resources. Most commonly used with www pages. For example, the home page for the Natural History Museum is: http://ww.nhm.ac.uk/

Veronica
Very Easy Rodent Oriented Net-wide Index to Computerised Archives! A catalogue of Gopher sites which allows you to search for menu items containing keywords, and then builds a menu of those sites.

Vlog
Video blog (see Blog above).

VRML
Virtual Reality Modelling Language. An extension of HTML which gives virtual reality effects.

WAIS
Wide Area Information Server. Allows a client to perform searches simultaneously on multiple databases.

WAN
Wide Area Network.

WAP
Wireless Application Protocol. Intended to be an industry standard protocol and service profile for use with digital mobile phones, pagers, personal digital assistants and other wireless terminals. A standard to enable mobile device users to view web pages easily. It is intended to simplify wireless access to e-mail and voicemail and enable transactions to be carried out.

Web site
An individual's or company's presence on the World Wide Web; web sites can be highly interactive and consist of complex design and data content and are often developed and maintained by third-party developers and hosted on third-party servers. Others are a mere text and picture brochure with no reader interaction.

Wi-Fi
An internet access service enabling access without use directly of a modem when using a particular device which is wi-fi enabled and in the Internet of Things may be any kind of device even a product such as a kettle. Wi-Fi is a group of wireless network protocols based on a group of standards based on IEEE 802.11 standards. It enables nearby digital devices to exchange data by radio waves.

Winsock
A standard interface within the Windows operating system, which resides between applications and network protocols. Used if you require access to the Internet from a Windows application.

WML
Wireless Markup Language. This allows web sites to tailor the information format to fit the screen and limited capacity of mobile devices.

WWW
World Wide Web. Also known as the Web. The generic name given to the entire inter-linked HTML documents on the Internet, which are accessible via browsers such as Netscape. The part of the Internet which has single-handedly contributed to its major growth over recent years. First developed by an Englishman, Tim Bemers-Lee.

XML
Extensible Mark-up Language. Similar to HTML in that it describes the contents of a web page. XML also enables the interpretation of the value or nature of the data being described.

ZIP
A way of compressing files to minimise transmission times over the Internet. Programs are available to ZIP files up (compress them) and UNZIP them (restore them to their original form) after transmission across the Internet.

Part I
Introduction

1 Understanding software licence agreements

1.1 WHAT IS A SOFTWARE LICENCE AGREEMENT?

At the core of software and software contracts is the legal concept of copyright. Copyright (as it applies to software) is the right for the owner or licensed proprietor to prevent anyone from copying their software without paying something for it. Since the use of software requires copying to occur, then any user of software must have permission to use and thereby copy such software.

A software licence agreement authorises someone to do something with software which would otherwise be an infringement of copyright. The party granting this authorisation is known as the 'licensor' while the party receiving the authorisation is known as the 'licensee'. Even where software is hosted online and the user uses a Software as a Service (SaaS) service to pay regular fees to access the software, rather than a one-off fee for a perpetual licence with the software held on the user's computer systems under the traditional licensing model, a licence or right to use is granted. In both types of arrangement, the user is given right or permission to use the software.

The licensor may own all rights to the software, or may have the permission of the owner to enter into licence agreements with others. The licensee may be:

- a user of the software;
- a distributor of the software;
- a publisher of the software;
- a website owner or host;
- a party who modifies, translates, or adds codes to the software;
- a party who makes copies of the software for its owner or a distributor;
- an original equipment manufacturer;
- a value added reseller;
- a joint venture partner;
- an independent maintenance company;

- a facilities management company;

- a technology escrow agent;

- an independent training company; or

- an independent sales representative or agent.

In general, if the software in question is protected by copyright the licence agreement allows the licensee to deal with the software as specified in the licence grant provision of the agreement without infringing the licensor's copyright. The agreement addresses other topics as well, such as payment and warranties. Sometimes maintenance and training will be addressed in the licence agreement and sometimes they will be covered by separate agreements. Whatever its other terms might be, the agreement will virtually always specify the rights conveyed to the licensee and the restrictions imposed on the licensee regarding the licensed software.

An agreement that licenses one or more copies of software is different from an agreement that sells one or more copies. When copies of software are sold, the purchaser takes title to the copies. One analogy is the purchase of a book at a bookshop. The purchaser can do many things with the purchased book, for example, they can resell the copy, lend it to a friend, or give it away. However, the purchaser cannot reprint the book, and cannot sell or make copies if the item is protected by an intellectual property law such as copyright. Such a reproduction and distribution would constitute copyright infringement if the purchaser did not have the permission of the copyright owner to reproduce the item and sell it commercially. Thus, when goods that are protected by copyright are purchased, title to the copy purchased does not give the purchaser complete freedom to do whatever they desire with the copy. There is an invisible, legal string attached to such goods that makes certain actions involving the purchased copy illegal.

In contrast, when copies of software are licensed, the licensee often does not obtain title to the licensed copy. Instead, the licensee obtains possession of one or more copies of the licensed software and gains certain specified rights to deal with the licensed copy or copies under the terms of the software licence agreement. There are exceptions to the general rule about the licensee not taking title to a licensed copy of software which are explained later. For this introduction, it is sufficient to note the general key difference between a software sale or assignment agreement and a software licence agreement: the former passes title while the latter does not. In addition, because licence agreements often contain limitations on the licensee's ability to deal with licensed software, the legal string mentioned above is usually strong when affixed to licensed copies.

One related point is important to our introductory discussion. There is a major difference between purchasing the intellectual property rights in software, on the one hand, and purchasing or licensing or accessing a copy of software, on the other. If the software is protected by copyright, to continue our book analogy, then the difference is between purchasing the copyright in the book and purchasing a copy of the book. In other words, the copyright owner can sell and you can buy copies of an item protected by copyright, but that purchase does not make you the copyright owner. Owning a copy of a book or software is not the same as owning the copyright for the book or software. Copyright is an asset of its owner and can be disposed of in the same manner as other assets, for example, when you sell assets of a company or sell all shares or stock in a company.

To continue further the book analogy, if there is copyright in a book written by one author, then the writing on the pages is the expression of the idea or creativity behind the book, but there is also copyright in the creativity or style if it can be expressed in writing. To this end the printed pages are like object code and the creativity, style and idea are like source code.

You should be aware that there is a difference between a software developer, a software publisher and a software distributor. A software developer is a party that creates software. A software publisher may create software, may acquire it from developers, or may do both. In any event the publisher will reproduce copies of the software or have them reproduced, will stock inventory of the software, and will promote its distribution. Most publishers distribute software as well. A software distributor acquires software from publishers and usually stocks an inventory, but always distributes copies by one or more methods, for instance, sales representatives, mail order, etc.

These differences have close parallels in the book publishing industry. A software publisher acquires its rights to the software in question from the developer just as a book publisher acquires its rights to books from authors. One difference between book publishers and software publishers is that book authors are rarely employed by the publishers of their books while it is more common for software developers to be individuals employed by the publishers of their software. It is also common for the developer to be an independent author like a typical book author. However, these independent developers are often corporations rather than individuals.. An independent software distributor is very much like an independent book distributor. Of course, there are exceptions to these general arrangements.

1.2 WHAT TYPES OF SOFTWARE AND DATABASES ARE DISTRIBUTED UNDER CONTRACT AND WHAT LAWS PROTECT THEM?

1.2.1 Software

Most computer software is distributed under a contract, and the source code is also confidential information/protected by trade secret law. The UK's Patents Act 1977 provides that computer software may not be patented 'as such', so copyright protection is used instead. However, where software is part of an underlying invention in the UK, EU and US it may be possible to patent the invention and indeed the computer industry has large numbers of patents for inventions. Contract law provides protection because such software is typically licensed to users.

1.2.2 Contracts

Almost all software is licensed for use, either through a standalone signed agreement or an end user licence agreement accepted in various ways by the user without a signature being applied. Software is protected by copyright law although the contract terms also provide even wider protection for the licensor.

1.2.3 Commercially available software

Trademark and unfair competition law (in the UK the common law of 'passing off') are important to the businesses of software, computer and database providers, for example, as to their identity, quality image, and sales; but trademark law and unfair competition law do not directly protect the content or expression of products as does copyright and database right law, except perhaps in some misappropriation situations, for example, the misappropriation and publication of news in a database before it is published by the source of the news.

1.2.4 Commercially available databases

Databases generally available to the public for a fee are protected by various bodies of law and contracts depending upon circumstances such as the method of dissemination, the value, user rights, etc, for example:

- If printed copies or reports are marketed, copyright and database right protection often is used exclusively. If the data is licensed, trade secret law/confidentiality and contract protection may be attempted.

- If a disk or a CD-ROM is the medium (rare these days), often copyright protection is used, especially if the data access code is recorded on the disk or CD-ROM. Usually the data is licensed under the terms of a licence agreement.

- If the data is downloaded and software hosted online, usually copyright protection is used and usually the data is licensed. The information is probably also confidential so the laws relating to confidentiality and trade secrets are also used.

- If the data is made available through the internet or online networks usually copyright and database right protection is used and usually the data is licensed under contractual terms and conditions often contained in the online terms/end user licence agreement with the user must accept before proceeding. Rights of confidentiality may also be used.

EC Directive 96/9 on the Legal Protection of Databases[1] introduced a *sui generis* right of protection known as a database right of 15 years in addition to copyright. This Directive will be discussed in Part II, section **4.6**. This right continues as at 2023 notwithstanding the fact the UK has left the EU.

1 OJ 1996 L77/20.

1.2.5 Non-contract protection

Tort law and/or criminal law offer some redress for the theft, disruption or destruction of software or databases under certain circumstances. For example, many jurisdictions have adopted computer virus legislation that makes a variety of types of computer tampering a criminal offence. In the UK the Computer Misuse Act 1990 specifically addresses the question of hacking in that three offences exist namely:

*   unauthorised access to computer material;

*   unauthorised access with intent to commit or facilitate the commission of further offences; and

*   unauthorised modification.

Further civil and criminal law remedies for infringement of copyright in computer programs is available under the Copyright, Designs and Patents Act 1988.

1.3 GENERAL COMMENTS

While the primary focus of this work is software licence agreements in the context of a major acquisition, distribution arrangement, development project or conversion project, many comments are offered regarding computers and databases accompanied by licensed software. Advice is given in relation to other types of computer contract such as maintenance and support agreements, outsourcing agreements and escrow, and numerous parallels are drawn between software providers on the one hand and computer and database providers on the other. The term 'provider' is preferred in this work because software is available from different types of sources: apps which can be downloaded such as via the Google store, developers, publishers, distributors, retailers, computer vendors, database publishers etc. 'Provider' encompasses all sources. As used in this work, either the type of provider in question will be clear from the context, or the term will have a typical meaning of publisher, distributor, computer vendor that distributes software, etc.

References in this work to a customer's 'technical staff' or 'technical personnel' are meant to refer to members of a company's data processing staff, programming staff, consultants in technical areas, or management information services department, and are intended to encompass their managers, directors, etc. 'Customer' is used in this book rather than 'user', except on occasion, because customer has a broader meaning. For example, a publisher may be a customer for a software developer, but not a user of the developed software. The context in which 'customer' is used should make its meaning clear. 'Price' as used herein is meant to include purchase price, licence fee, service charge, etc, depending on the context.

1.4 GOALS AND PURPOSES OF PARTIES TO A SOFTWARE LICENCE AGREEMENT

1.4.1 In general

The goals and purposes of the parties to a software licence agreement vary according to a number of factors, but some generalisations can be made. Software providers are motivated by profit. Software costs money to develop and distribute. A new computer business application may cost half a million pounds or many times that amount to develop and market. Mainframe programs often cost even more.

Software licensees are not uniform in their goals and purposes. Commercial users of application programs, operating systems, databases, and computers, generally want results. That is, such users have more or less specific results in mind when they acquire a new application, or switch to a new operating system. The desired results may be processing customer orders faster, inventory control, e-mail, improved secretarial efficiency, improved response times, a more capable system that does new things, reduction of current processing costs, etc. These desired results are the business and/ or technical reasons for licensing commercially used software. Of course, many commercial users also desire maintenance-free software that requires little or no operator training and hope for a good relationship with the software provider, but some problems in these and other areas usually will be tolerated if the more specific major business or technical results are produced.

In contrast, the traditional position of both software and computer providers is that they provide solutions which the customer is responsible for selecting and operating so as to produce whatever results are desired. The goal of the commercial customer to receive results and the purpose of software, database and computer providers to furnish a solution are inconsistent even though some solutions sometimes provide the desired result. This insight is important to your understanding of software, database and computer transactions.

Licensee-distributors have different goals from licensee-users. A distributor falls into the category of profit-motivated software providers. Like others in this group, the licensee is interested in moving products out of the door and into the hands of the user. Thus, you can see that the goals and purposes of all licensees are not the same because different types of licensees deal with software in different ways.

Another major goal of parties to a software licence agreement merits attention. Software providers want to minimise potential liability. A liability determination in litigation may lead to bad publicity that hurts business. Damages awards can wipe out profits and push a company into bankruptcy. Minimising the risk of legal liability is a goal of the software provider in software licence agreements.

In contrast, a software user wants quietly to enjoy his licensed software free of any concerns about liability arising from its operation. Sophisticated software users ensure that their licence agreement makes the software provider responsible for the most likely risks of legal liability arising from the exercise of the users' licensed rights.

There are other goals and purposes that could be mentioned, but these suffice to illustrate the differences in the parties' outlooks.

In general, the software provider wants to make profit from supplying a solution to the customer's needs (with software being the medium and the object of the solution) and without incurring the burden of ongoing responsibility and liability to the customer. The customer wants to get their needs satisfied fully by the software they are obtaining and for which they are paying with the maximum performance and ongoing support from the provider.

1.4.2 Why are software licence agreements required by many software providers?

As we observed earlier, software is an asset. It can be protected by contract provisions, patent law (sometimes), copyright law (often), and trade secret law (fairly often). Assuming the software in question is protected by copyright law, the owner of a copy is allowed to transfer that copy to others without the copyright owner's permission or knowledge. If all software were sold, the owner of each copy could deprive the copyright owner of much needed revenue by transferring his copy to another after a period of use. If the software could not be transferred, the second user would have to acquire a copy in the marketplace, thereby improving the copyright owner's profits. The only way the copyright owner can prohibit such a transfer under current law is by means of contract restrictions on a licensee. The desire to maximise revenue leads a copyright owner to license his software rather than sell copies.

In addition, if object code is distributed rather than source code, the owner can claim trade secret protection for his program. Unfortunately for the owner, trade secret law (ie, the English common law of confidentiality) allows reverse engineering through disassembly or decompilation as what can be discovered through such process is not confidential, albeit it may be hard to uncover. The trade secret owner can, subject to certain statutory exceptions in EU Member States and the UK, prohibit reverse engineering of distributed copies through restrictions in licence agreements. The desire to prohibit reverse engineering leads the owner to license his software rather than sell copies.

This desire to prohibit reverse engineering is prompted by the realisation that the ideas discovered from a decompiled or disassembled program can be used by a current or future competitor in a competing product, and can be disseminated to users by trade publications or online, any one of which reduces the owner's revenue flow. The software business is hard enough without giving away your trade secrets.

While there are other reasons, such as minimising legal risks through protective contract provisions, these are two of the main reasons why software licence agreements are required by many software providers.

In the case of *Microsoft Corporation v Commission* case T-201/04,[1] the Court of First Instance rejected the appeal by Microsoft against the European Commissioner's decision in 2004 that Microsoft had abused its dominant position under what is now Article 102 of the Treaty on the Functioning of the European Union.

The case originated from a complaint from Sun Microsystems that Microsoft had refused to provide it with interoperability information which Sun required in order to develop its server products so as to operate effectively with Microsoft's Windows PC operating system. After several years of investigation, the Commission adopted a Decision, finding that Microsoft had abused its dominant position in the marketplace and in particular that Microsoft's refusal to make available interoperability information was anticompetitive. Microsoft, amongst other things was fined €497,192,304 and ordered to cease its anticompetitive practices.

Microsoft's appeal to the Court of First Instance was based on a number of points but in essence Microsoft claimed that the Commission had been incorrect in its assessment of the law relating to interoperability and bundling and further, that the imposition of a fine was illegal.

For the computer industry, the issues surrounding the abuse of dominant position and also that of interoperability data are important.

At a time when many software companies are moving to more open solutions, it is unusual for a major software vendor totally to ring-fence its products and use intellectual property rights as a mechanism to prevent competitors or perceived competitors from interfacing their products.

The right to reverse analyse where interoperability data is necessary is an enshrined right under EU law in the EU software directive (and UK legislation made under it) and arises because the European Commission recognised many years ago that dominant technology companies could stifle competition and innovation by ring-fencing their technology and refusing to make interoperability data available to other developers. Microsoft's refusal to make data available to Sun was in itself anticompetitive as confirmed by the Court of First Instance.

The *Microsoft* court decision requires detailed analysis but for present purposes it is sufficient to say that the licensing practices of software companies continue to require audit and analysis in order to ensure compliance with English (and where applicable EU) law. The UK has the equivalent of Article 102 in the Chapter II prohibition of the Competition Act 1998 which prohibits abuses of a dominant position.

While there are other reasons, such as minimising legal risks through protective contract provisions, these are two of the main reasons why software licence agreements are required by many software providers.

1   [2007] ECR II-3601.

1.5   SOME DIFFERENCES BETWEEN SOFTWARE SALE, LEASE AND LICENCE TRANSACTIONS

1.5.1   Legal concepts and characteristics

As the introduction explained, there are significant differences between software sales and software licences. A software lease is also different from both and these days is often the norm with users paying monthly fees with software hosted by the licensor rather than downloaded and installed to the licensee's computer as with traditional software licensing. It is important that you understand the basic differences and similarities of these transactions. The following chart summarises their fundamental characteristics and compares them to similar transactions.

Subject Matter Activity	Sale	Lease/Rental	Licence
Property	Legal title, risk and possession passes	Leasehold title, risk and possession passes; freehold does not	Limited right of use granted only; risk and possession passes
Equipment	Legal title, risk and possession passes	Possession and risk passes, but the title does not	Limited right of use granted only; risk and possession passes
IPR	Legal title to copyright, trademarks, patents and risk and possession passes	N/A	Limited right of use granted only; risk and possession passes
Copy of Software Product	Legal title and risk in the media and possession passes, but IPR and title in software remains with setter/owner	Possession and risk passes on strict terms for a fixed period subject to regular payments	Limited right of use of copy granted only; risk and possession passes

1.5.2   Legal concept of sale

Nature: a sale conveys title or ownership, which is a property interest. The rights to possess and use the purchased item are part of the ownership rights, as are the rights to resell or otherwise dispose of the purchased item.

• **Sell equipment:** title passes to purchaser.

- **Sell intellectual property rights:** title to copyright, patent, trademark, or trade secret passes to purchaser.

- **Sell a copy of software:** title to the copy passes to the purchaser, but the seller retains ownership of the intellectual property rights in the copy, for example, patent, copyright, trademark, etc.

1.5.3 Legal concept of lease

Nature: a lease conveys the right to possess and use, but not to resell or otherwise distribute the leased item. No title passes. A lease is primarily a financing arrangement that conveys property interests. Thus it could be argued that a lease is a mixed property law and financing concept.

- **Property lease:** transfers a leasehold title to property giving the right to occupy the premises upon payment of rent. Title does not pass but an option to purchase the freehold may be included in the lease.

- **Equipment lease:** conveys a personal property right to possess and use the leased equipment upon payment of rent. Title does not pass but an option to purchase may be included in the transaction.

- **Software lease:** conveys a personal property right to possess and use the leased software upon payment of rent. Title does not pass as a part of the lease transaction. If the software is protected by copyright and trade secret law, the lessee should also have an express or implied intellectual property right licence to possess and use the intellectual property or protected technology in the software. The lessee often obtains this licence directly from the intellectual property right licensor who may or may not be the lessor as well. Independent, third-party software lessors are increasingly noticeable in the marketplace, as are financing companies who finance software licence fees receivable.

The personal property right to possess and use a copy of software under a lease is theoretically different from a right to possess and use all intellectual property in the software. This may sound like a difference without a distinction. If the lessor and the licensor are the same party, or the lessor has permission from the licensor to license the software to the lessee-licensee, then the theoretical difference is not noticeable as a practical matter. Also, a lease can be viewed as conveying an implied licence. To illustrate, assume that the software is a mainframe program protected by trade secret law and that the lessee-user finances possession and use of the software under a lease, but does not obtain the trade secret owner's permission to possess and use the trade secrets in the software under a licence. The very existence of a lease can easily be viewed to imply that it conveys to the lessee-user both personal property and intellectual property rights to possess and use the leased software. Also, the lessor may convey both types of rights expressly or by implication in the lease. If the lessor owns the trade secrets or has the permission of the trade secret owner to grant the user licence, then there is no problem. However, independent lessors who convey express or implied licences must be careful to obtain permission to do so.

One situation where the trade secret licensor may argue that the lessee has no right to possess and use its intellectual property in the leased software arises when the original lessee-licensee-user subleases the software to a third party, for example, a company spun off from the lessee-licensee, with the approval of an independent lessor, but without the knowledge or contractually required approval of the trade secret licensor. Generally speaking, the owner of trade secrets must know who has copies and grant permission for their possession and use in order to preserve their status as trade secrets.

1.5.4   Legal concept of licence

A licence conveys a personal privilege or right to do one or more things with the licensed item, for example, to possess it; to use it; to make or reproduce it; to distribute one or more copies by specified means (for example, sale, license, etc); publicly to display or operate the licensed item; to prepare modified versions or translations of the licensed item; etc. A licence agreement usually incorporates payment terms and hence is like a financing arrangement, but it can be used to convey more than the rights to possess, use, resell or otherwise dispose of the licensed item. For example, a licence of software can convey to the licensee the right to prepare a foreign language translation of the software, or a right to make many copies of the software and distribute them commercially. In the absence of a licence grant authorising them, the purchaser or the lessee of a copy of copyrighted software cannot do these things without infringing the copyright in the software.

- Property licence: grants limited right to use and not possess, real property. No property right is conveyed as a part of this privilege of use. This privilege is revocable but unassignable except for prior written agreement.

- Software licence: assuming the software is protected by intellectual property law, the licence grant conveys permission for possession and specified conduct with respect to the software. Use may or may not be allowed, depending on the type of licence agreement. For example, a distributor may be licensed to distribute copies supplied to him, but not licensed to use a copy of the software in his business.

1.6   WEAKNESSES OF THE SOFTWARE LICENCE CONCEPT

Many legal concepts are defeasible concepts. In other words, they are capable of being defeated by certain circumstances. For example, the concept of a contract is defeated if there is no consideration to support the parties' agreement. The concept of a software licence embedded in a contract called a software licence agreement is likewise defeated, or nullified, if the agreement is not valid. Generally speaking, an offer, its acceptance, and consideration are required to create a valid contract.

The existence of a software licence can also be destroyed by other circumstances. A software licence agreement may qualify as a valid and enforceable contract in every legal sense, but it may be characterised by a court as a valid and enforceable sale contract rather than a valid and enforceable licence agreement. For example, a licence grant in a software licence agreement can be adulterated to the point of destruction by sale language in the agreement. In its pristine form the concept of a licence does not pass title. A sale passes title. If a software licence agreement contains the terms 'sale' or 'purchase' or 'purchaser', the licence concept underlying the licence grant is adulterated. One, or more, uses of such terms anywhere in a software licence agreement may cause a court to characterise the contract as a software sale agreement.

Another example of massive licence grant and underlying concept adulteration is a perpetual term in a software licence agreement. If the licensee can keep the software forever after payment of a fee, a court may decide that there is no major difference for practical purposes (although big differences legally) between the so-called licence agreement and a sale agreement as will be discussed later in this section in the case of *UsedSoft GmbH v Oracle International Corp.*[1]

Mass-market software such as shrink-wrapped business software and leisure or entertainment software often contain licence grant terms such as 'a perpetual royalty free non-exclusive transferable licence' and is 'sold for a once only retail price'. Notwithstanding that the only part of the product which is a 'good' is the media upon which or within which the software is embodied, to all intents and purposes the whole item is perceived as a 'good' which in consumer terms involves a number of implied statutory rights (but only where true 'goods' are sold) which might not be included in a 'supply' or true licensing situation.

Similarly, a licence grant can be destroyed by the actions of the licensor. If the licensed software is advertised or promoted as software that is sold or purchased, such advertising or promotion is inconsistent with the legal concept of a licence that underlies the grant provision in a software licence agreement. It serves as a notice that the licensor really believes they are selling copies, and creates customer expectations that title to a copy will be acquired when a copy is acquired. Almost any advertising or promotion of sold or purchased copies contaminates the licence grant sufficiently that a court might characterise the software licence agreement as a software sale agreement.

Courts pay heed to substance over form, and substance includes more than the title given to a contract. The case of *St Albans City and District Council v International Computers Ltd*[2] has amongst other things, but only 'obiter' incidentally) inferred that software is 'goods' where it is supplied on physical media such as a disk, unless the language of the licence agreement clearly specifies that the media is 'sold' and the program and the user manual is 'licensed and supplied' only.

Thus, in order for a software licence agreement to be analysed by a court as such, the agreement must be a valid, unadulterated, and uncontaminated contract. The legal concept of a sale is stronger than the legal concept of a licence and they are inconsistent concepts. The concept of a licensed copy of software will be overcome by the concept of a sold copy of software if the software licence agreement is invalid (defeated), adulterated (not genuine), or contaminated by actions outside of the agreement's terms (not pure, ie not treated as a software licence transaction).

In contrast, the concept of a software lease is consistent with the concept of a software licence. Where the licence is a licence to possess and use, a software lease is virtually identical to a software licence although often these days entered into by way of a monthly rental as 'software as a service' (SaaS) hire. The lease conveys a personal property right to possess and use the leased item and the licence conveys an intellectual property right to possess and use the licensed intellectual property. The very existence of such a lease may be interpreted as conveying such a licence. However, the concept of a software licence is broader than the concept of a software lease because the licence concept is not limited to usage: it can cover reproduction, distribution, etc. In addition, a software licence agreement is not always a financing vehicle. Royalty-free licences are granted in some situations where non-monetary consideration is involved. The traditional lease financing of large value computer systems is a different idea from the SaaS service for standard software products so perhaps is a fourth category.

In mass-market software products the language of the transaction and marketing invariably includes the words 'sale', 'product', 'sale price', 'goods'. However, this is often an inaccurate description to which the courts are unlikely to give much weight when deciding if statutory rights attaching to the sale of goods rather than the supply of resources and materials apply.

As referred to above the judgment in *UsedSoft GmbH v Oracle International Corp* confirms that the author of software cannot oppose the resale of 'used' licences allowing the use of such programs downloaded from the internet where the licences were granted on a perpetual basis rather than for a fixed term. The exclusive right of distribution of a copy of a computer program covered by such a licence is exhausted on its first sale for such perpetual licences. Briefly the facts were that Oracle developed and distributed online computer programs functioning as 'client/server software'. The customer of such a program was entitled to download it on the basis of a licence agreement for an unlimited period exclusively for the customers' internal business purposes. UsedSoft was a German business which marketed software licences acquired from customers of Oracle by which customers of UsedSoft were able to download a copy of the program from Oracle's website after acquiring a 'used' licence. Oracle brought proceedings against UsedSoft in the German courts seeking an order for it to cease its marketing and sales practices.

In its judgment the European Court of Justice explained that 'the principle of exhaustion of the distribution right applies not only where the copyright holder markets copies of his software on a material medium (CD Rom or DVD) but also where they distribute them by means of downloads from his website. Where the copyright holder makes available to his customer a copy – tangible or intangible – and at the same time concludes, in return for payment of a fee, a licence agreement granting the customer the right to use that copy for an unlimited period, that right holder sells the copy to the customer and thus exhausts his exclusive distribution right'. The case was purely about perpetual licences and how competition law might affect restrictions on the 're-sale' of such licences even where the licence is personal to the licensee only. It does not apply to licences where the software is licensed or hired for a limited time.

The case above indicates, amongst other things, that perpetual licences will almost certainly be perceived as a sale however purely in relation to the issue of enforceability of clauses restricting assignment within the licence, rather than a licence and software owners should consider licensing on a fixed-term basis in order to prevent the exhaustion of the distribution right.

1   Court of Justice of the European Union 3 July 2012 judgment in case C/128/11.
2   [1996] 4 All ER 481.

2 Some general types of software licence agreements

2.1 DEVELOPER-PUBLISHER LICENCE AGREEMENTS

A developer-publisher licence agreement is an important type of software licence agreement for all categories of software: mainframe. These contracts are commonplace but vary in their approach to significant terms. For example, the licence grant may transfer the developer's copyright interest to the publisher, or the publisher may acquire an exclusive licence to distribute the software during the term of the licence agreement. Often such agreements cover several programs and it is not unusual for such agreements to cover several machine types or versions of each program, for example, an Apple Mac and Windows Mac or PC) version of each program developed.

Sophisticated developers require minimum royalty payments in these agreements plus an advance royalty payment that is returned at a rate of less than 100% of all royalties earned so that the developer receives some incremental revenue from initial copies distributed. Sophisticated developers will limit the geographical scope of the licence grant and reserve the right to market some machine types, media types, or foreign language translations directly or through other publishers.

Sophisticated publishers will set milestones for the development of each version of each program and insist that royalty advances are divided into payments that are tied to the milestones, for example, that become due only upon the publishers' acceptance or approval of the developers' work product or progress required by the milestones. Negotiations also occur over advance payments that are not recoverable as advance royalties.

In these agreements publishers must be careful to obtain the rights they need to distribute the programs as planned, to obtain warranties on all programs, to address maintenance responsibilities, to address enhancement development, etc. Developers must be careful to retain rights to their libraries or 'tool kits' of software. For example, a developer may write a component of a program known as an 'engine' for use in many programs, intending for each program ordered by various publishers to contain the engine. This component should be licensed on a non-exclusive basis so that it can be licensed to many publishers. An exclusive licence or assignment precludes multiple uses of such a component.

In the large mainframe software arena, computer vendors often assume the role of software publishers contracting with developers and customers for publication rights. Mainframe computer users commonly write or have their computer vendor's programmers write or assist in the development of unique applications or utilities. Sometimes the computer vendor will desire marketing rights for such programs in order to enlarge its libraries of software offered to other customers. Here the customer often retains ownership of the new program and grants distribution rights to the vendor. The vendor may pay a royalty, but more often provides the customer with 25-50% discount on future purchases up to a specified ceiling of discount pounds or for specified equipment or service purchases.

There are many other situations, patterns and exceptions in the general area of software development and publishing. Changes in these patterns occur from time to time and these customs are not uniform throughout the world. In general, however, developer-publisher licence agreements exist because one party develops or contracts for the development of software but has no interest in attempting to market the software developed, while another party wants to market new programs as part of its mainstream business but would not undertake internal development of the program in question for one or more reasons.

Remember that development projects are seldom completed on schedule, that they often generate disputes and that litigation often arises in relation to failure to deliver on time or failure to match specification. Developer-publisher arrangements are complex transactions that call for careful thought, attention, and negotiations by both parties. It is highly desirable to build dispute resolution mechanisms into the software development agreement rather than ignore the potential for problems in developer-publisher relationships. Also, acquiring outside help in negotiating and drafting the agreement is often prudent and well worth the cost.

Finally, it is important to ensure from the customer's point of view that the contract contains a rolling transfer of the ownership during and after development of the program where it is agreed title to the program will pass. If the publisher needs ownership of IPR in the program it needs this in the part-developed program as well as the finished program, because if the publisher has to terminate the contract before the program is completed, say for persistent failure of the developer to 'hit milestones' then the publisher needs title to the part-developed program in order to get the work completed elsewhere. To the extent that core technology of the developer will never be released, perhaps a source code escrow needs negotiating so that underlying technology can be used to complete the program.

2.2 PUBLISHER-DISTRIBUTOR LICENCE AGREEMENTS

2.2.1 Domestic distributors, OEMs and VARs

UK software publishers typically distribute copies of software through various means. Mainframe software publishers employ representatives to market their products directly to users.

Microcomputer software publishers can afford the overhead costs of an extensive in-house representative force only if many of their products are relatively expensive. Such programs might have licence fees ranging between £5,000 and £30,000, for example. Most microcomputer software publishers market less expensive products and hence cannot support many, if any, in-house representatives. As a result of this factor and others, such as an understandable desire to maximise market penetration, recover research and development costs, and maximise profit, many microcomputer software publishers market their products through original equipment manufacturers ('OEMs'), value added resellers ('VARs'), and distributors with their own sales forces. National accounts are also of major importance to many microcomputer software publishers. Large retailers with chains of outlets in several regions are the typical account for such publishers. In fact, one of the major decisions facing such publishers in the context of marketing strategy is whether to distribute their products exclusively through distributors, through distributors and OEMs or VARs, through national accounts as well as distributors, OEMs and VARs, through mail order, through independent sales representatives, or through some other mechanism or combination of means.

One of the recurring legal problems arising from the use of multiple distributors, OEMs, VARs, national accounts, independent sales representatives and combinations of these and others to market software is the publisher's failure to keep the contracts with each of these parties consistent. Contracts are written so that national accounts encroach on distributors' territories, so that OEMs and VARs violate sales representatives' exclusive rights to market to specified types of customers, etc. In the EU and UK certain exclusive distribution arrangements may be in breach of competition laws. Often these inconsistencies arise because of a lack of attention to such details by management, but they are notorious as the source of problems for microcomputer software publishers, microcomputer manufacturers, CD-ROM database publishers, etc. In-house or outside legal and administrative personnel can help maintain consistency in such agreements and cost less than the damages awarded or settlements paid when no one oversees contract consistency.

Another major area of concern in domestic distribution arrangements of many types is protection of the publisher's intellectual property rights. Without a carefully drafted software licence agreement for the arrangement, a publisher could find the trade secrets embedded in their code entering the public domain, they could lose their rights in their trademarks on the product, and they could lose the ability to recover copyright infringement damages from software pirates. Intellectual property law protections available for the protection of software assets function under specific conditions, limitations and restrictions. Software publishers who desire to protect their assets should gain a basic understanding of these legal protections and employ competent help to safeguard their software assets.

Distributors have their own legal concerns, such as ensuring proper calculation and receipt of payment through clear payment terms in their agreements with publishers. One of the growing items of concern for distributors, OEMs, VARs, and others who market software published by others is the possibility of product liability claims against the distributor as well as the publisher in connection with certain types of software, for example, software that operates medical examination or treatment equipment, software used to design buildings, etc. Product liability insurance and carefully drafted contracts that protect the distributor from such claims as much as possible are increasingly important.

2.2.2 Foreign distributors, OEMs and VARs

UK software publishers often have the opportunity to distribute their products abroad during the first few years of operation. Mainframe software publishers vary in their approach to international distribution. Some companies work through agents, distributors, or joint ventures in foreign countries.

Microcomputer software publishers use widely diverse means to distribute their products abroad. Only a small percentage of such publishers can afford to pay a sales staff in foreign countries so it is common for UK microcomputer software to be distributed to foreign nationals by mail, telecommunications, distributors, agents, OEMs, VARs, joint ventures, etc.

Another factor unique to foreign distribution arrangements is the impact of the laws of the countries of the software users and of some international treaties on the validity of international distribution contracts, on the effectiveness and operation of specific terms and conditions, and on the protection of UK publishers' intellectual property rights in their software. Patent, copyright and trademark treaties can help UK software publishers protect their programs in countries that are signatories to the treaties provided the requirements of local laws are satisfied. The United Nations Convention on the International Sale of Goods (of which the UK is not a part) can influence not only computer and software sales, but also some software distribution and user licence agreements. In general, UK software publishers can be unpleasantly surprised by foreign laws and the operation of treaties on their international transactions as easily as they can be pleasantly surprised if they do not learn how these laws and treaties affect their business before they distribute their products abroad.

Other major factors that may influence foreign disseminations of software in some countries include foreign tax requirements, statutory requirements for extra-contractual termination payments, restrictions on the repatriation of funds, and limitations on the validity of exclusive relationships, to name a few.

2.3 USER LICENCE AGREEMENTS

2.3.1 Signed licence agreements

User licence agreements typically give a computer user a conditional right to use the licensed software and no right to distribute it as contracted with VAR/distributor and OEM arrangements. The common conditions on continued use include timely licence fee payments, continued compliance with a prohibition on reverse engineering (but always stating this limited as required by EU and UK law), continued compliance with restrictions on the transfer of the licensed copy, use of the software on only one computer, at only one computer site, etc. Mainframe software publishers typically require signed licence agreements with their customers before they deliver programs. These agreements may be negotiated on one or more points prior to customer acceptance, and they are often valid and enforceable contracts. Even if these contracts are pre-printed documents that are signed unchanged, they will normally be enforceable against a mainframe computer user. Of course, there are noteworthy exceptions to this general rule.

2.3.2 Shrink-wrap licence agreements

Many software publishers distribute their products under different types of contracts. Publishers of expensive microcomputer programs can afford to have employees call on prospective customers, negotiate terms and obtain signatures on contracts.

More common business applications, educational and entertainment programs rarely generate sufficient revenue to support a nationwide field sales force. Such programs are generally marketed through sales staff, distributors, VARs, OEMs, etc. Attempts to have retail clerks obtain signatures on licence agreements were failures. Users shopping in retail stores and these days online usually preferred to acquire another package whose publisher did not require a signed licence agreement or to acquire the same package in another store whose assistants did not insist upon a signed contract as a condition to its acquisition. To increase the likelihood of research and development cost recovery, to maximise licence fees, and in an attempt to maximise legal protections, publishers of business applications and utilities employed 'shrink-wrap' licence agreements. The most common version of a shrink-wrap licence agreement appears was on the outside of the box or container for the software and could be read through a clear plastic wrapper around the box or container. These days it is rare to buy software in a box and much of it is licensed after being 'hired'/licensed online for a monthly fee or on a perpetual licence basis for a one-off fee. There is no box although the licensing concept is similar but better- users 'click' to accept the terms.

In contrast, most publishers of educational and entertainment software programs elected to sell copies of their software and ignored the use of a shrink-wrap licence agreement. Thus, buyers might buy copies of such programs in the same way they would have bought copies of books in a book store. Such programs are typically distributed in object code and protected by copyright law. The use of software locks, keys and dongles as an added safeguard against piracy are common.

Shrink-wrap licence agreements attempt to accomplish many of the same things that signed licence agreements attempt to accomplish. Payment terms, restrictions on usage, and prohibitions on licensee transfers, loans, rentals, etc, of the licensed copy of software are common to both types of agreements. Prohibitions on reverse engineering, limited warranties, limitations of liability, consequential damages exclusions, and limitations on recoverable damages are also common to both types of agreements. The major difference between a signed licence agreement and a shrink-wrap licence agreement is that the latter is not signed by the user, hence the validity of the shrink-wrap licence agreement is more open to question than the typical signed licence agreement.

Shrink-wrap licence agreements typically provide that opening the package or using the software constitutes acceptance of the agreements' terms and conditions. The problem with this concept is not that one's actions cannot signify contract acceptance, rather that there is probably no 'meeting of the minds' between the licensor and the user. Users typically believe they are purchasing copies of software bearing shrink-wrap licence agreements. At least some users would not acquire such software if they thought they were not purchasing the copy acquired. Actions signifying a meeting of the minds between two parties can constitute contract acceptance, but generally the actions must clearly signify that meeting of the minds before a valid contract is formed.

Another traditional criticism of shrink-wrap licence agreements is that they are contracts of adhesion. In other words, when one party has a far superior bargaining position and can force contract terms on the other by adopting a take-it-or-leave-it stance, a court may decide it is against public policy to enforce such a contract of 'adhesion'. Such decisions are most common when the party in the inferior bargaining position is a consumer and the party in the superior bargaining position is a merchant. Because the party acquiring microcomputer software bearing a shrink-wrap licence agreement is sometimes an individual who has no opportunity to negotiate the agreement, the possibility of an adhesion contract analysis was foreseen.

In an attempt to avoid meeting-of-the-mind and adhesion contract attacks on shrink-wrap contracts, many microcomputer software publishers allow customers to return unopened packages for a full refund. Nevertheless, conventional wisdom among computer law practitioners is that the simple shrink-wrap licence, unsupported by statute or other mechanisms, is likely to be deemed a sale agreement upon judicial analysis. The Consumer Rights Act 2015 contains protection for those who make digital downloads of products such as software (in addition to containing consumer warranties where physical goods are purchased). This was a new development under UK law in 2015 but is only applicable to consumers buying from businesses.

Before online purchase became so common, in those days the absence of validating legislation, some microcomputer software publishers had adopted the tactic of repeating the licence agreement's terms and conditions on initial screens of the microcomputer software program and requiring the user to press the return or enter key to signify his acceptance of the terms and conditions. This approach may not have been sufficient to create a valid and enforceable contract. For example, if the licence agreement is placed on 'optional' screens that can be avoided by the operator, or that do not appear unless the operator selects a menu item that makes them appear, then the operator is likely to avoid the licence agreement-bearing screens and never signify acceptance to its terms and conditions. Even if the screens are 'mandatory' or cannot be avoided, a user could press the return or enter key without reading or accepting the terms and conditions. Sophisticated software publishers will not only place the licence agreement's terms and conditions on mandatory initial screens following the 'splash' or first screen, but will also require the user to add a statement to the effect that they have read and accepted the terms and conditions and require the insertion of the user's name. If either is not inserted, the user should not be able to move on to the main menu or next screen. While this approach is not foolproof, it seems to be the best variation of the screen approaches.

Sophisticated software publishers will not stop here, however, in their attempts to ensure the validity of their shrink-wrap licences. Another approach in the old days was to include a response card with the microcomputer software program that addresses not only the availability of enhancements and other programs, but also states that by signing the response card the user accepts the terms and conditions of the shrink-wrap licence agreement. Signing of the card is couched as an alternative to the other actions of opening the package or using the software, any one of which signifies acceptance. Of course, one problem with this approach is that the user can nullify it by simply failing to sign and return the response card. Screens bearing the shrink-wrap licence (two or more are usually needed to capture all of the terms and conditions) and response cards are not the only options available to microcomputer software publishers to validate their shrink-wrap licence agreements. Whenever an organisation desires numerous copies of the software, the publisher can supply a signed master agreement covering all copies acquired. Such an agreement could be complete as to every detail, repeating and superseding relevant provisions of the shrink-wrap licence agreement as well as adding others, in which case the agreements packaged with any copy received by the user might be irrelevant. On the other hand, the master agreement could leave the shrink-wrap licence agreements' terms and conditions operational by simply incorporating them by reference as parent of the master agreement, in which case the user organisation's execution of the master agreement would signify acceptance of both the master agreement and the provisions of the shrink-wrap licence agreements accompanying copies of the software received by the user organisation.

Two cases in 1996, *Beta Computers (Europe) Ltd v Adobe Systems (Europe) Ltd*[1] under Scots law, and *PRO CD Inc v Zeidenberg*[2] under US Law have both reinforced the validity of shrink-wrap licence agreements provided the customer has the opportunity to read and, if necessary, reject the terms by returning the product within a reasonable period.

Of course, the reality that returns might so occur must be an issue addressed between the provider and the dealer who actually distributes the product to the customer.

The reality is that since the early editions of this book were published the physical purchase of software on a disk has become very rare for most users and instead the software is downloaded (or for more sophisticated products installed by the licensor) on the licensee's computer and usually there is no doubt at all that the licence terms apply. Indeed, most consumer buyers of software are unable to proceed to payment unless they have clicked to accept the terms (see **2.3.3** below – Click-wrap licence agreements). Where the buyer is a business and uses purchase orders to purchase but with no signed licence agreement or software as a service contract then the licensor has the same issues as in the days of shrink wrapped under English common law as the licensor needs to ensure its terms apply so will need to ensure that is achieved eg, by rejecting terms on a licensee/buyer's purchase order and responding with its own terms.

1   [1996] FSR 367.
2   No 95-C-0671-C (US 7th Cir CA, 20 June 1996).

2.3.3   Click-wrap licence agreements

As seen above these are digital variations of the shrink-wrap licence agreements and are becoming almost universal by 2023 electronic e-commerce, cybertrade and web-site shopping where no paper contract precedes or follows the making of a contract by the provider and customer.

Where demonstration software, databases, e-journals or internet shopping malls are accessible in a provider's web-site the customer must scroll through an on-screen licence agreement and can only make a purchase after reaching the end of the licence and signifying acceptance by e-mailing acceptance to the provider or sending his credit card details or clicking a particular key, this confirming agreement to the licence terms.

Because such click-wrap licence agreements are in standard forms and are accessed remotely by the customer, there is little or no room for negotiation. The UK's Consumer Contracts (Information, Cancellation and Additional Charges) Regulations 2013 which in the UK replaced the earlier EC Directive on Distance Selling[1] (discussed in part II, **section 4.9**) will also apply as will the Consumer Rights Act 2015 in the UK and the EC Directive on Unfair Contract Terms in the EU[2] so that suppliers will have to ensure such agreements are clearly written, contain no unfair terms and provide 'cooling off' periods.

The US case of *i.LAN Systems, Inc. v Netscout Service Level Corporation*[3] has confirmed that a click wrap licence agreement is enforceable but, under Massachusetts law would be interpreted under the Uniform Commercial Code.

In addressing the case Chief Judge Young said:

'Has this happened to you? You plunk down a pretty penny for the latest and greatest software, speed back to your computer, tear open the box, shove the CD ROM into the computer, click on "install" and, after scrolling past a license agreement which would take at least fifteen minutes to read, find yourself staring at the following dialog box: "I agree." Do you click on the box? You probably do not agree in your heart of hearts, but you click anyway, not about to let some pesky legalease delay the moment for which you've been waiting. Is that "click wrap" licence agreement enforceable? Yes, at least in the case described below.'

Of interest in this case was that i.LAN Systems were a reseller of Netscout's products. i.LAN had signed a detailed value added reseller agreement. i.LAN having signed the VAR agreement, then placed a purchase order for software products. The software products as delivered to i.LAN were subject to a click-wrap agreement which included language to the effect that nothing in the click-wrap agreement would affect any pre-existing agreements between Netscout and its licensee.

The click-wrap agreement contained the usual limitation of liability clauses and limited warranty clauses which the court held i.LAN had accepted when it clicked 'I agree'. In reaching this decision the court followed the leading US case on enforceable shrink-wrap contracts, namely *ProCD, Inc. v Zeidenberg*.

1   [1997] OJ L144/97/7.
2   [1993] OJ L95/93/13.
3   183 F.Supp.2d 328.

2.4   ESCROW AND TTP AGREEMENTS

Software or technology escrows sometimes involve a licence agreement. Software escrows historically become important when the software user licenses an important or critical application in object code and there is no commercially available substitute that could be acquired and placed in use on short notice and at a reasonable cost. If the software publisher fails to maintain and enhance the software as required by the licence agreement, or if the publisher falls into bankruptcy, the user would need the program's source code and technical information about the source code in order to continue to maintain and enhance the important or critical program. The frequency with which software publishers have liquidated or fallen into bankruptcy over the years helps to give rise to such concerns.

Of course, users are not the only parties who demand the creation of software escrows. Distributors, OEMs, VARs, joint venture partners, and others worry about the non-performance, liquidation or bankruptcy of software publishers. Any of these parties could inquire about or demand a source code escrow arrangement.

Software escrows are a subset of a broader type of escrow known as the technology escrow. The major difference between the two is that a software escrow arrangement is limited to software and related items including updates, enhancements, technical documentation, user documentation, flow charts, etc; while technology escrows are used for non-software as well as software technology. Technology escrows are used by inventors and participants in research and development joint ventures to substantiate the creation of their inventions and the timing of those inventions, by government contractors to comply with the demands of procurement RFPs, and by others. The inventions or technology of such parties may or may not involve or include software.

There are various approaches to software escrows. The software publisher may establish an escrow in advance of customer demand, or in response to customer demand. The escrow may serve more than one customer or only a particular customer. The escrow agent may be one of the party's banks, insurance companies, accountants or attorneys, or it may be an independent escrow company whose primary business is escrow service. Generally speaking, sophisticated users prefer an independent escrow provider to an agent of one of the parties.

The reason the parties cannot simply provide in a contract between licensor and licensee that if the licensor goes into liquidation the software source code will be handed to the licensor for repair purposes only. is because UK insolvency legislation under the Insolvency Act 1986, s 178 allows administrators and liquidators to disclaim onerous contracts. By entering into what is often a tripartite agreement between licensor, licensee and an escrow agent such as the NCC and lodging the source code with that agent the user can obtain a copy of the software without the risk that the onerous contracts provision can be used by the liquidator. Another reason is to ensure the licensee can obtain access to the source code relatively quickly in such a case.

The escrow arrangement typically requires the software publisher to transfer a copy of source code to the escrow service provider who is required by contract to deliver a copy of the source code to one or more users upon the failure of the publisher to maintain the program licensed by the user(s) in executable code form, or upon the bankruptcy of the publisher. The escrow service provider may hold a copy of the source code under a licence agreement with the publisher, or may take title to a copy of the source code. The user may receive a copy of the source code from the escrow service provider under a licence from the provider, or under the terms of the user's executable code licence agreement. Alternatively the user may own the copy of the source code received from the source code provider, or other arrangements could be worked out. In any event, licence agreements between publishers and escrow service providers, and licence agreements between escrow service providers and software users are both considered escrow licence agreements.

Of course, one option to a source code escrow arrangement is for the publisher to give the user a copy of the source code, but many publishers are understandably reluctant to do so. Another alternative is for the user to plan on acquiring a commercially available substitute program if the original program crashes and is not fixed or otherwise becomes unusable in part or in whole. This approach makes an escrow unnecessary but requires confidence by the user that such substitutes will be available and capable of being quickly utilised whenever the need for them arises.

The UK's leading escrow agency, the National Computing Centre (NCC),[1] has published a range of escrow agreements.[2]

Trusted Third Party (TTP) agreements are a variation upon escrow agreements and are becoming used in the area of cryptography and e-commerce. In order to provide certification or authentication of cryptographic keys and digital signatures used in cybertrade transactions a number of corporations and bankers are offering their services as TTPs who hold in escrow algorithms and keys of the cybertraders in order to provide if requested a verification service.

The terms upon which they are licensed to hold such information and materials are contained in a TTP agreement.

1 NCC Group plc (previously National Computing Centre and NCC Escrow International Ltd), XYZ Building 2 Hardman Boulevard Spinningfields Manchester M3 3AQ.
2 https://softwareresilience.nccgroup.com.

2.5 RUNTIME LICENCE AGREEMENTS

Runtime licence agreements typically arise in the context of a microcomputer software developer or publisher developing a new program that incorporates a component or elements from another developer, for example, the code comprising the 'engine' of the program. Copies of the new program containing code from both developers will be distributed to users. The engine, which enables the new program to operate on a microcomputer, is licensed from its developer in an agreement that allows the new program creator to use the engine in his development work and then to reproduce and distribute copies of the new program containing the engine and the creator's code. This licence agreement also allows the new program creator's customers to operate or 'run' the engine portion of the new program under the creator's standard user licence agreement for the entire program. Sometimes the engine developer will require all users to sign a separate licence agreement with the engine developer in addition to licensing the remainder of the program from its creator under a signed or shrink-wrap licence agreement. Some engine developers do not require a separate user's agreement but insist that the program creator's standard user agreement contain certain protective provisions that benefit the engine developer as well as the program creator. In any event the engine developer often charges a royalty for every copy of the new program distributed as well as a fee for the program creator's acquisition, use, and reproduction of the engine code.

2.6 MANUFACTURING LICENCE AGREEMENTS

A manufacturing licence agreement can be distinguished from a typical user licence agreement in that the former allows the licensee to make or reproduce numerous copies while the latter allows the user to operate or use a single copy of the licensed product and may allow the user to make one or a few backup copies. These days as software is not being copied on to disks, any distributor/VAR/OEM arrangement is likely to provide that the licensee is given by the distributor access to the licensor's product and the distributor does not make copies of it.

The manufacturing licence agreement was used long before software was invented and is still used by patent owners for all types of patented devices and formulas. The patent owner would license another party to make the patented invention and perhaps to sell units as well. When patent attorneys and inventors of patented devices talk about licence agreements they often mean this type of manufacturing licence agreement. If a patented device includes software, then software reproduction and perhaps distribution is covered by such a licence.

For non-patented software the closest thing to a manufacturing licence agreement is a licence from a software publisher to a 'reproduction house' or distributor to reproduce copies of the software on magnetic or other media such as CD-ROM. A reproduction house is the equivalent of a printer printing copies of a book which are forwarded to the publisher's order fulfilment warehouse. In contrast a distributor will reproduce, stock, and distribute copies of the software.

In each context the right to make or reproduce copies of the item in question is separate from the right to sell or otherwise distribute copies of the item and the licence will have only those rights granted in the licence agreement.

2.7 CROSS-LICENSING AGREEMENTS

Cross-licensing agreements traditionally arise in the context of two or more patent owners licensing other(s) to make, use, or sell their respective patented inventions. Such agreements can also arise in the context of patented or non-patented software, for example, where two software publishers license the other to distribute their respective programs to a type of customer or in a territory that the licensor has not penetrated.

The key to a cross-licensing agreement is that part or all of the consideration for the agreement is the reciprocal licence grant for each party's products. Cross-licensing agreements may be most common where the parties are located in different countries or have a different customer base in the same country, but they typically arise where the parties' respective rights block the other in the marketplace or where both parties want to distribute the other's products. Always check for compliance with the Competition Act 1998 in the UK and Articles 101 and 102 of the Treaty on the Functioning of the European Union in relation to cross-licensing to ensure there is no breach of competition law in such arrangements, particularly if the two parties are competitors. For example paragraph 12 of the EU's IPR Guidelines (2014 version in force 2023) state: 'For instance, where two undertakings established in different Member States cross licence competing technologies and undertake not to sell products in each other's home markets, (potential) competition that existed prior to the agreement is restricted.'

Paragraph 20 also says

'Technology is an input, which is integrated either into a product or a production process. Technology right licensing can therefore affect competition both upstream in input markets and downstream in output markets. For instance, an agreement between two parties which sell competing products downstream and which also cross license technology rights relating to the production of these products upstream may restrict competition on the downstream goods or services market concerned. The cross licensing may also restrict competition on the upstream market for technology and possibly also on other upstream input markets. For the purposes of assessing the competitive effects of licence agreements it may therefore be necessary to define the relevant product market(s) as well as the relevant technology market(s).'

There is a lot of detail on cross-licensing in the above mentioned IPR Guidelines which are useful even for copyright licensing, albeit that the EU's Technology Transfer Block Exemption Regulation 316/2014 (which still applies in the UK despite Brexit, as at 2023) only applies to exempt certain patent and knowhow licensing agreements from EU/UK competition law.

2.8 JOINT VENTURE LICENSING AGREEMENTS

Joint venture licensing agreements often arise where one party has a distribution capability for a product which its developer lacks, or where two or more parties join in a research and development effort to create new technology that both can use and/or distribute. In the former context, the parties share costs and profits in some defined manner. Thereby the agreement is distinguishable from a simple distribution arrangement where there is little if any cost sharing and the distributor typically receives a fee regardless of the publishers' profits or lack thereof.

In the context of a research and development joint venture, mutual investment and established technology contributions are commonplace. The new technology developed by the joint venture's personnel is usually shared by the investors for their use and often may be incorporated in their products. Cost and risk sharing are key elements in this context.

Again, with joint ventures particularly between competitors, always consider the competition law implications. For competitors even forming the venture may breach competition law. For non-competitors the issue is more likely to be whether any-competitive restrictions have been included in the agreement between the parties forming the joint venture.

2.9 CORE TECHNOLOGY LICENCE AGREEMENTS

The core technology of a company is the technology that generates or allows the generation of the bulk of the company's revenue. A core technology licence agreement typically allows another party to either use or distribute the core technology. The licence agreement must be carefully negotiated and drafted and the consideration paid to the licensor should justify the risks inherent in licensing core technology. Sometimes government agencies insist on such licences. Also, these licences are found most frequently where the technology in question is near the end of its useful or market life, or where the licensor is desperate for funds or plans to sell his company.

2.10   SOFTWARE CONVERSION AGREEMENTS

Software conversion agreements arise in various contexts and may involve virtually any type of software. Conversions from one computer to an incompatible computer fairly often involve both data and software conversions from one data format and software operating system environment to another. Data conversions are virtually inescapable in this context, but the user can avoid a software conversion by deciding to utilise new software on the new computer. Readers will know the differences that can arise between apps which will run on an iPhone but not on an Android mobile telephone and vice versa, although often versions are issued for both kinds.

Software conversions also arise where the user retains an existing computer but wants to acquire a program that will not operate on the existing computer. Here the user may contract for the conversion work. Another context in which conversion work is common is in the development context. For example, a microcomputer software developer might be asked to develop a new program that would operate on a Windows PC and other, incompatible computers such as a Mac PC or in the case of games software for Xbox or Nintendo Switch. In this context, the developer might develop one program and convert the others from the first. The other programs are frequently called 'conversions'. In contrast, in the mainframe software arena, the process of changing the software and/or data is known as the 'conversion'. Thus, in some contexts a conversion means a program, and in others a conversion means a transaction.

Conversion transactions are among the most complex transactions involving software. They rarely progress without glitches. They often generate heated disputes and cost overruns. Carefully planned conversion transactions that are captured in carefully drafted contracts are most likely to be successful, and minimise the risk of cost overruns and disputes. Conversion transaction agreements are thrown in file drawers after execution like most other contracts, but conversion agreements rarely stay in the file because they are working project documents, because of the extreme likelihood of cost overruns and because of the frequency of disputes.

2.11   DATABASE AND ACCESS SOFTWARE LICENCE AGREEMENTS

Databases distributed on floppy disks or compact disks such as CD-ROMs are often accompanied by access programs that permit the user to gain access to their contents. These days it is quite rare for software and databases to be supplied otherwise than via a download however. Commercially available online databases also require access codes, and such programs are distributed separately or are built into custom-made terminals supplied by the database publisher.

These access programs are often distributed under shrink-wrap licence agreements for a nominal charge. While online database providers do not necessarily want competitors to reproduce and distribute portions or all of their access code, many feel that copies should be distributed freely or at a nominal charge in the hope or expectation that usage of their databases might increase. Hence, some are willing to give away unlicensed copies of their access programs or dispense with the traditional shrink-wrap licence agreement and employ an online agreement purportedly accepted by some action of the user.

Publishers of databases distributed on floppy disks, compact disks, or tapes are usually more concerned about protecting their access programs. They may require a signed licence agreement that covers both their databases and their access software. Reverse engineering of their access software or its piracy is a sensitive issue for these publishers because their major assets, the databases, may become accessible by competitors or unlicensed users if the access software is penetrated and used in an unauthorised manner. If the databases are recorded on compact disks, and the data is arranged in a proprietary format, the access code can take considerable time and money to develop and may be a major asset of the database publisher.

2.12 MAINTENANCE SERVICE LICENCE AGREEMENTS

It is common for the software owner to license the software and also provide maintenance service. However, independent maintenance providers have slowly grown in importance to software users for several reasons. Sometimes these service providers offer a lower cost alternative to the vendor's maintenance service. In addition, many software companies have gone out of business and hence are not available to provide maintenance service. Independent maintenance service providers may fill the void, especially when the user's data processing staff has neither the time nor the knowledge required to maintain the system.

Software providers commonly discontinue standard maintenance on old releases of programs at or near the end of their market life. The alternatives for users of such programs are either to try to maintain the systems themselves, pay the software provider for maintenance service on a time and material basis or contract with an independent maintenance house for the service. The last alternative may be the most sensible and economical, assuming a suitable escrow agreement is already in place.

The same situation arises concerning old releases of a program still marketed in a current release several steps advanced from the user's old release. Software providers will offer a standard maintenance contract and fee for the current release and perhaps the one or two latest releases before the current edition of the software, but will not indefinitely continue to offer standard maintenance service and charges for early releases of the program. Here again the independent maintenance service provider may fill the void.

Whatever may trigger the use of an independent software provider, maintenance will be virtually impossible without a copy of the source code for the program. The independent maintenance service provider will need to obtain a copy of the source code from someone, either the user, an escrow agent or the software provider. If the source code is obtained from the latter source, the software provider is likely to license its use to furnish maintenance service. If the source code is obtained from an escrow agent, the agent may require the maintenance company to sign a licence agreement. Such agreements are examples of maintenance service licence agreements.

2.13 FACILITIES MANAGEMENT AGREEMENTS

Facilities management ('FM') or outsourcing agreements are very common within the computer industry particularly as companies believe it will save them money or have 'returned to their core activities'.

Many companies have decided it is more cost effective and more manageable to sub-contract to a third party some or all of the information technology services previously handled in-house.

Many computer providers have for years offered bureaux services and indeed a number of companies built their entire reputation upon such services and then diversified to other areas.

The facilities management agreements are either negotiated during the life of an existing computer system so that the hardware and software as they exist are transferred to the FM company with or without all of the transferor's personnel or are negotiated at the start of the installation of a new system where the outsourcing service is often provided by the provider itself.

Often the more crucial part of a facilities management agreement relates to the level of service to be provided by the FM company but inevitably the issue of intellectual property rights and software licensing becomes part of the negotiations and where outsourcing takes place during the life of an existing software agreement, problems will occur where the existing software licence does not provide for the right to assign and the FM company therefore cannot get the right that it needs in order to carry out the service that it has sought to negotiate for.

Facilities management agreements and outsourcing agreements in general are a complex area and are subjects worthy of entirely separate consideration from this book. However, many of the legal and commercial issues relative to software licensing are as equally relevant to facilities management agreement negotiations.

2.14 WEBSITE AGREEMENTS

As more businesses engage third-party developers and internet service providers to build and manage interactive websites for the internet, so licence agreements are becoming more sophisticated in relation to the development of the site and its interactivity, the licensing rights and the provision of ongoing maintenance and support.

In complex websites where the full range of audiovisual material is used, the developer may be required to procure third-party rights to use certain material, may develop specific application software programs and incorporate third party authorising tools, all of which the customer will require licensing to.

In the event that the developer fails adequately to maintain the website or goes into liquidation, then the customer will require an escrow agreement in respect of source code.

2.15 OPEN SOURCE LICENCES

2.15.1 Introduction

What if you had the right to obtain a free upgrade whenever your software needed it? What if, when you switched from a Mac to a PC, you could switch software versions without incurring an additional charge? What if the software does not work or is not powerful enough, you can have it improved or even fix it yourself?

What if the software were maintained even if the company that produced it went out of business? What if you could use your software on your office workstation, your home desktop computer, and your portable laptop, instead of just one computer? These are some of the rights that Open Source gives you.

The Open Source Definition is a bill of rights for the computer user. It defines certain rights that a software licence must grant you to be certified as Open Source. Programs like the Linux operating system and Netscape's web browser have become extremely popular, displacing other software that has licences that are more restrictive. Companies that use Open Source software have the advantage of its very rapid development, often by several collaborating companies, and much of it contributed by individuals who simply need an improvement to serve their own needs.

Programmers feel comfortable contributing to Open Source because they are assured of the following rights:

- the right to make copies of the program, and distribute those copies;

- the right to have access to the software's source code, a necessary preliminary before you can change it; and

- the right to make improvements to the program.

These rights are important to the software contributor because they keep all contributors at the same level relative to each other. Anyone who wants to is allowed to sell an Open Source program, so prices will be low and development to reach new markets will be rapid.

Anyone who invests the time to build knowledge in an Open Source program can support it, and this provides users with the option of providing their own support, or the economy of a number of competing support providers. Any programmer can tailor an Open Source program to specific markets in order to reach new customers. People who do these things are not compelled to pay royalties or licence fees.

2.15.1.1   Open Source – A Warning

However plenty of business buyers of software commissioning programs from a provider want to own copyright and include clauses prohibiting any open source being used in the resultant product so this is not such a similar issue as open source is always best, not least because the open source licences are not a free for all but instead often contain tight restrictions on future use which those commissioning software do not want to find applies to their software in any way. See **2.15.5** below for more details.

2.15.2   Historical analysis of the Open Source movement

Richard Stallman has popularised free software as a political idea since 1984, when he formed the Free Software Foundation and its GNU Project. Stallman's premise is that people should have more freedom, and should appreciate their freedom. He designed a set of rights that he felt all users should have, and codified them in the GNU General Public Licence or GPL. Stallman christened his licence the 'copyleft' because it leaves the right to copy in place. Stallman himself developed seminal works of free software such as the GNU C Compiler, and GNU Emacs.

The Open Source Definition started life as a policy document of the Debian GNU/Linux Distribution. Debian, an early Linux system and one still popular today, was built entirely of free software. However, since there were other licences than the copyleft that purported to be free, Debian had some problem defining what was free, and they had never made their free software policy clear to the rest of the world.

2.15.3   The Open Source Definition

The Open Source Definition is not itself a software licence. It is a specification of what is permissible in a software licence for that software to be referred to as Open Source. The Open Source Definition was not intended to be a legal document. To be Open Source, all of the terms below must be applied together, and in all cases. They should be applied to derived versions of a program as well as the original program. It's not sufficient to apply some and not others, and it is not sufficient for the terms to only apply some of the time.

Open Source does not simply mean access to the source code. The distribution terms of an Open Source program must comply with the following criteria:

2.15.3.1   *Free redistribution*

The licence may not restrict any party from selling or giving away the software as a component of an aggregate software distribution containing programs from several different sources. The licence may not require a royalty or other fee for such sale.

This means that you can make any number of copies of the software, and sell or give them away, and you do not have to pay anyone for that privilege. The 'aggregate software distribution containing programs from several different sources' was intended to fit a loophole in the Artistic Licence, a rather sloppy licence originally designed for Perl. Today, almost all programs that use the Artistic Licence are also available under the GPL.

2.15.3.2   *Source code*

The program must include source code, and must allow distribution in source code as well as compiled form. Where some form of a product is distributed without source code, there must be a well-publicised means of downloading the source code, without charge, via the internet. The source code must be the preferred form in which a programmer would modify the program. Deliberately vague source code is forbidden. Intermediate forms such as the output of a pre-processor or translator are not allowed.

Source code is a necessary preliminary for the repair or modification of a program. The intent here is for source code to be distributed with the initial work, and all derived works.

2.15.3.3   *Derived works*

The licence must allow modifications and derived works, and must allow them to be distributed under the same terms as the licence of the original software.

The intent here is for modification of any sort to be allowed. It must be allowed for a modified work to be distributed under the same licence terms as the original work. However, it is not required that any producer of a derived work must use the same licence terms, only that the option to do so be open to them. Various licences speak differently on this subject – the BSD licence allows you to make modifications private, while the GPL does not.

2.15.3.4 Integrity of the author's source code

The licence may restrict source code from being distributed in modified form only if the licence allows the distribution of 'patch files' with the source code for the purpose of modifying the program at build-time.

Some authors were afraid that others would distribute source code with modifications that would be perceived as the work of the original author, and would reflect poorly on that author. This gives them a way to enforce a separation between modifications and their own work without prohibiting modifications. Some consider it un-aesthetic that modifications might have to be distributed in a separate 'patch' file from the source code. Linux distributions like Debian and Red Hat use this procedure for all of the modifications they make to the programs they distribute.

Note also that this provision says that in the case of patch files, the modification takes place at build-time. This loophole is employed in the Qt Public Licence to mandate a different, though less restrictive, licence for the patch files, in contradiction of section 3 of the Open Source Definition. There is, however, a proposal to clean up this loophole in the Definition while keeping Qt within Open Source.

The licence must explicitly permit distribution of software built from modified source code. The licence may require derived works to carry a different name or version number from the original software.

This means that Netscape, for example, can insist that only they can name a version of the program Netscape NavigatorTM while all free versions of the program must be called Mozilla or something else.

We generally accept that when we have to pay for a licence to use software then we are bound to observe the software licence and acknowledge the copyright of the software owner. However, it is often presumed that if software is free then copyright and licence terms are no longer applicable.

That is not the case and indeed has recently been confirmed in the US in the case of (1) *Jacobson v Katzer* and (2) *Kamind Associates Inc*, 13 August 2008. The above case from the US Appeals Court confirms that where a royalty free Open Source software product was used in breach of its licence the breach was not only of contract but also of copyright. The Court rejected the argument that because the software was distributed on a royalty free basis the copyright owner had no economic rights to enforce and confirmed that the law of copyright applies to Open Source licences as much as it does to freeware.

This US case highlights that whilst copyright in software generally denotes the licence to use copyright in return for some economic benefits, it does not preclude the economic benefit from being generated other than by money. In other words, Open Source licences which allow royalty free use in return for the ability to generate market share through brand awareness or reputation need to be supported by not only contract terms but also the law of copyright.

2.15.3.5   No discrimination against persons or groups

The licence must not discriminate against any person or group of persons.

2.15.3.6   No discrimination against fields of endeavour

The licence must not restrict anyone from making use of the program in a specific field of endeavour. For example, it may not restrict the program from being used in a business, or from being used for genetic research.

2.15.3.7   Distribution of licence

The rights attached to the program must apply to all to whom the program is redistributed without the need for execution of an additional licence by those parties.

The licence must be automatic, no signature required. Unfortunately, there has not been a good court test in the US of the power of a no-signature-required licence when it is passed from a second party to a third. However, this argument considers the licence in the body of contract law, while some argue that it should be considered as copyright law, where there is more precedent for no-signature licences.

2.15.3.8   Licence must not be specific to a product

The rights attached to the program must not depend on the program's being part of a particular software distribution, if the program is extracted from that distribution and used or distributed within the terms of the program's licence. All parties to whom the program is redistributed should have the same rights as those that are granted in conjunction with the original software distribution.

This means you cannot restrict a product that is identified as Open Source to be free only if you use it with a particular brand of Linux distribution, etc. It must remain free if you separate it from the software distribution it came with.

2.15.3.9   Licence must not contaminate other software

The licence must not place restrictions on other software that is distributed along with the licensed software. For example, the licence must not insist that all other programs distributed on the same medium must be Open-Source software.

2.15.4 Examples of licences

The GNU GPL, BSD, MPL, X Consortium, and Artistic licences are examples of licences that are considered conformant to the Open Source Definition.

2.15.5 Analysis of licences and their Open Source compliance

To understand the Open Source Definition, we need to look at some common licensing practices as they relate to Open Source.

2.15.5.1 Public domain

A common misconception is that free software is public domain. This happens simply because the idea of free software or Open Source is confusing to many people, and they mistakenly describe these programs as public domain. The programs, however, are clearly copyrighted and covered by a licence, a licence that gives people more rights than they are used to.

A public-domain program is one upon which the author has deliberately surrendered their copyright rights. It cannot really be said to come with a licence; it is the holder's personal property to use as they see fit.

If you are doing a lot of work on a public-domain program, consider applying your own copyright to the program and re-licensing it. For example, if you do not want a third party to make their own modifications that they then keep private, apply the GPL or a similar licence to your version of the program. The version that you started with will still be in the public domain, but your version will be under a licence that others must heed if they use it or derive from it.

You can easily take a public-domain program private, by declaring a copyright and applying your own licence to it or simply declaring 'All Rights Reserved'.

2.15.5.2 Free software licences in general

One can be forgiven for the mistaken belief that programs on a Linux disk are your own property. That is not entirely true. Copyrighted programs are the property of the copyright holder, even when they have an Open Source licence like the GPL. The licence of the program grants you some rights, and you have other rights under the definition of fair use in copyright law.

It is important to note that an author does not have to issue a program with just one licence. You can GPL a program, and sell a version of the same program with a commercial, non-Open Source licence. Many people who want to make a program Open Source and still make some money from it use this exact strategy. Those who do not want an Open Source licence may pay for the privilege, providing a revenue stream for the author.

All of the licences have a common feature: they each disclaim all warranties.

2.15.5.3 *The GNU General Public Licence*

This licence is simple: everyone is permitted to copy and distribute verbatim copies of this licence document, but changing it is not allowed. An important point here is that the text of the licences of Open Source software are generally not themselves Open Source. Obviously, a licence would offer no protection if anyone could change it.

The provisions of the GPL satisfy the Open Source Definition. The GPL does not require any of the provisions permitted by paragraph 4 of the Open Source Definition, Integrity of the Author's Source Code.

The GPL does not allow you to take modifications private. Your modifications must be distributed under the GPL. Thus, the author of a GPL-ed program is likely to receive improvements from others, including commercial companies who modify his software for their own purposes.

The GPL does not allow the incorporation of a GPL-ed program into a proprietary program. The GPL's definition of a proprietary program is any program with a licence that does not give you as many rights as the GPL.

There are a few loopholes in the GPL that allow it to be used in programs that are not entirely Open Source. Software libraries that are normally distributed with the compiler or operating system you are using may be linked with GPL-ed software; the result is a partially free program. The copyright holder (generally the author of the program) is the person who places the GPL on the program and has the right to violate his own licence. However, this right does not extend to any third parties who redistribute the program – they must follow all of the terms of the licence.

In early 2007 The Free Software Foundation (https://www.fsf.org/) published a discussion draft of version 3 of the GPL (and of LGPL – see below) in order to address certain commercial issues arising from an agreement between Microsoft and Novell under which Microsoft agreed to refrain from asserting its patent rights against Novell customers in the event that Microsoft patents were found in Novell's software.

2.15.5.4 *The GNU Library General Public Licence*

The LGPL is a derivative of the GPL that was designed for software libraries. Unlike the GPL, a LGPL-ed program can be incorporated into a proprietary program. The C-language library provided with Linux systems is an example of LGPL-ed software – it can be used to build proprietary programs, otherwise Linux would only be useful for free software authors.

An instance of an LGPL-ed program can be converted into a GPL-ed one at any time. Once that happens, you cannot convert that instance, or anything derived from it, back into an LGPL-ed program.

The rest of the provisions of the LGPL are similar to those in the GPL – in fact, it includes the GPL by reference.

2.15.5.5 The X, BSD and Apache licences

The X licence and its relatives the BSD and Apache licences are very different from the GPL and LGPL. These licences let you do nearly anything with the software licensed under them.

The most important permission, and one missing from the GPL, is that you can take X-licensed modifications private. In other words, you can get the source code for a X-licensed program, modify it, and then sell binary versions of the program without distributing the source code of your modifications, and without applying the X licence to those modifications. This is still Open Source, however, as the Open Source Definition does not require that modifications always carry the original licence.

Many other developers have adopted the X licence and its variants, including the Berkeley System Distribution (BSD) and the Apache web server project. A feature of the BSD licence is a provision that requires you to mention (generally in a footnote) that the software was developed at the University of California any time you mention a feature of a BSD-licensed program in advertising.

Keeping track of which software is BSD-licensed in something huge like a Linux distribution, and then remembering to mention the University whenever any of those programs are mentioned in advertising, is somewhat of a headache for business people. The Debian GNU/Linux distribution contains over 2,500 software packages, and if even a fraction of them were BSD-licensed, advertising for a Linux system like Debian might contain many pages of footnotes! However, the X Consortium licence does not have that advertising provision.

2.15.5.6 The Artistic Licence

Although this licence was originally developed for Perl, it has since been used for other software.

Section 5 of the Artistic Licence prohibits sale of the software, yet allows an aggregate software distribution of more than one program to be sold. So, if you bundle an Artistic-licensed program with another of the licensed program you can sell the bundle. This feature of the Artistic Licence was the cause of the 'aggregate' loophole in paragraph 1 of the Open Source Definition.

The Artistic Licence requires the programmer to make modifications free, but then gives a loophole (in section 7) that allows modifications to go private or even place parts of the Artistic-licensed program in the public domain!

2.15.5.7 The Netscape public licences and the Mozilla public licence

NPL was developed by Netscape when they made their product Netscape Navigator Open Source. Actually, the Open Source version is called Mozilla; Netscape reserves the trademark Navigator for their own product.

An important feature of the NPL is that it contains special privileges that apply to Netscape and nobody else. It gives Netscape the privilege of re-licensing modifications that you have made to their software. They can take those modifications private, improve them, and refuse to give you the result. This provision was necessary because when Netscape decided to go Open Source, it had contracts with other companies that committed it to provide Navigator to them under a non-Open Source licence.

Netscape created the MPL, or Mozilla Public Licence, to address this concern. The MPL is much like the NPL, but does not contain the clause that allows Netscape to re-license your modifications.

The NPL and MPL allow you to take modifications private.

Many companies have adopted a variation of the MPL for their own programs. This is unfortunate, because the NPL was designed for the specific business situation that Netscape was in at the time it was written, and is not necessarily appropriate for others to use.

2.15.6 Choosing a licence

2.15.6.1 Do you want people to be able to take modifications private or not?

If you want to get the source code for modifications back from the people who make them, apply a licence that mandates this. The GPL and LGPL would be good choices. If you do not mind people taking modifications private, use the X or Apache licence.

2.15.6.2 Do you want to allow someone to merge your program with his own proprietary software?

If so, use the LGPL, which explicitly allows this without allowing people to make modifications to your own code private, or use the X or Apache licences, which do allow modifications to be kept private.

2.15.6.3 Do you want some people to be able to buy commercial-licensed versions of your program that are not Open Source?

If so, dual-license your software. Use the GPL as the Open Source licence; then find a commercial licence appropriate for the code you add to the program.

2.15.6.4 Do you want everyone who uses your program to pay for the privilege?

If so, perhaps Open Source is not for you.

The table below gives a comparison of licensing practices:

Licence	Can be mixed with non-free software	Modifications can be taken private and not returned to you	Can be re-licensed by anyone	Contains special privileges for the original copyright holder over your modifications
GPL	NO	NO	NO	NO
LGPL	YES	NO	NO	NO
BSD	YES	YES	NO	NO
NPL	YES	YES	NO	YES
MPL	YES	YES	NO	NO
Public Domain	YES	YES	YES	NO

2.15.7 The future

With more and more software hosted in the cloud and collaboration between software developers online, Open Source is likely to continue to be an important area. Although the UK's large project 'UK-GOV Verify' (which UK readers may know if they have an on-line government gateway account, eg, for tax returns) was started before the UK Government's new policy *Coding in the Open,* open source is not within that new policy, since that project has moved to an open source basis – see https://technology.blog.gov.uk/2019/02/18/opening-the-gov-uk-verify-hub-source-code/.

This is illustrative of what many state and private sector bodies have done in recent years.

2.16 APPLICATION SERVICE PROVIDER LICENCES

At the end of the last century a new phenomenon in the field of software licensing was the development of the application service provider concept ('ASP'). Computer software owners began licensing their products to independent intermediaries who then loaned or rented for specific periods and/or specific purposes the original licensor's software to end users. An ASP enables customers to avoid the expense of purchasing licences for indefinite periods when they might only want to use the licensed product for a short period. For example, a user might permanently require Microsoft Office products such as Word and PowerPoint but might only occasionally require Excel or Publisher.

In a strict ASP scenario the licensor, the software owner, usually licenses the ASP the right to provide customers with the right to use on a 'rented' basis, the licensor's software. This is almost a 'pay as you go' concept., hire.

A number of ASPs have found themselves in breach of the owner's rights, because they have not put in place appropriate licences from software owners to rent out the use of the software to customers.

In many ASP scenarios, the customer may uplift its data to the ASP's website and, using the ASP server, carry out data processing tasks. One of the difficulties here is that the processing activities will be carried out on the ASP server and not the customer's server and may, therefore, put the customer in breach of any obligations it may have under UK GDPR/the Data Protection Act 2018 in relation to personal data that is being processed by or on third-party systems.

Other than the hosted aspect of the ASP licence terms and the payment mechanisms, most of the ASP licence terms will be the same as in any other software licence agreement.

2.17 SOFTWARE AS A SERVICE (SAAS)

In the past 20 years or so there has been a move from customers outsourcing their licensed software management to third parties (such as applications service providers) offering their solutions on a hosted basis to customers.

SaaS has itself moved into the Web 2.0 community where applications can be used on an almost 'pay as you go' basis with customers using services hosted outside their office environment, small software vendors providing hosted services through large application providers such as Google and providers such as Google offering hosted services to corporations large and small. This complex web of software services is often referred to as 'cloud computing'.

Many SaaS solutions are provided on a 'one too many' basis and as a consequence many of the solutions are generic and not tailored to individual users' requirements. The mass market nature of SaaS means that licences are standardised and negotiation is limited to key issues.

Whereas outsourcing did not preclude tailoring of software and services, SaaS solutions are generally not bespoke but therein lies a risk. The 'day-by-day' nature of many SaaS solutions means that the concept of a fixed product does not exist and the importance of support becomes critical. The software and solutions that SaaS providers make available are regularly updated and intellectual property rights remain with the SaaS provider. By 2023 this is the most common method for most standard software products such as Microsoft Office including Word to be licensed to office workers and indeed home users with a personal computer or laptop. However not all users prefer this. It is indeed by analogy whether a user prefers to buy a car out right or have it in effect on hire with fees continuing forever. There are advantages and disadvantages of each approach.

Whereas in outsourced arrangements the software remained in the 'ownership' of the customer, in a SaaS situation ownership remains with the SaaS provider and on termination of any contractual arrangement the customer has little or no opportunity to 'port' to another solution. Back-up is therefore critical as are issues over data protection and information security. The following checklist may be useful to consider for SaaS/Cloud agreements:

- Basic charges.

- Licence fees.

- Charge per user.

- Configuration and integration.

- Consultancy issues.

- Support and maintenance.

- Escrow.

- Data protection.

- Information security.

- Transfer of services.

- Applicable law.

- Warranties and indemnities.

Part II
Laws and regulations

3 Introduction to laws relevant to software contracts

3.1 OVERVIEW

Every jurisdiction has its own national laws which vary for protecting intellectual property rights. In the UK the law which applies includes the Copyright, Designs and Patents Act 1988, the Patents Act 1977 and the Trade Marks Act 1994. In the US the Patent Act, the US Commercial Code, the Copyright Act, the Uniform Trade Secrets Act and various state laws all apply to intellectual property in computer programs.

Intellectual property is a bundle of rights including patents, copyright, design rights, trademarks registered and unregistered designs and topographies for semiconductor products and such rights attach to a variety of inventive or creative efforts such as music, literary works, designs and, amongst other things, computer programs. Allied to IP rights, but not an intellectual property right, are rights in confidential information/trade secrets.

On occasions some if not all of the bundle of intellectual property rights may relate to a software licence and the major areas of law which apply domestically and internationally to software licence agreements and other software contracts are discussed below.

Warning: Always take advice from lawyers qualified in the relevant jurisdiction under which a contract's laws are based.

3.2 PATENT LAW

Most foreign countries have an absolute novelty standard that requires the patent application in that country to be filed before any sale of the invention or offer to sell it and before any publicity, advertising, or distribution of promotional literature that describes the invention sufficiently to disclose it to the public. Disclosing the invention without a confidentiality agreement also nullifies your ability to obtain a patent in many of these countries. Note that these disclosures may be in the US or elsewhere, not only in the foreign country in question, and they will be sufficient to preclude you from obtaining a patent in the foreign country. Also, in most foreign countries the first to file the application for an invention or discovery will obtain the patent. The US moved from 'first-to-invent' system where a subsequent filing claiming an earlier discovery or invention date would obtain the patent to first to file from 16 March 2013 by virtue of the America Invents Act.

Under English law an inventor may patent an idea (or invention) but copyright only protects the expression of the idea. The idea or the invention to be patentable must be new, involve an inventive step, be capable of industrial application and must not be one of the statutory exceptions of which a 'computer program' is one and 'a method of doing business' is another.

Whilst patent protection in the UK has not always been regarded as appropriate for computer software, there have been a number of applications. However, these have generally been unsuccessful because the Hearing Officer has either regarded the application as being in respect of a computer program and thereby excepted, or the result of the use of the program is merely a method of doing business, thereby being also excepted (see Merrill Lynch's Application (1989)). A good summary on software patenting in the UK is at https://www.govgrant. co.uk/knowledge-hub/can-you-patent-software-in-the-uk/. In the UK, software cannot be patented 'as such'. However it is part of an overall invention it may be capable of patent protection. However, patents expire after 20 years so the longer protection of copyright and the fact there are no copyright fees in the UK is not always a disadvantage; although to prove breach of copyright, copying must be shown, which is not a requirement to show breach of patent.

Warning: Never write a patent. This is a specialist skill even intellectual property solicitors in the UK would never do. Patent agents/attorneys who are members of a separate profession and often members of the Chartered |nstitute of Patent Attorneys (CIPA) and have science degrees and have trained for years in patent drafting are the ones to write a patent. Many an inventor has lost their rights forever by trying to write a patent without such professional help.

Following the US case of *State Street Bank & Trust Co v Signature Financial Group Inc*,[1] it has become important to consider the value of patenting software.

In the *State Street Bank* case the court addressed Signature Financial Group's patent which was directed to a data processing system for its 'hub and spoke financial services configuration' which was an investment structure in which mutual funds ('Spokes') pooled together assets in an investment portfolio ('Up') which operated as a partnership. It was claimed that the structure achieved economies of scale and the tax benefits of a partnership. When negotiations for a licence between the State Street Bank and Signature Financial broke down, the bank sued to have the patent declared invalid on the basis that it was 'a method of doing business' which under US Patent Law was an invalid subject matter for a patent.

The Federal Circuit in abandoning the 'method of doing business' exemption found that since the software produced a useful concrete and tangible result, it was inventive enough to be the subject matter for a patent application.

With so many web products being driven by software technology it becomes important to view patent protection as a more valid route than was previously the case. It becomes equally as important for any business to carry out patent searches to establish at as early a date as possible the fact that their developments do not infringe already filed patent applications for third parties.

The European Patents Convention enables a single application to be made for designated patents in signatory countries or to the European Patents Officer in Munich which permits patents for software where its application has a novel technical effect although its members may not all permit such patents under their national laws. In the European Patent Office guidelines it is stated that, amongst other things, 'a computer program claimed by itself or as a record on a carrier is unpatentable irrespective of its content. The situation is not normally changed when the computer program is loaded into a known computer but patentability should not be denied merely on the ground that a computer program is involved in its implementation'.

The UK Patents Act 1977 provides patent protection for 20 years and for countries which are signatories to the European Patent Convention the term is for the same period. Whilst it may appear harder and, therefore, less desirable to obtain patent protection in the UK than it may be in other countries such as the US, this is still no reason to discount patent protection as a means of securing suitable rights for software.

The Court of Appeal delivered an important judgment on the rights of employers to claim ownership of employee inventions. The claimants lost and their employer was held to own the inventions (which were US inventions further to complicate matters and which would not be patentable in the UK.) The decision in *LIFFE Administration & Management v Pavel Pincava (1) and De Novo Markets Ltd (2)*[2] was at the time the first Court of Appeal judgment on the employee invention provisions in nearly 30 years. It is of particular relevance given the widespread development of inventions which may not be patentable as such in the UK, notably computer software, business methods and so-called 'blue sky' research. The importance of these types of inventions to business is increasing given the increased reliance on computer software and automated business processes which were of course of significantly less importance to business when the Patent Act 1977 came into force. The current case demonstrates the importance of careful drafting of employment contracts and employment policies for businesses in relation to employee inventions, intellectual property and confidentiality provisions.

The UK Patents Court has ordered compensation to be paid to two employee inventors as compensation for the outstanding benefit of the patent to the employer, but held they did not own the inventions.

Section 40(1) of the Patents Act 1977 provides that compensation may be awarded to an employee where it appears to the Court that:

'(a) the employee has made an invention belonging to the employer for which a patent has been granted,

(b) having regard among other things to the size and nature of the employer's undertaking, the invention or the patent for it (or the combination of both) is of outstanding benefit to the employer, ...'.

All inventions by employees (during the course of their employment and within their normal duties) belong to the employer. However, there may in very limited cases be an entitled to some compensation under s 40. in the case of a patent of 'outstanding benefit' but the benefit must flow from the invention not eg, the excellent marketing skills of the employer.

More recently in *Shanks v Unilever PLC and others* [2017] EWCA Civ 2 (Court of Appeal) it was held by the Court in 2017 that Unilever was such a large company that an employee's – Professor Shanks' – invention was de minimis by comparison and no compensation was due. Section 40 refers to the need for the benefit to be relative to the 'size and nature of employer's undertaking'.

In the earlier decision in this long-standing litigation which only ended in 2017, in *Shanks v Unilever Plc & Others* [2014] EWHC 1647 (Pat) the Court held that Professor Shanks, an ex-Unilever employee could not recover damages for an invention under these provisions. In an even earlier decision in the case, the Court of Appeal had ruled on an initial issue that he could not recover what Unilever might have made from the invention had it properly exploited it and only a share of what it did make. In the event, he was found to be entitled to nothing. Shanks assumed that Unilever should have made at least US$1 billion but in fact it made only £23 million from the invention. A good summary of the 2017 judgment is on line at http://ipkitten.blogspot.co.uk/2017/02/too-big-to-pay-employee-inventor.html.

The above decision makes it clear that it is very hard in the UK (in contrast with other countries like Germany) for inventors who are employees to claim compensation under s 40. Their monthly salary from their employer is regarded as their payment for the work they do not matter how well the employer does out of the said work.

Talented and creative employees are extremely valuable to many companies and employers use not only contractual controls and restrictions on those employees to ensure that their creativity benefits the employer, but also induce loyalty by share option schemes, incentive schemes and compensation arrangements particularly in the field of research and development. What is interesting is that the level of compensation payable to an employee as a result of a patent of outstanding benefit may be in addition to any existing employee benefits. It is quite common for inventors employed by companies to be given small prizes and in universities sometimes there is a formal scheme where inventors may be paid up to 10% of the profits the university claims, under the terms of a specific contract between the employee and the university.

On 18 May 2009 the Intellectual Property Office published a Decision under the Patents Act 1977 in favour of Fisher-Rosemount Systems, Inc on the issue as to whether or not four particular patent applications numbered GB 0419580.6, GB 0419583.0, GB 0724070.8 and GB 0724072.4 were excluded from patentability as a program for a computer by s 1(2)(c) of the Patents Act 1977.

The four applications related to reconfiguring a process control system associated with a process plant. The process control system of the invention included workstations which stored and executed applications used to configure and monitor a process plant, a configuration database which stored configuration data generated at the workstations and the number of process devices throughout the process plant.

The Patents Act 1977 indicates that a patent may be granted only for an invention in respect of which the grant of patent is not excluded by s 1(2) (c)— namely that invention must not be 'a scheme, rule or method for performing a mental act, playing a game or doing business, or a program for a computer'.

The general approach to deciding whether an invention is excluded from patentability is the four-step test laid down by the Court of Appeal in *Aerotel /Macrossan*[3] namely:

1. properly construe the claim;

2. identify the actual contribution;

3. ask whether it falls solely within the excluded matter; and

4. check whether the contribution is actually technical in nature.

In the *Fisher-Rosemount* Decision the hearing officer, applying the four step test, reached the conclusion that the use of the computers did not exclude the inventions from patentability and in particular that the invention, albeit utilising computer software, made a technical contribution.

The *Fisher-Rosemount* Decision continues to reinforce the fact that computer generated inventions or inventions that rely upon computer programs should seriously be considered for patent protection notwithstanding the relatively restrictive regime in the UK.

There have been a number of software patent cases since, and in 2023 the UK Government has been consulting on some intellectual property issues arising from artificial intelligence – see https://www.gov.uk/government/consultations/artificial-intelligence-and-ip-copyright-and-patents/outcome/artificial-intelligence-and-intellectual-property-copyright-and-patents-government-response-to-consultation which in part concluded that it would not allow commercial companies to breach copyright in harvesting data online.

It looked at:

● copyright protection for computer-generated works (CGWs) without a human author;

● licensing or exceptions to copyright for text and data mining (TDM), which is often significant in AI use and development;

● patent protection for AI-devised inventions.

In early 2023 the UK Minister for Science, Research and Innovation stated in Parliament that the government will not be proceeding with an extension to the UK's text and data mining exception to copyright infringement which would have allowed more access to materials needed for machine learning and to train AI systems. This is consistent with current UK copyright law.

1 149 F 3d 40368 (Fed Cir 1998); Cert denied 1999.
2 [2007] EWCA Civ 217.
3 Sub nom *Aerotel Ltd (A Company Incorporated Under the Laws of Israel) v Telco Holdings Ltd, Telco Global Distribution Ltd, Telco Global Ltd* [2006] EWCA Civ 1371.

3.3   COPYRIGHT AND DATABASE LAWS

Copyright is at the core of intellectual property right protection for computer software and globally is recognised as the main protection for the rights of the owner.

Copyright arises in the expression of an idea whereas patents arise in the idea itself. Therefore, the concept or idea behind a piece of software may not necessarily be protected by copyright until such time as it is reduced to written form.

Until recent years in many countries computer software was not specifically referred to in statutes as having its own right to protection for copyright purposes. Certainly in the UK in the Copyright Act 1956 there was no mention of computer programs and therefore copyright was deemed to apply to computer programs because they were 'written' and therefore might well be regarded as 'literary works' which were specifically referred to in the Copyright Act 1956.

The Copyright, Designs and Patents Act 1988 (CDPA 1988) replaced previous UK copyright statutes. CDPA 1988 specifically refers to computer programs as being a literary work and, therefore, being entitled to copyright protection. However, copyright only subsists under CDPA 1988 if the work is original, whether or not the work is generated by human or computer provided that there is writing which is defined as 'any form of notation or code', whether by hand or otherwise and regardless of the method by which, or medium in or on which, it is recorded!

The author, that is the person who creates the work, is generally regarded as the copyright owner except that where the software program is made by an employee in the course of their employment the employer is the first owner of copyright.

If the work is created by an employee under a contract of employment but outside the normal course of their employment, the work may not necessarily belong to the employer (eg, someone writing a novel in their spare time) and if the work is created by a sub-contractor, such as a freelance programmer, then since that person is not an employee again ownership will remain with that freelance programmer. It is, therefore, extremely important to ensure that there is some contractual arrangement whereby work which is carried out by an employee outside of their normal duties or is commissioned as between software publisher and freelance programmer is vested in the employer, otherwise difficulties may occur in the future. There is an assumption that where a company commissions the writing of computer software upon payment of the appropriate fee, title in the computer work vests in the commissioner. This is not the case, as has been learnt to the cost of many businesses.[1] Programmers who are contracted to major companies and institutions through agencies are usually signed to agreements whereby all intellectual property rights are owned by the company but as more and more work is 'done on the move' or by means of 'teleworking' there is always the risk that work created outside the usual company's offices may not always belong to the company but may remain with the programmer.

It should be remembered that copyright prevents third parties from copying the work of the copyright owner and copyright will attach to the work, not to the idea that underlies the work. It should, therefore, be remembered that where the idea for a particular piece of software is generated the idea as such does not have the benefit of copyright protection until it is reduced to written form.

The case of *Kabushi Kaisha Sony Computer Entertainment v Edmunds (trading as Channel Technology)*[2] shows that UK copyright law in the guise of the Copyright, Designs and Patents Act 1988, s 26 will enable copyright owners to successfully prevent copy protection devices from being used in the UK. In this case, Sony successfully obtained summary judgment against the defendants on the ground that they were importing into the UK from Russia a computer chip which allowed users to circumvent the copy protection codes implemented in Sony's Playstation 2 consoles.

On an international basis it is important for the provider and the customer to have agreed specific contractual licensing provisions because the degree of protection afforded to software varies from jurisdiction to jurisdiction. The Berne Convention is the most widely observed international treaty relating to copyright. No formalities are necessary to obtain copyright protection.

The Universal Copyright Convention is another international treaty where, for protection to exist, a copyright notice must appear on published works and in certain jurisdictions a deposit of the work or its registration is necessary before protection applies.

In the 1990s a number of EU member states introduced a voluntary registration system for software programs, namely, Italy, Spain and Portugal, where deposit of a software program in its object code form and upon payment of a small fee may provide the copyright holder with certain presumptive rights of ownership which may be of use in infringement proceedings.

A voluntary registration scheme has existed in the UK since 1911 whereby a copy of the copyright work (the program) may be deposited upon payment of a fee with the Register of Copyright at Stationers' Hall in London and a certificate is issued to the copyright holder thereby asserting their copyright. This scheme has become more popular in recent years with the increase in piracy and as a means of further reassurance for the copyright owner in infringement proceedings. At the beginning of 2000 Stationers' Hall ceased to offer its registration scheme. There is no need nor possibility to register copyright under English law. In the US where it is possible it is usually only done when litigation is in prospect.

Whilst it is not necessary to display any statement or wording regarding copyright on a software product in order to obtain copyright protection it is generally felt good practice to display a copyright statement as an assertion of copyright ownership and statement to the world at large as well as to the licensed user. Therefore, where the owner of a computer program wishes to assert or further enforce copyright ownership, the statement that is usually suggested is as follows:

'© [name of copyright owner] [year of first publication]'.

Often the words 'all rights reserved' are added to the copyright statement. These words are intended to mean that apart from copyright, all other intellectual property rights are reserved or retained by the copyright owner.

The usual places to display the above copyright statement are:

- on all packaging for the software product;

- on the front cover or inside front cover of any accompanying documentation and user manuals;

- as an opening page on the first loading of the program so that the copyright statement is clearly displayed as the program is 'scrolled through'; or

- physically on the media within which or upon which the program is embedded or incorporated.

The extent to which copyright arises in the 'look and feel' of a computer program or part of a computer program has been the subject of much litigation in the US, although no Supreme Court rulings have been given on the issue. There have, however, been a considerable number of Circuit Courts of Appeal decisions but their analyses have not been uniform.

In the US, copyright protection extends to the literal elements of a computer program such as the source code and object code but there is no clear decision on how much of the non-literal 'look and feel' of a computer program can be protected by copyright.

The first test, a simple 'sweat of the brow' test was applied in the case of *Whale Associates Inc v Jaslow Dental Laboratories Inc*,[3] but this test was subsequently replaced by the 'abstraction-filtration-comparison' test developed by the Second Circuit in *Computer Associates International Inc v Altai Inc*.[4] This test employs first, a consideration of the computer program at all levels of abstraction, thus permitting a detailed analysis of all of the structural components of the program from the general functions of the program to specific line by line coding. The test also involves a filtration step to attempt to define elements which are protectable for copyright purposes as being expressions of an idea from those elements which comprise the concept of the idea of the program itself. Finally, the comparison test compares the protected expression of the idea within the computer program to the allegedly infringing program using a 'substantial similarity' test.

The Computer Associates test found favour in the Tenth Circuit case of *Gates Rubber CO v Bando Chemical Industries Ltd*.[5]

The First Circuit's decision in *Lotus Development Corpn v Borland International Inc*[6] took a slightly different view of testing what is capable of copyright protection and proposed that first, one should analyse and identify the idea, concept and methodology involved in the program and thereafter examine to see which of those elements were essential to the expression of the idea and which were not. The court then proposed that it should be considered whether or not the unessential elements were capable of copyright protection.

Under UK law the first 'look and feel' decision was given in the case of *John Richardson Computers Ltd v Flanders and Chemtec Ltd*[7] where the US approach was followed drawing on the *Computer Associates* test. However, in the case of *IBCOS Computers Ltd v Barclays Mercantile Highland Finance Ltd*,[8] the reliance upon US tests was criticised by the court and the test to be applied as laid down by Jacob J is:

(1)   what are the work(s) in which copyright is claimed?;

(2)   is each work original?;

(3)   was there copying from that work?;

(4)   if there was copying, has the substantial part of that work been reproduced?

The European Court of Justice (ECJ) decision in *British Horseracing Board v William Hill*[9] has narrowed the *sui generis* database right, the right which protects database owners against unlawful extraction and manipulation of the contents of databases. The right exists where there is 'a substantial investment in obtaining, verifying, or presenting the contents of the database'.

The ECJ has ruled that an 'investment ... in obtaining ... the contents' of a database refers to 'resources used to seek out existing materials and collect them in the database'. Crucially, 'it does not cover the resources used for the creation of materials which make up the contents of a database'. 'Substantial' must now be assessed qualitatively as well as quantitatively in relation to the investment placed in that acquisition for the right to exist and is relative to the database from which data is being taken.

This could affect all databases viewed outside the business (either by licence or published in the public domain). In order to ensure the commercial value of such databases is fully protected, it may be wise to seek alternative means, such as:

- electronic rights management;
- rigorous licences/agreements;
- separating data collection and database creation (management between arm's-length commercial entities).

It would also be prudent to consider the means of audit trailing in cases where data 'theft' is suspected.

The look and feel sometimes is protected by copyright or even design right law so consideration should be given to all IP rights in trying to protect look and feel.

The major issue exists in relation to the 'ownership' of the data placed into the database. The database right exists only if there was substantial investment in the obtaining, verifying or presenting data forming the contents of the database. The investment is at the stage of the creation of the database and not the original creation of the data (whether prior or subsequent to that).

In terms of infringement, the amount extracted or re-utilised, has to be 'substantial' for the right to be infringed. 'Substantial' in this instance is measured against the database from which the data is taken. When measured against the database from which extraction or re-utilisation occurred, what is taken may be insubstantial but of significant economic value relative to the remnant. This could affect the value of the database as an asset, which may be disastrous for smaller publishers. The *sui generis* right would no longer offer protection.

There are two main courses of action:

- increasing the likelihood of successful litigation with the rights currently available; or
- prevention.

Although the decision has reduced the potential protection available under the *sui generis* database right there are other sources of protection. Under the Copyright, Designs and Patents Act 1988, as amended, databases are expressly protected under copyright as a literary work, using the same definition as for the database right. Despite the classification of originality imposed, the right subsists for longer (the author's life plus 70 years) and is supported by a body of case law. Databases which are sufficiently creative are protected by copyright law (and database right). Those which are not may be protected just by database right.

The careful drafting of end user agreements, licences and contracts dealing with the database or a part thereof can aid in the control of the use of data, ensuring its value to the owner.

Digital Rights Management is becoming of great importance to many industries. The means of controlling access to certain sources of data, permitting particular modes and time of access (from mere viewing through to download) and even the control of its use post-download has grown with the explosion of electronic data management. This may involve additional expense but is a relatively robust mechanism.

Finally, if the separation of data creation and acquisition with the aim of constructing a database is the key, then the separation could be achieved by ensuring an arm's-length relationship, perhaps by the creation of a new subsidiary company to undertake database creation and management, with associated agreements as to the rights. However, this is not a tested route and subsequent ECJ judgments or jurisdiction interpretation may decide otherwise (or confirm it as an option).

One low cost option is the use of auditing processes by which infringements can be traced. This at its simplest may consist of seeding data.

In a decision[10] that will be of interest to data-owners and data-users, the Court of Appeal has ruled that the British Horseracing Board (BHB) was not in breach of competition laws aimed at preventing abuse of a dominant position, by insisting on a licence agreement put in place for the supply of data, despite the fact that the data (or at least some of it) was not protected by database rights.

Attheraces Ltd (ATR) and the BHB entered into negotiations for a licence for the supply of data, including pre-race data. At the same time a dispute arose between the BHB and William Hill in which the BHB alleged that William Hill was infringing BHB's database rights in the pre-race data that was the subject of the negotiations with the ATR. That dispute was ruled in favour of William Hill and the effect of the judgment was to deny BHB database rights in the pre-race data. The decision undermined the ATR/BHB negotiations and BHB threatened to cease to supply ATR unless ATR entered into a licence and paid sums claimed to be due. In April 2005 ATR brought proceedings, claiming amongst other things that the BHB was abusing its dominant position by refusing to supply it data.

The High Court initially found in favour of ATR, ruling that the BHB's refusal to supply ATR data amounted to an abuse of its dominant position. The BHB appealed against the finding of abuse (but not that it had a dominant position). The Court of Appeal found in favour of the BHB and found that there was no abuse.

When considering the intellectual property aspects of ATR's claim (ie that the BHB's insistence on a licence to access data was unjustified in light of the decision in the *William Hill* case that the pre-race data was not protected by database rights), the Court of Appeal examined the draft agreements that were in negotiation between ATR and the BHB. It noted that at no time during the negotiations had ATR raised the issue as to whether the definition of 'data' should only include data in which the BHB had database rights. Had ATR raised these sorts of arguments, and the BHB been adamant or unreasonable in its response (perhaps by refusing to remove pre-race data from the definition of 'data'), then the outcome might have been different. However, ATR had not done so and in the overall context of the case, ATR had not established that the BHB's insistence on a licence constituted an abuse of a dominant position.

ATR was in an unusual position in this case as it was able to rely on a decision directly relating to the issue of whether database rights existed in specific data or not. In most cases it will be difficult to advise with absolute certainty whether database rights exist in specific data. Therefore, data-owners are best advised to continue to insist on licences to use their data, although where they have a particularly large market share they will need to pay heed to arguments from licensees that certain data is not protected by database rights or risk a competition law claim. Even where there are no database rights, however, there may be perfectly valid reasons for requiring a licence (eg the data being of a confidential nature) and legal advice should be sought. It is the abuse of a dominant position with which the law is concerned, not the creation and holding of the dominant position itself.

In the case of *Navitaire Inc v (1) Easyjet Airline Co (2) Bulletproof Technologies Inc*[11] Navitaire claimed that Easyjet and their software developers had infringed copyright in Navitaire's ticketless booking program by developing a similar system based on their computer language, computer commands, screen layouts, icons and business logic.

Although Navitaire did not suggest that the new Easyjet ticketless booking program had copied the underlying software of Navitaire's system they did claim that copyright had been infringed by, amongst other things, non-textual copying.

The Court held that under the Copyright, Designs and Patents Act 1988, computer languages were not in the copyright protection afforded to computer programs and that ad hoc languages such as user command interfaces were not protected by copyright either. In addition, the Court held that, as a matter of policy, business logic of a computer program should not be protected through literary copyright.

The Court did find, in this instance, that Easyjet's computer development partners, Bulletproof Technologies Inc, had infringed copyright in certain icon drawings which had been copied exactly by Bulletproof Technologies Inc.

The Court of Appeal Judgment in *Nova Productions v Mazooma Games & Ors*[12] will be of immense interest and potential concern to software developers and the owners of copyright in computer programs. In its Judgment, the Court of Appeal, following the *Easyjet* decision, confirmed that:

- it is not an infringement of copyright to make a computer program which emulates another program (including its look and feel) but which does not copy the other program's code or graphics;

- ideas which underlie computer programs are not protected by copyright; and

- no additional copyright protection, over and above protection as individual graphic works, is given to a series of images displayed in a computer program.

If a computer program is protectable by copyright but other aspects of it including computer language and commands and business logic are not so protected by copyright then, perhaps, other methods of protection should be considered, such as, patent, trade secrets and stricter licensing terms.

In the case of *Cyprotex Discovery Ltd v University of Sheffield*,[13] the UK Technology and Construction Court was faced with deciding on who was the owner of copyright in a computer program that was developed by an employee of Cyprotex as part of a Research Agreement with the University of Sheffield.

The University had developed a database known as Simcyp and in 2000, Cyprotex and the University agreed to collaborate in the creation of an improved software program based on Simcyp, but utilising more user friendly operating systems such as Windows. As part of the funding for the program Cyprotex provided the services of one of its employees. The contract that the parties entered into was poorly drafted and there was no clear definition as to who was to be the owner of copyright in not only the finished developed program, but also the developments themselves. When relationships between the parties broke down, a dispute over ownership arose, since each of the parties argued the terms of the Research Agreement gave them copyright in the program.

Part of the difficulty that the court faced was that the Research Agreement clearly expressed that copyright ownership would vest in the improvements to the computer program and also indicated that the University was allowed to license third parties and sponsors to use the resulting intellectual property in the computer program. To this extent, no statement was made about who would have ownership in the computer program itself, as opposed to the improvements to it.

The court stated that notwithstanding the common law position (that in the absence of an agreement to the contrary copyright vests in the party developing the work, in this case Cyprotex), the intention of the parties must clearly have been that the developed program and the program itself would belong to the University and therefore, were satisfied that either by virtue of the express terms of the Research Agreement or by necessary implication, ownership of copyright of the software vested in the University.

Following the Court decision, Cyprotex appealed to the Court of Appeal but once again the Court of Appeal held that the Research Agreement contemplated and indeed required that the University should recruit a programmer to produce the software, and whether or not the work was carried out by an employed programmer or a sub-contracted programmer the intention of the parties must have been that ownership would pass to the University.

It would be wise not to rely upon a court making such a decision in the future. Businesses are urged to define as clearly as possible, where ownership of copyright and all other intellectual property rights will vest under any research development or programming agreement. Moreover, businesses should remember that unless work is carried out by an employee in the course of employment, then ownership of intellectual property rights will vest in the person that carries out the work. Given the amount of use of third party developers, designers, consultants and outsourced companies, it is most important to ensure that ownership is addressed by a properly drafted and legally enforceable contract.

Following the UK case of *St Albans City & District Council v International Computers Ltd,*[14] the High Court opined (but only obiter so not part of the binding judgment) that a computer disk containing intangible software might fall within the description of 'goods' to the same extent as the tangible medium on which the software was supplied. After drawing an analogy between the tangible hardware (the disk) on which the intangible program (the software) was delivered, Sir Iain Glidewell stated that 'If the disk is sold ... but the program is defective ... there would prima facie be breach of the terms as to quality and fitness for purpose implied by the 1979 Act or the 1982 Act'. It follows that the mode employed to deliver the software ie encoded onto a disk, is just as important as the software licence terms which govern the use of the software by the licensee.

This classification has since been echoed in a number of European jurisdictions, notably by the Finnish Supreme Court[15] and in two German Courts of Appeal decisions.[16]

The legal concept of copyright is pivotal to software and software contracts. Copyright law provides the mechanisms for the controlled commercial exploitation of an author's work whilst ensuring the extensive circulation of the copyright work.

Products rich in intellectual property rights which are sold are subject to both the Sale of Goods Act 1979 and the Copyright, Designs and Patents Act 1988.

In certain circumstances, the Supply of Goods and Services Act 1982 will govern the contractual relationship between the software supplier and the end-user. This would be the case where software has been designed and developed as a result of a commissioned project. A contract of this type would be for the provision of services as opposed to the sale of goods and the supplier in this scenario would have to comply with the implied terms under the Act as well any explicit contractual terms in the supply agreement.

An important distinction needs to be drawn between the sale of intellectual property rights in the software as opposed to the sale or licence of the copy version of the software. The distinction becomes apparent between the sale of a tangible product such as a CD-ROM versus the sale of the copyright in the CD-ROM. The pivotal issue to this distinction is one of ownership of the copyright.

What is the status of software? The judiciary across the European Union appear unanimously to agree that software may indeed be classified as 'goods', as exemplified in the cases cited at the beginning of this chapter. The apparent 'consensus of the judiciary' to decree that software may be classified as goods is an alarming development for software vendors and the software industry as a whole. 'According to at least one English judge, sheer commercial expediency dictates that software be treated as "goods" lest it fall through the cracks in consumer protection legislation'. However, in the UK the Consumer Rights Act 2015 now contains specific protection for consumers where they buy a 'digital download' with slightly different warranties implied than for supply of goods or services and EU law since Brexit has continued down a similar path. Whether software is goods needs to be considered in a particular context as whether or not it is may depend on the legislation being considered. For example, under English and EU law, commercial agents who often sell on a commission basis are entitled to large lump sums of compensation or indemnity on termination of an agency agreement in the UK under the Commercial Agents (Council Directive) Regulations 1993. However this only applies to agents marketing goods, not software. In 2021, in a reference before Brexit to the CJEU from the English courts, the CJEU confirmed that downloaded software with a perpetual licence is sale of goods under agency law – *The Software Incubator Ltd v Computer Associates UK Ltd,* Case C-410/19. The CJEU ruled that the electronic supply of computer software, licensed for an unlimited period in return for payment of a fee, is a 'sale of goods' under the Commercial Agents Directive 86/653 (under which the UK's 1993 Regulations were made). The 2019 UK Supreme Court hearing can be watched online at https://www.supremecourt.uk/watch/uksc-2018-0090/280319-am.html.

Nevertheless, the intangible status of software can work to a software vendor's benefit and avoid the goods classification, providing the delivery mechanism of the software is addressed. If the software is delivered in a downloadable intangible form or is installed by the supplier on the customer's server, and the terms of the software licence uses language that indicates licence and supply, then the classification of software as goods is avoided.

If judicial consensus for classification of goods as software is a growing trend, what is the impact of the doctrine of exhaustion of rights on software distribution? Most companies will be at the mercy of this doctrine due to its significant influence over the 'extent to which the distribution of goods protected by their intellectual property can be controlled'.

The doctrine is founded on the premise that the intellectual property right holder 'exhausts' their right following the first sale of the software product. The doctrine operates on three distinct platforms: national exhaustion, regional exhaustion and international exhaustion.

The 'regional exhaustion' applies to the confines of the European Union (and since Brexit as to exports from the EU to the UK (but not vice versa)) and states that the intellectual property right holder cannot obstruct any subsequent resale of that software copy after the initial sale has been concluded.

In the decisions of the Courts of Appeal of Frankfurt am Main and Munich, the Courts based their opinion on section 69c, no. 3 of the German Copyright Act which is the result of the direct implementation of Article 4(c) of the

EU Computer Software Directive 1991 (The Directive) (which is now codified without changes into directive 2009/24/EC). The Directive states that the first approved sale of a software copy, by the intellectual property right holder within the European Union, exhausts any further distribution rights of the intellectual property right holder in relation to that software copy. The exception to this is the right to control subsequent rental of the software copy.

Software vendors supplying into the European Union and UK need to re-examine their standard end user licences to ensure that their software does not fall foul of being classified as 'goods'. Furthermore, delivering software in an intangible form or installing as part of commissioning is crucial to ensuring that the goods classification is not applicable. Such a classification will almost certainly open up Pandora's box and the grasp of the doctrine of exhaustion will not be far behind.

In the US case where an enterprising US university student imported copyright protected US textbooks sold from the US to Malaysia and then made US$700,000 exporting them back to the US, he was held to be allowed to do so as the US (unlike the EU) has worldwide exhaustion of copyright under its first sale doctrine. The starting point is always that national intellectual property statutes state that importation of even genuine non counterfeit product is a breach of IP rights. The second question is whether the rights are exhausted or not. This case was *Kirtsaeng v John Wiley & Sons Inc* (see further at: http://en.wikipedia.org/wiki/Kirtsaeng_v._John_Wiley_%26_Sons,_Inc and the article on the case in *IT Law Today* (February 2014)). For the EU see *Honda Giken Kogyo Kabushiki Kaisha v Maria Patmanidi SA* (Case C-535/13) and summary at https://ipkitten.blogspot.com/2014/08/honda-v-patmanidi-cjeu-quietly-gives.html. This held that under EU law trade marked products could be prevented from being imported from outside (as the EU does not have international exhaustion of rights).

The European Court of Justice (ECJ) decision in *British Horseracing Board v William Hill* has narrowed the *sui generis* database right, the right which protects database owners against unlawful extraction and manipulation of the contents of databases. The right exists where there is 'a substantial investment in obtaining, verifying, or presenting the contents of the database'.

Two cases have further explored the application of copyright to software and software contracts. The first case is the case of *UsedSoft GmbH v Oracle International Corp*[17] (discussed in more detail in Part 1 Section 1.6.).

The second case is *SAS Institute Inc v World Programming Ltd* [2013] EWHC 69 (Ch).[18] In 2009 the SAS Institute, creators of the SAS system, brought litigation against World Programming Ltd (WPL) on the basis that WPL had infringed copyright of SAS in both its software program and accompanying manuals. WPL did not dispute the fact that it had obtained a licensed copy of the program but relied upon the fact that, in producing a competing program that achieved the same functionality of that of SAS, it had not infringed copyright since there was no copyright in the underlying ideas of the SAS program. The case was first heard in the

High Court of England and Wales[19] where it was held that WPL infringed copyright in the SAS manuals by substantially reproducing them in the WPL manual but had not infringed copyright in the SAS software. The matter was referred to the Court of Justice of the European Union where full judgment was handed down on 2 May 2012.[20] In essence the ruling from the EWHC was that 'Article 1(2) of Council Directive 91/250/EEC' of 14 May 1991 on the legal protection of computer programs (now consolidated into Directive 2009/24/EC) must be interpreted as meaning that neither the functionality of the computer program nor the programming language and the format of data files used in a computer program in order to exploit certain of its functions constitute a form of expression of that program and, as such, are not protected by copyright in computer programs for the purposes of that Directive. Further 'Article 5(3) of Directive 91/250' must be interpreted as meaning that a person who has obtained a copy of a computer program under a licence is entitled, without the authorisation of the owner of the copyright, to observe, study or test the functioning of that program so as to determine the ideas and principles which underlie any element of the program, in the case where that person carries out acts covered by that licence and acts of loading and running necessary for the use of the computer program, and on condition that that person does not infringe the exclusive rights of the owner of the copyright in that program. Further 'Article 2 (a) of Directive 2001/29/EC' of the European Parliament and of the counsel of 22 May 2001 on the harmonisation of certain aspects of copyright and related rights in the information society must be interpreted as meaning that the reproduction, in a computer program or a user manual for that program, of certain elements described in the user manual for another computer program protected by copyright is capable of constituting an infringement of the copyright in the latter manual if – this being a matter for the National Court to ascertain – that reproduction constitutes the expression of the intellectual creation of the author of the user manual for the computer program protected by copyright.

1 *Saphena Computing Ltd v Allied Collection Agencies Ltd* [1995] FSR 616.
2 [2002] A11 ER (D) 170 (Jan).
3 609 F Supp 1307,225 USPQ 156 (ED Pa 1985).
4 23 USPQ 2d 1241 (2d Cir); amended 982 F 2d 693 (2d Cir 1992).
5 9 F 3d 823,28 USPQ 2d 1503 (10th Cir 1993).
6 49 F 3d 807, 34 USPQ 2d 1014 (1st Cir 1995).
7 [1993] FSR 497.
8 [1994] FSR 275.
9 (C-203/02) [2009] Bus LR 932.
10 *Attheraces Ltd v The British Horseracing Board* [2007] EWCA Civ 38.
11 [2004] EWHC 1725 (Ch).
12 [2007] EWCA Civ 219 (14 March 2007).
13 [2004] EWCA Civ 380.
14 [1996] 4 All ER 481.
15 (KKO 2003:88).
16 Decision of Courts of Appeal of Munich of February 12 1998 – 28U 5911/97 and the Decision of Courts of Appeal of Frankfurt am Main of November 3 1998 – 11U 20/98.
17 Court of Justice of the European Union 3 July 2012 judgment in case C/128/11.
18 *SAS Institute Inc v World Programming Ltd* [2013] EWHC 69(Ch).
19 [2010] EWHC 1829(Ch).
20 *SAS Institute Inc v World Programming Ltd* case C-406-10.

3.4 TRADE SECRET LAW

Trade secret protection may have originated in the 1851 English case of *Morison v Moat*,[1] and later it may have been first recognised in the US in a Massachusetts case, *Peabody v Norfolk*.[2] One goal in the judicial development of trade secret law has been to discourage unfair competition and trade practices. A second goal has been to encourage research and innovation.

Trade secret and the law of confidence are not designed to protect secrecy so much as to protect against the misappropriation of a secret exploited in commerce and the effort or investment required to develop the secret. The EU has a Directive 2016/943 in this area which applies to some trade secrets but not all confidential information. In the UK this was implemented by Trade Secrets (Enforcement, etc.) Regulations 2018 SI 2018/597. This did not substantially change the English law on confidentiality but does make it more important to document trade secrets to help prove infringement in litigation.

Regulation 2 of the UK 2018 regulations defines a trade secret as

"'trade secret' means information which—

(a) is secret in the sense that it is not, as a body or in the precise configuration and assembly of its components, generally known among, or readily accessible to, persons within the circles that normally deal with the kind of information in question,

(b) has commercial value because it is secret, and

(c) has been subject to reasonable steps under the circumstances, by the person lawfully in control of the information, to keep it secret;'.

As this is narrower than what English law protects as confidential information, some information will be under the above regulations but also protected by the common law of confidence and others will simply be protected by English common law.

Historically the question of how mass-marketed software could be distributed to thousands without the loss of its trade secrets was among the first generation of legal issues faced by computer law practitioners. Publishers of such software quickly decided to distribute executable code, not source code, and to attempt to license their programs just like their colleagues who published minicomputer and mainframe software.

In theory the life of a trade secret can be permanent so long as the elements of the relevant statutory or common law definition continue to be satisfied. The writer's confidentiality agreement for example usually extend without limit as to time as so much technology is secret for decades.

The types of items that may contain trade secrets and be protected by trade secret law include algorithms, source code and private databases as well as the more traditional business plans, customer lists, etc. Trade secret protection has been recognised for software, printed program instructions and magnetically recorded information.

The inadvertent disclosure of a trade secret will destroy its status as a secret as easily as an intentional disclosure might and either may result in the loss of trade secret protection.

Of course, trade secrets can be preserved through the use of valid licence agreements. Trade secret law allows reverse engineering by a party that legitimately acquires an item containing the secrets. Reverse engineering the item to discover its embedded trade secrets is a well-used practice in many industries and is used by some regarding software. A valid licence agreement with confidentiality obligations and perhaps a reverse engineering prohibition serves to preserve the status of the trade secrets as secrets.

Many foreign countries do not have trade secret laws and some who have such laws have only a very weak version of them in comparison to the UK and US. Thus contract protection for trade secrets is important in international transactions. In the UK trade secret law and confidential information applies to a wide variety of matters but computer programs, algorithms, designs for hardware, user manuals and expressions of ideas may all be regarded as being confidential information provided they are not already in the public domain and, further, that when such matters are communicated the person wishing to have the protection of trade secret laws conveys to the other party an indication that the matters concerned are treated by him as being confidential.

As has been previously stated, in the UK as well as in the US, copyright does not extend to the idea behind the software but only to the software itself whereas trade secret law may apply to the idea as well as to the expression of it, but it not an IP/property right. For example, an employee who creates a program during the course of employment will be bound under their common law duty of good faith to their employer to maintain the idea as confidential as well as the expression of the idea, namely the resulting computer program and will have created a copyright protection which, generally speaking, will pass to the employer. For confirmation that the obligation of confidence covers concepts or ideas see *Fraser v Thames Television Ltd.*[3]

As has previously been stated, the importance of the role of contractual protection as a means of controlling trade secrets law cannot be understated and wherever trade secrets or confidential information are being imparted it is extremely important to indicate clearly that such matters are regarded as being secrets and confidential information.

Despite the existence of the common law concept of trade secrets, in the software industry there has been a difficulty in recent years in preventing unauthorised access to computers or 'hacking' as it is commonly known and, whilst the Data Protection Act 1984 in the UK in its day (now UK GDPR/ Data Protection Act 2018 which may in their turn be amended by the draft Data Protection and Digital Information (No. 2) Bill 2023 when in force) did much to address the issue of protecting the confidentiality of computer stored information about individuals, it was not until the Computer Misuse Act 1990 became statute that criminal law protection against the unauthorised access to confidential information stored on computer was provided.

The Police and Justice Act 2006, amongst other things, amended the Computer Misuse Act 1990 extending the scope of a number of computer misuse offences.

The Computer Misuse Act was drafted at a time when hacking was hardly a word in common use and when denial-of-service attacks and similar activities were not envisaged.

The Police and Justice Act 2006:

- extends the scope of the hacking offence by amending the Computer Misuse Act Section 1(1) to read 'A person is guilty of an offence if (a) he causes a computer to perform any function with intent to secure access to any program or data held in any computer *or to enable any such access to be secured*; (b) the access he intends to secure, *or to enable to be secured*, is unauthorised...';

- provides for a person found guilty of hacking to be subject on summary conviction to imprisonment for a term of up to 12 months or a fine not exceeding the statutory maximum or both and on indictment, up to two years' imprisonment or a fine or both;

- amends the Computer Misuse Act to make it an offence to carry out any activity with the requisite intent or knowledge which causes an unauthorised modification of the contents of any computer (note that this wording falls short of what many security experts require to address denial-of-service attacks or the distribution of malicious code);

- provides for a new offence of making, supplying or obtaining articles for use in activities of computer misuse.

One of the difficulties, not only in the UK but on a more global basis, for businesses is that as systems become more 'open' the instances where confidential information can be easily accessed become almost limitless and whilst there is little UK litigation on this area of the law, at present, there undoubtedly will be more in the future.

1   (1851) 9 Hare 241.
2   98 Mass 452 (1868).
3   [1984] QB 44, [1983] 2 All ER 101.

3.5 TRADEMARK LAW

Trademark rights arise from commercial use or the intention to use them commercially followed by commercial use. Trademarks may be registered or not, but registration gives some advantages and is usually preferable to not registering your mark. If a mark is registered, the registration must be renewed from time to time. The duration of trademark protection is potentially unlimited. The trademark owner's exclusive rights to use the mark with respect to certain goods and services may continue as long as the trademark owner uses the mark in commerce; uses it correctly, for example, as a trademark rather than a generic name; controls the quality of the products bearing the mark; and as long as customers continue to perceive the mark as an indicator of source or sponsorship of the products bearing the mark.

While it is beyond the scope of this book to discuss trademarks and trademark law at length, it should be noted that trademark rights may be lost through abandonment or misuse of the mark.

In the UK trademarks are protected by statute under the Trade Marks Act 1994. They can be registered for protection of marks used in relation to goods and to services.

Under the existing law trademarks may be applied for in respect of computer programs generally speaking under Class 9 for the program itself and under Class 16 for accompanying user manuals. One difficulty which many software houses have is that they tend to use descriptive marks as trademarks which may be unregisterable although the Trade Marks Act 1994 is considerably more lenient than the previous UK legislation. It is now possible to register not only names and words but also distinctive shapes and configurations.

One of the difficulties with trademark protection is that whereas in some countries trademarks may have protection even if unregistered in other countries there may be no protection at all (in the UK, sometimes claims for passing off where trade marks are unregistered (and indeed where registered) may be possible) and, therefore, whilst a prudent company may wish to register trademarks in connection with a particular program, this can be an expensive process since it may be necessary to register a trademark in every jurisdiction where it may be used.

The European Trade Mark (previously called the Community Trade Mark ('CTM')) which applies to Member States of the EU (but not now in the UK due to Brexit) came into force in 1996.[1] The European Trade Mark Office is based in Alicante, Spain, and provides a harmonised trademark application system by means of one application for all Member States. Usually for new trade marks companies in Europe would register in the UK (if they propose use there) and in the EU now that the UK is no longer part of the European Trade Mark system.

1   Council Registration (EC) (No 40/96 of 20 December 1993).

3.6   CONTRACT LAW

As previous sections of this work indicate, contract law is very important to software licences and the differences between software sale, lease, and licence agreements.

The rules as to whether a contract is validly formed differ between jurisdictions. What constitutes an enforceable contract under one legal system may not apply in another. A new area that is emerging particularly relates to digital signatures since many contracts are now being formed through e-commerce where no handwritten signature exists at all.

In English law it is necessary for there to be some consideration passing between the parties (unless the document is signed as a deed) as well as there being an offer and acceptance. A promise to carry out a contract where there is no other consideration will not lead to a valid contract under English law. However, whilst agreeing to keep an offer open for a certain length of time would not be binding under English law it would be in other legal jurisdictions such as Scotland.

The Contracts (Rights of Third Parties) Act 1999 applies in the UK to contracts which are entered into on or after 11 May 2000. The Act enables a third party to enforce contractual rights as if it were a party to the contract. This was a big leap forward for customers who wish to seek the benefit of warranties in third-party licensed products as well as in reseller and integration contracts where many of the software products licensed are licensed on a 'back-to-back' contract basis. The parties to a software contract needs to consider when and whether third parties are to have rights or not. If third-party rights are to be excluded then such exclusion must be expressly referred to in the contract terms. Sometimes the first page and a half of a software licence taken by a large group will consist of clauses about the extensive third party rights given to all companies in the group both to use and sue under the contract often using the 1999 Act as a base as well as additional contractual rights of enforcement. On the other hand, most licensors will want licences limited to one company and almost universally exclude the 1999 Act by a contract term to that effect.

In the US where the transaction relates to a sale, then the Uniform Commercial Code applies and in many parts of Europe specific civil codes apply to contracts for sale. However, in Scotland, many European countries and parts of the US such rights can be conferred. This is significant where software is distributed by OEMs, VARs and other resellers appointed by the original provider. Care needs to be taken if the provider is to create a right to enforce rights against a licensee or receive the protection of any limits of liability in the sub-licence.

In 1999 the US passed the Uniform Computer Information Transactions Act (UCITA) which a number of states have now adopted. UCITA is intended to clarify the issues of online software contracting and provide statutory guidance as to how a click-wrap contract can be effectively made. More importantly UCITA is intended to clarify how the law applies to relationships between the software publisher and the end user. UCITA is, however, only of value when it is enforced as part of state legislation. At the beginning of 2002 UCITA was the subject of continued criticism and is the subject of redrafting, particularly in relation to sections of the legislation which presently allow software vendors to install disenabling devices into the software which are activated when licence fees are not paid or are not kept up.

3.7   REGISTERED DESIGNS

Directive 98/71/EC of the European Parliament and of the Council of 13 October 1998 on the legal protection of designs (OJ L289, 28.10.1998) was implemented throughout the EU by virtue of the Community Design Regulation (CDR) (OJ L3, 05.01.2002) whilst the UK was still in the EU. At the end of 2006 the European Council confirmed that the EC will become a signatory to the Geneva Act of the Hague Agreement concerning the International Registration of Industrial Designs, and this will then allow applicants to obtain registered designs across the EU as well as in non-EU countries that are also signatories of the Geneva Act. On 13 June 2018 the UK became an individual signatory of the Hague Agreement in advance of Brexit and in readiness for it.

In the UK the CDR caused amendments to the Registered Design Act 1949 and has now generally made the registration as designs of computer icons, graphical user interfaces and web pages, a real opportunity for software developers and program owners.

Before the CDR, the UK, like many other member states, defined 'design' in terms of 'features of shape, configuration, pattern or ornament applied to an article by any industrial process ...' and the definition of 'article' was defined as 'any article of manufacture and includes any part of an article if that part is made and sold separately'. This set of definitions meant that computer generated images and icons were prevented from being protected.

Under the Registered Design Act 1949 (before amendment) in the United Kingdom, the narrow definitions of registered designs meant that in the case of computers, icons and symbols could only be protected if they were displayed directly as a result of information used to define and generate those symbols and therefore icons produced by software such as word processing programs were not capable of registration as they were not an integral part of the computer. Apple computers were successful in obtaining UK registered design no. 2094032 for 'computer display screens with computer generated icon' but this was after an appeal tribunal hearing.

The CDR as now implemented means that the definition of design under s 1(2) of the UK Registered Designs Act 1949 as amended reads '... the appearance of the whole or a part of a product resulting from the features of, in particular, the lines, contours, colours, shape, texture or materials of the product or its ornamentation'. Moreover, product is now defined as 'any industrial or handicraft item other than a computer program: and in particular, includes packaging, get up, graphic symbols, typographic typefaces and parts intended to be assembled into a complex product'. This continues despite Brexit.

The UK law and no doubt laws in other EU member states are now able to provide greater registered design protection for computer designers and computer vendors. It is possible to register all sorts of images generated by computer, displayed on screens, mobile phones, digital watches, digital cameras and MP3 players.

It has been suggested that the range of examples of what may be included within the definition of 'product', including 'get-up', 'graphic symbols' and 'typographic typefaces' shows that the term is to be interpreted broadly. Whilst computer programs are excluded from the definition of product this is only as regards the computer programs themselves (ie the lines of code and the functionality). Specific graphics which are produced by computer programs, such as icons, are likely to be considered protected as symbols.

It must be remembered that for graphics or symbols to be registered they must also be new and have individual character. This means that the design must not be identical to an existing design but there are no barriers to the registration therefore of new computer icons, graphical user interfaces, webpage designs or other computer generated symbols which were previously unregistered on the grounds that they were not applied to an article.

A registered design once granted lasts for 25 years and is an aggressive method of protection.

In the Intellectual Property Act 2014 the UK changed designs law to ensure the default position on ownership of registered and unregistered designs became like that in regards to copyright. There were other changes to designs law not so relevant here in the Act too. As to the ownership point, the Explanatory Notes states at Section 6:

> 'Subsection (1) amends section 2 of the RDA so that, in the absence of a contract to the contrary, where a design has been commissioned, the designer will be the initial owner of the design, and not the person who commissioned it. This brings UK law into line with the EU Regulation. It also aligns the treatment of UK designs with the way commissioned works are treated under UK copyright law, and means that the default position is that the initial ownership of closely related rights will no longer end up with different parties'.

3.8 MORAL RIGHTS

Many jurisdictions which recognise that the inventive and intellectual efforts of authors are entitled to legal protection divide that protection between economic rights on the one hand and moral rights on the other. Whilst economic rights are intended to provide the means for the inventor or author to secure remuneration for exploitation of their works, the moral rights are concerned with the author's personal and professional reputation and are seen as quite separate to, for example, copyright.

France introduced express copyright protection for computer software in 1985 and, at the same time, modified the application of moral rights to this type of copyright work. Moral rights include first, the right to control disclosure of the work, secondly the right to determine when and in what matter the work is to be attributed to the author, thirdly the right to withdraw the work from publication and fourthly, the right to prevent modification of the work and to prevent its destruction.

In the UK moral rights were first introduced into our statutory law by the Copyright, Designs and Patents Act 1988, ss 77–79.

Moral rights do not apply to computer programs in the UK but they will apply to other material accompanying computer programs, such as user manuals, specifications and so on, and since quite often works produced by employees for employer licensors or by sub-contracted programmers will be vested in the licensor then it is certainly necessary to provide, for contractual provisions, to deal with the question of moral rights which will not necessarily pass over to the employer or commissioner. The best protection for the employer or commissioner is to ensure that the employee/freelance programmer waives moral rights but where such a waiver cannot be obtained then specifically there must be agreement as to precisely what moral rights are to be exercised or may be exercised.

They have little importance in the UK and most copyright agreements waive moral rights. However sometimes website designers want their name/credit on a website and will include an express clause to that effect. Occasionally where a software product modifies another product (even in the area of internet memes) a breach of a moral right not to have copyright work subject to derogatory treatment may occur.

4 EU and UK EU-derived legislation

4.1 OVERVIEW

Although the UK is not a member of the EU, this chapter has been retained as at 2023 many EU laws are still in place despite plans to 'sunset' 600 existing EU laws which remain part of English law by 31 December 2023 unless expressly retained and about 3,400 others in due course (see Retained EU Law (Revocation and Reform) Bill). However as there are so many changes in EU law this chapter does not contain all of them and simply provides an update on those which are also part of English law. For example, the latest copyright directive and Digital Services and Digital Markets Acts of the EU which do not apply in the UK are not addressed.

At the core of the laws of the EU is the Treaty of Rome (now updated into the Treaty on the Functioning of the European Union (TFEU), or Lisbon Treaty), which provides for the establishment of a common European and economic market and each member state of the EU is subject to the Treaty of Rome and the laws which emanate from the European Commission.

When the UK joined the EC various laws were immediately incorporated into UK law without further parliamentary legislation, but since the UK left the EU on 31 January 2020.

Many of the competition laws and other laws of the EU are applicable to member states who are members of the EEA but are not in the EU.[1]

One of the main areas of EU law which affects computer contracts is in the field of competition where the TFEU, arts 101 and 102 (formerly Treaty of Rome, arts 81 and 82) relate to agreements between companies which, in effect, are distorting competition by creating monopolies or where the parties abuse their dominant position within the market place. These apply in the EU only, not the UK, but the UK has similar legislation such as the Competition Act 1998.

---

1   Ie the member states of the EU plus Norway, Iceland and Liechtenstein.

4.2   EU AND UK COMPETITION LAW

The competition rules of the EU are interpreted and applied by the European Commission so as to further the general economic and political policies of the member states to the ultimate benefit of the consumer. They are applied to distribution agreements, know-how agreements, joint ventures, mergers, acquisitions, patent licences etc.

Article 101 of the TFEU prohibits agreements which distort competition, for instance, where a licensor attempts to specify prices at which goods may be resold or imposes obligations on a licensee to automatically hand back to the licensor improvements made by a licensee during the course of an agreement. However, Regulation 720 (2022) (and the equivalent UK vertical block exemption 2022/516 – Competition Act 21998 (Vertical Agreements) (Block Exemption) Order 2022) – provides a general block exemption for vertical agreements which meet the requirements of the respective exemption regulations. Restricting the resale price at which a distributor resells goods to its customers breaches the block exemptions and is a hard core (void/banned) restrictions. Restrictions on territories and customers should be treated with care.

Importantly for software vendors, it is possible to impose 'non-compete' clauses on resellers provided the term does not exceed five years if the other requirements of the exemptions are met. However, there are certain minimal agreements to which the TFEU, art 101 (formerly Treaty of Rome, art 81) will not apply where, for example, the goods or services that the agreement relates to, together with the parties' similar goods or services, are less than 5% of the total market affected by the agreement and the parties' aggregate annual turnover does not exceed €300 million. The above rule (applying to minimal agreements), known as the 'de minimis' rule, changes over the years. The latest version of the EU notice in this area was in 2014. The de minimis rule arises as a result of the European Commission Notice on Agreements of Minor Importance which do not fall under article 101(1) of 2014 if they contain no hardcore restrictions.[1] In addition to the exemptions listed above, an agreement can also be exempted from art 101 either under individual or under block exemptions issued by the European Commission if certain conditions are met.

A block exemption is a regulation which automatically confers exemption on a particular type of agreement which complies with the terms of the exemption. For example, there is a block exemption relating to exclusive distributorships (vertical agreement) as mentioned above which, amongst other things, permits restrictions in exclusive distribution agreements to the effect that distributors are prevented from actively seeking customers outside their territory. However, if a distributor receives an unsolicited request from outside its territory it is entitled to respond. However, in an exclusive distribution agreement where there was a statement that a distributor 'shall not sell nor export whether directly or not the products to other countries and the territory without the "principal's" consent in writing', it was held that this was not protected by the block exemption since the terms of the wording were such that the distributor was effectively prevented from himself distributing outside the territory or indeed allowing anyone else to. This contravened the EU concept of free trade within the whole Community.

The European Commission has introduced a series of similar such block exemption Regulations to apply to technology transfers over the years. Technology transfers have been subject to European competition rules for many years, but have had the benefit of certain 'clearances' which automatically apply if the agreements either meet existing competition laws, or are of relatively minor importance and therefore do not materially affect free trade within the European Union.

The Technology Transfer Block Exemption Regulation ('TTBER')[2] provides a 'safe harbour' to businesses whose market share thresholds fall below certain levels – 20% combined for licensing agreements between competitors and 30% each for agreements between non-competitors. In other words, even if the terms of a licensing agreement could be seen as anti-competitive the agreement may not be subject to competition rules if the parties' market shares fall below the above levels.

In addition to the market share (or de minimis) exemption the TTBER provides a blacklist of hardcore anti-trust violations.

The TTBER affects not only patent and know-how licensing but also technology transfer agreements relating to design right and software. It does not, however, apply to R&D, technology pooling and sub-distribution agreements.

The TFEU, art 102 (formerly Treaty of Rome, art 82) seeks to prevent abuse of dominant position within the

marketplace where, for example, a dominant company forms cartels, refuses to supply or creates elements of over-charging.

In 1984 IBM was investigated by the European Commission who applied the Treaty of Rome, art 82 to the situation where IBM was found to have a dominant position in the supply of central processing units and basic operating and system software for IBM computers 360 and 370 on account of IBM's significant market share in the central processing unit market. It was alleged that IBM had abused its power because it had not provided other manufacturers with the technical information they needed in order for them to make competitive products compatible with 360 and 370 products. Proceedings by the Commission were suspended after IBM gave certain undertakings to supply the necessary interface information and to make available certain formats and protocols to third parties.

Two decisions are of relevance to aspects of the computer industry and, in particular, contractual provisions within the industry, because it is clear that the European Commission will not tolerate dominant companies maintaining a monopoly or abusing their power by restricting competition or the movement of goods and services within the EU (*Re Magill TV Guide/ITP, BBC and RTE,*[3] and *Re Tetra Pak II*[4]).

In relation to the Treaty of Rome, arts 81 and 82 it has only been possible to touch the surface of this complex area. However, the question of aspects of a software licence which might distort the opportunity of competition or restrict the movement of goods within the Community should be borne in mind, whether the parties are both within the UK or whether only one of the parties is within the EU.

There are often conflicts between the intellectual property rights monopoly that an owner has over its products on the one hand and the requirements of competition law for there to be free movement of goods on the other hand.

As a general principle, compulsory licensing of intellectual property rights is contrary to the notion of monopoly conferred by intellectual property rights, but on occasions the European Court of Justice recognises that there may be an obligation to grant licences where an intellectual property right either relates to an essential facility or is otherwise required for development of new markets.

1   [2014] OJ C291/1.
2   Reg 316/2-14 [2014] OJ L93/17 with accompanying Intellectual Property Guidelines OJ 2014 C89/3.
3   [1989] 4 CMLR 757.
4   [1992] 4 CMLR 551.

4.3   EC DIRECTIVE ON THE LEGAL PROTECTION OF COMPUTER PROGRAMS

The Software Directive[1] (officially known as the Directive on the legal protection of computer programs) harmonises copyright protection for computer programs throughout the EU so that there can be a more internationally effective basis for protection. As it was implemented in the UK about nearly 30 years before Brexit it has so far remained in place. However, the proposed 'sunset' of 600 EU laws on 31 December 2023 with more to follow mentioned above might potentially mean it is removed from UK legislation automatically unless it is expressly retained.

The Software Directive requires computer programs to be protected by copyright as if they were literary works, following what is already the case in the UK and is understood in the Berne Convention. The period of copyright protection under UK/EU copyright law for literary works such as software is the life of the author plus 70 years. In addition, the copyright holder is entitled to prevent unauthorised copying, but a licensee of the program is permitted to carry out any form of copying which is necessary for the program to be used or in order to make a security back-up, and is also allowed to carry out error correction for the purpose of enabling the program to run correctly. Furthermore, reverse engineering or decompilation is now possible where the licensee needs to understand the underlying code, copy and translate the program and investigate the functionality of the program in order to understand its ideas and principles and no consent of the copyright holder is here required provided, of course, that such information is not already available to the licensee. Attempts in a contract to exclude all decompilation (as is common in US contracts) is void. Therefore, it vital to ensure that clauses restricting decompilation and reverse engineering including wording such as 'save unless otherwise permitted by law' or words to that effect. If a clause which makes no such allowance is included the clause is void. It is not rewritten to accommodate the Directive.

The Software Directive is embodied in UK law by the Copyright (Computer Programs) Regulations 1992.[2]

The Software Directive has been the subject of judicial opinion and analysis in the case of *SAS Institute Inc v World Programming Ltd* (see discussion in **3.3**).[3]

1   2009/24 [2009] OJ L111/16 a consolidated version of 91/250 [1991] OJ L122.
2   SI 1992/3233.
3   *SAS Institute Inc v World Programming Ltd* [2013] EWHC 69 (Ch).

4.4   EC DIRECTIVE ON RENTAL AND LENDING RIGHTS AND CERTAIN RIGHTS RELATING TO COPYRIGHT

This Rental Lending Directive,[1] which came into force in 1994, introduced a right for the creators of copyright work to authorise or prohibit the rental and lending of originals and copies of copyright works. The Directive is implemented in the UK under the Copyright, Designs and Patents Act 1988.

1   92/100 [1992] OJ L346.

4.5   EC DIRECTIVE HARMONISING THE TERM OF PROTECTION OF COPYRIGHT AND CERTAIN RELATED RIGHTS

This Directive[1] harmonised the term of copyright protection as from July 1995 where the term is set at 70 years after the death of the author or after the work is made available to the public and for related rights 50 years from the point at which the copyright term begins. This is now in force from 1 January 1996 in the UK by virtue of the Duration of Copyright and Rights in Performances Regulations 1995.[2]

Another copyright Directive – Copyright in the Digital Single Market 2019/790 – is not addressed here as it does not apply in the UK due to Brexit, but sets out some modernisation of copyright in the EU.

1   93/98 [1993] OJ L290.
2   SI 1995/3297.

4.6   EC DIRECTIVE ON THE LEGAL PROTECTION OF DATABASES

This Database Directive[1] intended to harmonise, throughout the EU, the legal protection of electronic and manual databases.

The Directive defines a database as 'a collection of works, data or other independent materials arranged in a systematic or methodical way and capable of being individually accessed by electronic or other means'. Not only does the Directive contemplate electronic and digital databases, but it also states that protection under the Directive should also extend to non-electronic databases, thereby including paper databases within the Directive.

The Database Directive creates protection of both structure and content of the database with copyright protection applying to the structure and a *sui generis* right applying as a method of protection for the content.

For the structure as well as the content of the database to be protected by copyright, the creator of the database must have used skill and judgment in the selection of the content. The period of copyright protection is to be 70 years from the date of creation or publication. The *sui generis* right will apply where the content has been compiled without necessarily involving skill and judgment and its period of protection is 15 years, but renewable in the event of any major change to the database content.

It should be noted that the copyright protection will apply to the structure of the database notwithstanding that individual elements of the content of the database may also be subject to their own copyright protection.

Because of the EEA-centric nature of the Directive non-EEA database makers or database owners cannot benefit from the *sui generis* right. The UK has retained database right since Brexit.

A UK company which sub-contracts database development abroad is still regarded as the database maker and therefore has full protection.

A US company which acquires a database from a UK database maker will on the one hand purchase the database but on the other hand may not have any rights to enforce the *sui generis* right in the UK.

Often, this UK/EEA-centric issue is not a problem because foreign companies purchasing databases from the UK or EEA do so as a result of a share acquisition and therefore the database rights holder remains an EEA resident entity. However, where a foreign company makes an asset purchase (as opposed to a share purchase) the rights will be assigned to the foreign entity which, if copyright protection does not apply, will no longer be able to enforce the *sui generis* right within the EEA.

It is important that companies which are making acquisitions or taking licences of EEA or UK created databases should carry out due diligence as to the rights of the database maker in such databases (eg whether copyright or *sui generis* or both). Where the database being transferred is protected by *sui generis* rights then the foreign company should consider making such acquisition through an EEA or UK subsidiary.

1   96/9 [1996] OJ L77/20.

4.7   EC DIRECTIVE ON UNFAIR CONTRACT TERMS

This Directive,[1] which came into force at the end of 1994, protects consumers from unfair terms in pre-printed or standard form contracts. In the UK we already have the Unfair Contract Terms Act 1977 which has similar intentions but the European Directive is now in force in the UK by means of the Unfair Terms in Consumer Contract Regulations 1994[2] which were first replaced by similar regulations in 1999 and then now for sales to consumers by the Consumer Rights Act 2015 (the 1977 Act continues to apply to business contracts) and relates to a number of terms which may be considered unfair in contracts with consumers.

This Directive and the UK Consumer Rights Act 2015 are of particular interest to software suppliers who operate on standard terms of sale or supply and to sizeable purchasing companies who operate on standard terms and conditions of purchase in that where the parties are of considerably unequal bargaining power, and particularly where the other party is a consumer or end-user, then any ambiguity in the standard terms will be interpreted against the person who drew them up or, in the event that the terms are deemed to be unfair, then they will be struck out of the contract.

1   93/13 [1993] OJ L95.
2   SI 1994/3159.

4.8   EC DIRECTIVE ON E-SIGNATURES

In e-commerce and e-procurement it is important to be sure that any online contracts and licences are validly made and furthermore that the parties making them can be authenticated.

The E-signature Directive[1] was the result of various EU communications and research, in particular work carried out by DG XI11 and is an indication of the EU's desire to lead in the initiatives for globally secure e-commerce.

The Directive was a reaction to the demands and initiatives of business communities including the work of UNCITRAL, OECD, ICC and others.

The Directive has as its aim first, the framework for providing legal validity to e-signatures and, secondly, a framework for a hierarchy of certification authorities.

Since not all signatures which are created electronically are digital signatures (as later defined) the Directive accepts that there may be a need to define digital signatures and e-signatures separately (and indeed does so).

The Directive also addresses the issue of certification authorities. In paper contracts where high levels of authentication or verification are required, then the signature of the party to be bound to a contract is often witnessed and/or notarised. In electronic transmissions there is no automatic form of witness or notarisation and indeed there is usually an absence of this act or performance. Recently this lack of authenticity has been addressed by the use of certification authorities who attest to the identity of the person signing electronically and where such signature is achieved using a digital signature then the facility exists for a digital certificate to be supplied by a certification authority, giving further certification or verification to the e-signature as well as the message.

'E-signature' is defined so as to include digital signature but to include other 'data in electronic form'. The Directive recognises that there are other methods of e-signature such as biometric technology or signature digitisation technology which provide methods of authentication.

Where an e-signature is to be given force of law by being verified by a certification service provider, it is easier in the area of digital signatures to see how this can occur than it is in other forms of digitised signature because in general the creation of a digitised signature is carried out with the use of technology, whereas the creation of a digital signature is created by technology itself.

The definitions of 'e-signature' and 'advanced e-signature' compare favourably with other definitions in circulation.

The Directive also defines what is meant by 'certification service provider' as an accredited person or entity providing certification services. These services are not spelt out but would be likely to include not only the provision of e-certificates but also date and time stamping and other archiving and storage services, but not key escrow services where the private key, as opposed to the public key, is held by the certification service provider.

The UK government implemented the Electronic Signatures Regulations 2002.[2] These remain in force despite Brexit. Services like Docusign are now extensively used in the UK for business to business contracts and their use was significantly advanced during the Covid 19 (pandemic) lockdowns in the UK and elsewhere.

1   99/93 [1999] OJ L013.
2   SI 2002/318.

4.9   EC DIRECTIVE ON CONSUMER RIGHTS (DISTANCE SELLING OF GOODS AND SERVICES)

The Distance Selling Directive[1] on the protection of consumers in respect of distance contracts was published in June 1997. This was replaced by the Consumer Rights Directive 2011/83/EU which in the UK is implemented by the Consumer Contracts (Information, Cancellation and Additional Charges) Regulations 2013 (SI 2013/3134).

It should be noted that this legislation does not apply to contracts relating to financial services including banking and insurance.

The Directive applies to any contract concerning goods or services concluded between a supplier and a consumer under an organised distance sales or service scheme run by the supplier, who, for the purpose of the contract, makes exclusive use of one or more distance communications, up to and including the moment at which the contract is concluded. This specifically lists media by which such distance sales can take place which include digital transmissions via PC or television. In addition, the Directive also sets out requirements for contracts which are 'on premises' (made in a shop) and those made at someone's home which are not addressed in this book.

The Directive requires the supplier to give certain information to the consumer before a contract is concluded of at least 20 items set out in the legislation, including:

- the identity of the supplier;

- the supplier's address;

- description of the goods or services;

- details of payment;

- delivery costs;

- a right of cancellation; and

- for alternative conditions to be in clear and intelligible language.

The Directive lays down requirements relating to the right of withdrawal, including a 'cooling-off period' – ie, online shoppers in most cases have 14 days to cancel the contract even if there is nothing wrong with the goods or services or digital download.

In the UK the Consumer Contracts (Information, Cancellation and Additional Charges) Regulations 2013 (SI 2013/3134) are the most important set out requirements relevant to the selling online in a business to consumer manner and contain (as does the Directive) a large number of legal requirements and provisions should be included in the contract.

1   97/7 OJ 1997 L144.

4.10   EC REGULATION ON DATA PROTECTION – GDPR

English law protects privacy through the common law of confidentiality and the Human Rights Act 1998, but in addition, where personal data about living individuals is concerned data protection law sets out detailed requirements for those handling personal data. In the UK this is contained in the UK's amended version of the EU General Data Protection Regulation, known as UK GDPR with some provisions also in the Data Protection Act 2018 particularly as regards enforcement and the state sector. These are due to be amended by the draft Data Protection and Digital Information (No. 2) Bill 2023 when in force.

For those in the EU, it is the EU General Data Protection Regulation which is the relevant legislation. As at 2023, there are few material differences between GDPR and UK GDPR.

The UK brought into force its first legislation in this field in the Data Protection Act 1984 (DPA 1984) to enable the UK to ratify the Council of Europe's Convention for the Protection of Individuals with Regard to Automatic Processing of Personal Data.

4.10.1 Background to the Data Protection Acts of 1984 and 1998 and UK GDPR/ Data Protection Act 2018

In 1974 the Organisation for Economic Co-operation and Development (OECD) set up a Data Bank Panel, and a group of experts that succeeded the Data Bank Panel put together what have become known as the OECD Guidelines. These were a set of guidelines rather than compulsory regulations and they placed importance on:

- the need to harmonise the data protection laws of different countries;

- the need to ensure a free flow of information; and

- the necessity of guaranteeing rights where privacy and personal data were concerned.

Separately from the OECD the Council of Europe in the 1970s worked, amongst other things, on the preparation for an International Data Protection Treaty which was adopted on 28 January 1981 under the title of the Convention for the Protection of Individuals with regard to Automatic Processing of Personal Data. The Convention came into force on 1 October 1985 and is binding upon those Member States who have signed or ratified the Convention.

The UK, having ratified the Convention, incorporated its basic principles into the Data Protection Act 1984 (DPA 1984).

This was followed in the UK by the Data Protection Act 1998 which implemented the EC Directive on Data Protection (the 'Directive').[1]

This was replaced by the EU's General Data Protection Regulation known as GDPR and once the UK left the EU in the UK a UK version – the 'UK GDPR' amended to reflect the fact the UK is not part of the EU and accompanied by the Data Protection Act 2018 – was also then amended to reflect Brexit.

In both the UK regulations – the Privacy and Electronic Communications (EC Directive) Regulations 2003 (2003/2426) (due to be amended in 2023 by the draft Data Protection and Digital Information (No. 2) Bill 2023) – and the EU, there are also specific regulations on email marketing which at the EU level in 2023 are likely to be updated. The UK also plans to update its regulations through the draft Data Protection and Digital Information Bill which as of 2023 has not yet received Royal Assent and will make some changes generally to data protection law.

Under existing law in the UK entities which handle personal data in many cases need to notify their holding of data with the Information Commissioner's Office and most websites need a privacy policy in addition to the requirements for notifying anyone generally who does business with a company as to how their personal data will be handled.

For small businesses the cost of notification is an annual fee of £35 per annum.

Failure to comply with the law in some instances brings not only civil liability but also criminal liability and there may be personal liability for directors and officers too.

Compliance with UK GDPR (and GDPR) extends to the adherence to the various legal requirements including Data Protection Principles laid down by the legislation.

Article 5 of the UK GDPR sets out seven key principles. Article 5(1) requires that personal data shall be:

'(a) processed lawfully, fairly and in a transparent manner in relation to individuals ('lawfulness, fairness and transparency');

(b) collected for specified, explicit and legitimate purposes and not further processed in a manner that is incompatible with those purposes; further processing for archiving purposes in the public interest, scientific or historical research purposes or statistical purposes shall not be considered to be incompatible with the initial purposes ('purpose limitation');

(c) adequate, relevant and limited to what is necessary in relation to the purposes for which they are processed ('data minimisation');

(d) accurate and, where necessary, kept up to date; every reasonable step must be taken to ensure that personal data that are inaccurate, having regard to the purposes for which they are processed, are erased or rectified without delay ('accuracy');

(e) kept in a form which permits identification of data subjects for no longer than is necessary for the purposes for which the personal data are processed; personal data may be stored for longer periods insofar as the personal data will be processed solely for archiving purposes in the public interest, scientific or historical research purposes or statistical purposes subject to implementation of the appropriate technical and organisational measures required by the GDPR in order to safeguard the rights and freedoms of individuals ('storage limitation');

(f) processed in a manner that ensures appropriate security of the personal data, including protection against unauthorised or unlawful processing and against accidental loss, destruction or damage, using appropriate technical or organisational measures ('integrity and confidentiality').'

Article 5(2) adds that: 'The controller shall be responsible for, and be able to demonstrate compliance with, paragraph 1 ('accountability').'

4.10.1.1   Rights of individuals

The individuals' rights under this legislation relate to 'personal data'. Personal data is data which relates to a living individual who can be identified:

- from those data,

- from those data and other information,

- and includes any opinion about an individual and an indication of the data controller's intention towards that individual.

The definition of this may change when the UK's proposed new Data Protection and Digital Information Bill receives royal assent.

The UK GDPR provides the following rights for individuals:

1. The right to be informed.

2. The right of access.

3. The right to rectification.

4. The right to erasure.

5. The right to restrict processing.

6. The right to data portability.

7. The right to object.

8. Rights in relation to automated decision making and profiling.

4.10.2   Data security

It is difficult for a business which does not have in place adequate data security procedures to argue that it is in compliance with UK GDPR.

IT security is a huge issue for those involved in the IT sector both because of UK GDPR obligations but also more generally given the scale and amount of hacking taking place.

Businesses are advised to consider the implementation of the generally accepted security standard, set up by the British Standards Institute and endorsed by the Information Commissioner and the British Government, ISO 27001 (BS7799).

4.10.3   Transfer of data overseas

UK GDPR provides that personal data should not be transferred outside the UK unless certain conditions are met.

These include that the individual has consented to the data export. Another basis for lawful export is where the recipient abroad is in a country whose data laws have been deemed adequate (eg, the EU and UK both deem each other's laws adequate). A third possible basis is where the recipient signs Standard Contractual Clauses (Model Clauses) of the EU for exports from the EU or, in the UK, the UK's equivalent.

For those just exporting data from the UK the International Data Transfer Agreement (IDTA) is the best document to use.

However, if a UK business will also be exporting data to or from the EU then it should instead consider the UK amended version of the EU's standard clauses known as the Addendum.

Both the IDTA and the Addendum can be downloaded from the UK's ICO's website in word format at https://ico.org.uk/for-organisations/guide-to-data-protection/guide-to-the-general-data-protection-regulation-gdpr/international-data-transfer-agreement-and-guidance/. These are both also included as some of the precedents with this book.

The EU's Standard Contractual Clauses for International Transfers can be used for those exporting data from the EU and are available at https://commission.europa.eu/publications/standard-contractual-clauses-international-transfers_en. These are also included as part of the precedents with this book.

The EU and US have had various arrangements between them over the years permitting only those very few US companies who sign up to the schemes to receive data from the EU. However, these have been challenged over the years, eg, the Privacy Shield.

Finally, a handful of companies has thought it worthwhile having approval by the EU or UK of its data privacy arrangements – known as Binding Corporate Rules. This is quite a substantial task and most companies do not use this route for their data transfers.

4.11 EC DIRECTIVE ON WASTE ELECTRICAL AND ELECTRONIC EQUIPMENT (WEEE DIRECTIVE) (2012/19/ EC) AND EC DIRECTIVE ON THE RESTRICTION OF THE USE OF CERTAIN HAZARDOUS SUBSTANCES IN ELECTRICAL AND ELECTRONIC EQUIPMENT (ROHS DIRECTIVE) (2011/65/EU)

The objective of the WEEE Directive is to increase and encourage the amount of recycling of WEEE within the EU while minimising the disposal of WEEE as unsorted municipal waste. Manufacturers are encouraged to design products that can be easily disassembled, recycled and reused and that have minimal environmental impact. Broadly this is achieved by making producers of WEEE responsible for its collection and recycling and environmentally sound disposal. Original 2002 directives were replaced with modernised versions of 2012/2011. Despite Brexit the UK has so far retained its legislation in this field.

The RoHS Directive goes hand in hand with the WEEE Directive in limiting the amounts of specified potentially hazardous substances that may be contained in electronic equipment, since the content of hazardous components in electronics is seen as a significant barrier to recycling of WEEE.

Individual member states are responsible for implementing the Directives and it will be these local laws that must be complied with. As both Directives grant member states some discretion in how they may transpose, it is expected that local differences will pose a major challenge for businesses operating across different member states.

4.11.1 Type of products affected

The WEEE Directive applies to a wide range of electrical appliances, provided that they do not form part of another type of equipment that is not covered by the Directive, intended both for consumers and business users which are in ten broad categories:

- Large household appliances.
- Small household appliances.
- IT and telecommunications equipment.
- Consumer equipment.
- Lighting equipment.
- Electrical and electronic tools (with the exception of large-scale stationary industrial tools).
- Toys, leisure and sports equipment.
- Medical devices (with the exception of all implanted and infected products).
- Monitoring and control instruments.
- Automatic dispensers.

The RoHS Directive covers most of the categories listed under the WEEE Directive but does not include medical devices and monitoring and control instruments (although the possible inclusion of these two categories will be reviewed) but also covers electric light bulbs and household luminaries. The RoHS Directive does not apply to spare parts for the repair of EEE placed on the market before 1 July 2006 or to the reuse of EEE placed on the market before that date.

4.11.2 Key elements of the WEEE Directive

A 'producer' of WEEE, according to the Directive is any person who:

- manufactures and sells EEE under their own brand;
- resells EEE produced by other suppliers under their own brand; or

- imports or exports EEE on a professional basis into a Member State.

Under a notion of Individual Producer Responsibility, in each EU member state 'producers' will, *inter alia*, be responsible for:

- registering with the appropriate authorities;

- providing annual data on the quantity and category of EEE that they put onto the market;

- ensuring the equipment is marked with a crossed-out wheelie-bin symbol (this signals that the product is EEE for the purposes of the WEEE Directive and was placed on the market after 13 August 2005) and bears the mark of the producer;

- financing the collection, treatment, recycling etc of household WEEE from central collection facilities;

- financing the collection, treatment, recycling etc of non-household WEEE placed on the market before 13 August 2005 when supplying replacement products;

- financing the collection, treatment, recycling etc of non-household WEEE;

- demonstrating evidence that targets of recycling and reuse are being met;

- providing information to those involved in the collection, treatment, recycling and environmentally sound disposal of WEEE to enable them to identify various components and any hazardous substances;

- providing financial guarantees in respect of household EEE (by way of participation in a collective financing scheme, a recycling insurance or a blocked bank account).

Retailers and distributors of EEE to household consumers are required to provide free in store take-back to domestic customers when those customers are placing like-for-like replacement equipment.

It will be an offence and penalties will be imposed on those firms who fail to meet their responsibilities under the implementing member state law.

It is open to producers to comply individually or through a compliance scheme or a collective scheme which would handle registering and reporting as well as collecting, treating and recycling the waste according to the producer's needs.

4.11.3   Key elements of the RoHS Directive

While, in essence the WEEE Directive makes the WEEE producer 'responsible' for what they place on the market, the RoHS Directive places strict limits on the amount of lead, cadmium, mercury, hexavalent chromium and both polybrominated biphenyl (PBB) and polybrominated diphenyl ether (PBDE) flame retardants. Again, this responsibility falls on the 'producer' but will in practice be up to the manufacturer to ensure that the products are marketable in the EU.

In broad terms, producers of electronics will be prohibited from placing on the EU market EEE products which are non-compliant with the maximum concentration values. Failure to comply will be an offence (although there will be a defence of due diligence) and fines will be imposed by the regulatory authorities.

There are also numerous exemptions from RoHS (which will be reviewed every four years) for specific applications such as lead in glass of cathode ray tubes and fluorescent tubes, lead as an alloying element, lead in electronic ceramic parts, mercury in particular categories of fluorescent lamps, hexavalent chromium as an anti-corrosion of the carbon steel cooling system in absorption refrigerators. The European Commission is considering further possible exemptions for specific applications.

Although self-declaration will be the basis for compliance, producers must be able to demonstrate this by supplying enforcement agencies with technical information, when requested, as to the contents of the EEE. This information must be retained by the producer for a period of four years after the EEE is placed on the market. Failure to supply this information when requested will also be an offence.

4.11.4   Key dates

13 August 2005 was a key date in the EU in respect of the original WEEE – any products placed on the market after this date must bear the crossed-out wheelie-bin symbol and carry the producers mark. The key date for the original RoHS was 1 July 2006. EEE products placed on the EU market after that date must comply with the RoHS maximum concentration values.

4.11.5   Issues for the inbound and outbound supply chain

The WEEE and RoHS Directives have a combined impact on the entire supply chain. Component suppliers, OEM manufacturers, manufacturers, importers, distributors and business end-users are likely to be affected. The intended effect is that in order to comply with WEEE more easily, manufacturers will be encouraged to produce EEE that is durable and can be easily treated, reused or recycled. Important decisions at the design stage will therefore reduce end-of-life costs associated with WEEE.

In a typical scenario, a manufacturer of IT equipment that is sold in the EU will need to ensure that their component suppliers supply RoHS compliant components (this could involve a vast number of suppliers). The head manufacturer will require materials information and certificates of compliance. Manufacturers should also review their contractual relationships with suppliers to take account of the question of RoHS compliance. Likewise first tier suppliers will require certificates of compliance and materials information from their suppliers and so on. Information on the contents of components will be important in order to meet the RoHS requirements but also to be able to provide that information to recyclers and treatment facilities when those products reach end-of life as required by WEEE.

The IT manufacturer will have to adopt measures to comply with WEEE in individual EU member states – their approach will depend on how the products are sold (whether directly or via resellers or distributors) across the EU and whether the end-users are household consumers or businesses. As per RoHS considerations, the manufacturer will also need to review existing and proposed contracts with resellers/distributors and business end-users. This will involve collaborating with outbound supply chain participants, establishing company policies concerning WEEE and RoHS as well as making important business decisions.

Failure to take up the compliance challenge promptly will result in damaging consequences: suppliers of

non-RoHS-compliant parts risk being removed from supplier lists, non-RoHS-compliant products will be banned from sale in the EU and producers that have not addressed WEEE compliance will therefore be at a competitive disadvantage in the marketplace.

4.11.6   EU WEEE Changes

The UK has implemented the EU recast WEEE Directive 2012 (Directive 2012/19/EU on waste electrical and electronic equipment (WEEE) (recast)) by the Waste Electrical and Electronic Equipment Regulations 2013.

The recast WEEE Directive introduced a number of changes of which the main ones were:

* The introduction of higher member state collection and recovery targets and a changed methodology for calculating the WEEE collection rate;

* A wider scope for the range of products covered by the Directive;

* Lowering the regulatory and cost burdens on business through the introduction of an 'authorised representative' who can fulfil the obligations of the producer;

* Better controlling of the illegal international trade in WEEE; and

* A requirement for retailer take-back of very small WEEE in certain circumstances.

Part III
Preparing for negotiations

5 Understanding negotiating principles

5.1 INTRODUCTION

All of us negotiate on a daily basis because negotiation is an aspect of daily life.

We negotiate at home over what TV programme to watch, over what is for supper, over what we are doing at the weekend. We negotiate in the workplace with our superiors and our assistants, we bargain for pay rises and improved work conditions, we negotiate over when we can take holidays. We strike business deals both large and small and we negotiate when we buy a car, electrical goods, property and so on.

We are all capable of negotiation but not all of us are natural negotiators. We can, however, improve our negotiating skills by training and experience.

There are many excellent books and training courses on various aspects of negotiation and the fact that there is a proliferation of these indicates that the art of negotiation is of increasing importance.

Negotiation is as much a business practice as are team skills, management and quality control and, inevitably, aspects of negotiation find their way into many other business practices and management skills.

5.2 WHAT IS NEGOTIATION?

Negotiation is the process between two or more opposing parties to a deal or transaction by which each party seeks to obtain the maximum benefits and rewards from the deal that is struck or agreement that is reached.

Negotiation is a process which occurs in bargaining situations with no guarantee that a bargain will be reached.

Successful negotiation inevitably involves elements of compromise by the bargaining parties.

Negotiation occurs when we want something that someone else already has and may or may not be prepared to give to us.

Remember that there are some occasions where negotiation could occur but does not. Often this happens when someone introduces to us the opportunity to get something which we never knew we even needed and where, because of lack of preparation and lack of information, we are induced or bamboozled into buying something we had never contemplated. Opportunist sales, such as insurance, time-share, satellite dishes and the like, are examples of where experienced sales people will seek to strike a bargain with the innocent customer who, through lack of skill and preparation, is persuaded that the thing that is for sale is the very thing they have always wanted.

Perhaps the earliest negotiating and non-negotiating process occurred when the serpent persuaded Eve that the apple was the thing that she and Adam really wanted and poor old Adam ate the apple without ever inquiring about the terms of the deal, or attempting to negotiate a get-out clause.

5.3 WHY NEGOTIATE?

Why not negotiate! Unless you believe that you cannot improve the terms of the bargain that you are seeking to strike then there must be value in negotiating. Usually the other side are expecting you to negotiate anyway.

In many cases the other party is disappointed and even anxious if there is no element of negotiation in the deal.

Negotiation can be positive for both parties since, as compromise is reached and terms are disclosed, each party will learn positive information about the other and the deal reached may be better than either party had anticipated.

If you never try for the maximum you are never going to know how much you could achieve. The art of negotiation is to understand how to push for the maximum benefits, and at what point to push no further in case no deal is struck at all.

Shimon Peres said that 'all known solutions are dead ones. The art of negotiation is to invent and create and not to hang from the cliff of yesterday'. He also once said 'This is not a negotiation of give and take because [we have] something to give but nothing to take'.

5.4 THE GIVE/GET PRINCIPLE

METHOD I

PARTY A

GIVE/GET

PARTY B

GIVE/GET

Both parties are willing to give up points at issue in negotiation in order to get what they respectively want. This is a positive approach to reaching a compromise although the concessionary areas will be subject to variation. Since both parties have an attitude of compromise this method is likely to result in a good bargain for both sides.

METHOD 2

PARTY A

GIVE/GET

PARTY B

GET/GIVE

Here Party A approaches the negotiation with a willingness to give up in concessionary areas in return for something it wants. However, Party B is intending only to give up points if Party B gets what it wants. Party A may eventually revert to Party B's method and create a stalemate. Likewise Party B may keep getting without any intention of giving too quickly and create a stalemate again by forcing Party A to take a less positive approach.

METHOD 3

PARTY A

GET/GIVE

PARTY B

GET/GIVE

In this example neither party comes to the table prepared to give until a point is first won or received. This is confrontational aggressive positioning by both parties and unlikely to lead to a lasting solution. Indeed there is a real risk that both parties will have to walk away rather than conclude a deal.

5.5 WHAT IS A WIN-WIN DEAL?

Much emphasis is placed on achieving a win-win situation and many attempts have been made to define what makes for a win-win. A win-win occurs when both parties feel that not only have they achieved as good a result as possible, but that they have also helped each other achieve such a satisfactory result. If the parties genuinely believe that each party has gained more than lost, then they may be anxious to ensure that the agreement realises its potential during the life of the agreement. To be able to achieve a win-win both parties must understand the needs and goals of the other. This does not mean that the bottom line must be revealed by both sides, but that they should negotiate towards a mutual compromise and not a confrontational result. If either one or both sides intend to win at any cost or to 'score points' then it is unlikely that a win-win will be achieved.

It is important to appreciate that the real win-win deal must be capable of lasting throughout the life of the agreement. I have seen many situations where the parties to negotiation leave the table, both feeling that a satisfactory win-win agreement has been struck, only to find that six months down the line it is a win-lose deal at best and, at worst and more often than not, it is a lose-lose. This scenario often occurs when the parties are seeking to strike a 'point in time' deal where because of lack of flexibility, lack of long-term planning and short-term objective criteria the parties reach an agreement which they perceive a win-win at the time but which was never built to last.

Benjamin Franklin once said: 'Trades would not take place unless it was advantageous to the parties concerned.' Of course, it is better to strike as good a bargain as one's bargaining position admits. The worst outcome is when by overriding greed, no bargain is struck, and a trade that could have been advantageous to both parties, does not come off at all.

5.6 NEGOTIATING STYLES AND ETHICS

Your negotiating style is a combination of the personality and attitude you display during negotiations together with the approaches you adopt towards those negotiations. Your attitude and approach may remain consistent during negotiations, or one or both may change from issue to issue, from day to day, and so on. The following chart illustrates the interplay of attitudes and approaches often adopted. Some personality and attitude types are listed across the top of the chart, while common approaches appear in the left column. A discussion of ethics in negotiations follows the chart.

5.7 NEGOTIATING STYLES

PERSONALITY AND ATTITUDE TYPES			
A **P** **P** **R** **O** **A** **C** **H** **E** **S**	Co-operative/ Pleasant/ Professional/ Diplomatic/Polite	Coercive/ Combative/ Aggressive/ Arrogant/ Stubborn/ Confrontational/ Sarcastic	Mixed – Varies With Issue
Straightforward and honest			

Subtle, secretive or clever, but honest			
Slightly dishonest and/or somewhat devious			
Dishonest or dishonourable, and devious			
Mixed – varies with issue			

Many of these categories are self-explanatory, but a few require illustration. A dishonourable style of negotiation becomes evident when one party to the negotiations makes major, unqualified commitments and then refuses to honour them. Imagine a salesperson who gives a customer an unauthorised 'side letter' containing major concessions or assumptions of responsibility. Then imagine their employer refusing to honour the letter.

Another example is a party's negotiating team that agrees to positions on issues, and then reopens and renegotiates many of the issues, perhaps several times for some of them.

Other evidence of a dishonourable style is one party ignoring the content of the signed contract and continuing to negotiate as though no contract had been signed. Of course, this style is occasionally used by business people in emerging nations, not because these business people are dishonourable but more because few of them have any real experience of how Western-style business is conducted.

Dishonesty may or may not be detected in negotiations, but dishonourable behaviour will be noticeable as a general rule.

Perception plays a role in recognising your own negotiating style. For example, fairly often a dishonourable, devious, sarcastic and confrontational negotiating style used by one party's team in negotiating a major transaction or alliance will be perceived by that team as a straightforward, honest and co-operative style.

Those with a straightforward, honest and co-operative style have the tendency to feel that anyone with any other style is unethical or unprincipled. In fact, only those who are dishonest or dishonourable are generally perceived as unethical, and some who are slightly dishonest or devious might still be perceived as ethical. Literally speaking, all negotiators have principles, but those principles may or may not lead to ethical behaviour. Your feeling of trust for the other party, your perception of whether or not you obtained a fair win-win deal and your assessment of whether the other party is ethical may or may not coincide.

You might trust the other party to take only those actions that are in its short-term and long-term best interest, but you might feel that the other party is slightly unethical in its negotiating style.

A fair win-win deal can be obtained from an unethical or untrustworthy party if you know what you are doing before, during and after negotiations and if you have sufficient leverage at the negotiating table to get the concessions and the deal that you want.

The bottom line regarding ethics in negotiations is that each person decides whether or not to be completely ethical, or to engage in slightly or materially unethical conduct, and sometimes your perception of what constitutes ethical behaviour will not be shared by the other party.

It must be recognised that negotiation is unique and culture-specific. For example, in the UK we tend to negotiate on the basis of proposal and counter proposal, whereas in Asian and Far Eastern countries negotiations tend to solve problem areas from the information available. In the UK we will often accept a less than perfect position.

6 Preparing for negotiations

6.1 PROVIDER PREPARATIONS

6.1.1 In general

The degree to which some suppliers prepare for negotiations of major transactions is not well recognised by customers. In certain industries where there is a degree of ongoing maintenance and support, service revenue provides an increasingly large share of the suppliers' gross revenue, but even in these industries major transactions usually contribute most of the sellers' revenues as well as the bulk of sales commissions. Hence sales personnel, senior management, financial and treasury departments and staff and support groups and most hi-tech providers are oriented towards pursuing and securing major transactions. New accounts occupy a special place in the hearts of most suppliers because of their contribution to revenue growth and because new customers often become repeat customers. Discounts on add-on orders often are not as great as those on initial orders unless there has been careful negotiating by the customer. Hence new accounts are valued for likely future orders as well as the initial order. Sales personnel often receive bonuses and promotions based in part on their success in landing new accounts. With these incentives both new and existing customers who are major deal prospects are given much attention and thought.

6.1.2 Sales force training, customer qualification and negotiating experience

Long-established suppliers train new sales people in product characteristics, sales techniques and company policies. These new personnel are then assigned to a sales supervisor or manager, given a list of existing accounts and told to service the existing accounts and bring in new business through cold calls, referrals, existing contacts or prospects already identified. Periodic reviews of progress are conducted by the supervisor or manager, who usually visits any new or existing customer that contemplates any measurable order through the new sales representative. Large orders trigger a visit by the supervisor's or manager's superior. Each prospect for any measurable or significant order is continuously 'qualified', meaning that a series of stages are identified leading from an expression of interest to a signed contract, and the prospect is guided from one stage to the next by the sales staff. Each stage tests the continued interest of the prospect. Supervisor and manager visits are part of the testing process, which may also include product demonstrations, discussions with reference accounts, and sometimes a trial use of the desired product or an off-site benchmark test. Of course, some of these steps are also used by the prospective customer to 'qualify' the supplier.

When the time comes to close a major transaction the sales representative, their supervisor, and their manager may all attend the closing to help ensure contract signing. A contract administrator or in-house solicitor may join the sales personnel. Generally, the attention a transaction receives will depend upon its size. Most often the sales supervisors and managers, and any accompanying staff or support personnel, at negotiating sessions or closings are experienced, sophisticated negotiators. Their experience and skill usually exceeds the negotiating skill and experience of all licensee personnel. Thus the supplier almost always has an advantage in negotiations. One way a customer can neutralise that advantage is to bring an experienced negotiator into the negotiations.

Some suppliers in the IT sector train their negotiators to use unusual techniques. A few software publishers train their female sales representatives and contract negotiators to say 'Help me', whenever a deadlock or stalemate is reached. Opposing, older male negotiators often treat the younger female as they would treat their daughters and communicate the 'bottom line' of the customer that must be satisfied if the deal is to close. Usually the bottom line had not been disclosed prior to that point. Sometimes the older male on the customer's negotiating team goes further and suggests some creative problem-solving solution to the deadlock or stalemate. At least one US software publisher goes one step further and trains their female representatives or negotiators to cry and feign stomach illness when the customer gives a negative reaction to some important request by the licensor or when a deadlock or impasse is reached.

6.1.3 Standard charges

Virtually all substantial electronic and telecoms providers will publicly list their standard fees and charges for all off-the-shelf products and standard services. These fees and charges are calculated to provide profit and some room for discounts in appropriate situations. A 25%–50% profit margin in standard fees and charges is to be expected, but a 60% or greater margin is not unheard of, and each product will have a break-even quantity for recovery of development costs before it generates a profit. Standard fees and charges are usually accepted by prospective customers as a starting point for discount negotiations. Hence the provider has the advantage of being able to determine the starting point for financial discussions, and being able to concede modest or reasonable discounts while still making a profit on the transaction. Of course, this method of operation is standard in the computer and database industries as well as others, and is generally accepted as reasonable.

6.1.4   Standard, protective contracts

Prudent sellers prepare and employ standard, contract forms and offer them to customers for virtually all of their transactions. Most use terms with small print. Small type makes these agreements much shorter. Thus, they appeal to business people who prefer short contracts. More important to suppliers is the impact of such forms on negotiations and doing business. Blank lines or schedules will be used for product identification and statements of charges, but virtually no room is left for changes in contract terms, thereby creating an 'official' looking and intimidating document that discourages negotiation of non-price terms. Often this is sent in pdf format only rather than word in the hope that will make it less likely the other will amend the terms. Many business people have no interest in reading legal documents in general, much less documents in small print, thus review and negotiation of non-price terms is discouraged by the small print. Further, if a provider's form agreement is used, its general business policies, risk protections, and explanations of the transaction contained therein are likely to be accepted. Since providers do business with many customers, standardisation of contract terms is a logical administrative step and tends to minimise expenditures for contract administration. Custom-made contracts with many customers makes contract administration and its cost a major problem. Finally, provider form agreements give the provider an advantage in negotiations. The starting point for negotiations of many non-price terms in these form contracts will be slanted to some degree in favour of the provider, for example, by giving the provider flexibility in satisfying performance obligations. Thus there are many advantages inherent in the use of standard form contracts.

A customer must really want to negotiate before the time and energy necessary to review, analyse, discuss, and negotiate a fine-print contract is expended. Then changes, except for deletions, must be added via an addendum. Of course, the customer can insist upon the right to prepare a custom-made contract for its deal and indeed big IT buyers like state entities will often require the buyer's terms to be accepted as part of the process for tendering, and some do so, but these agreements are expensive and time consuming for the customer to prepare. Few customers have them prepared in advance other than large buyers, and even if they are prepared in advance or for a particular transaction, the customer must have sufficient bargaining power to insist successfully on the use of its form as the basic contract. Hence, most customers accept standard, printed, provider-protective contract forms and any changes are usually made via an addendum to the form. Of course, vendor printed-form contracts are used in many industries and are generally accepted as a reasonable way to do business.

Customers or buyers who engage in expensive transactions on a regular basis, or who license technology or services that are very important to their business more than a few times per year, should prepare and require most suppliers to use the buyer's standard form agreement. It can be difficult and time consuming to make all of the business decisions that are captured in these standard-form contracts, but the result is worthwhile for a number of reasons, for example, using the customer's standard-form contract helps to level the negotiating table that is otherwise slanted heavily in the seller's favour.

6.1.5 Pre-negotiation groundwork with customer

By the time the salesperson presents the provider's standard contract for a major transaction, he has had the opportunity for numerous meetings and telephone conversations with the customer's business or technical personnel, and these personnel are usually convinced that the proposed deal captured in the standard contract is the solution to their company's needs or problems. A member of senior management will normally sign major transaction contracts.

If the contract is forwarded to the company's lawyer before execution, it is typically forwarded with the message that some individual or group within the company wants to sign the document and has already negotiated the fee or charge to their satisfaction. If the company lawyer raises objections or concerns upon review of the contract, he may be viewed as an obstacle or 'deal killer'. While this is not true in every company, it is true in a measurable number of companies and providers are well aware of the perception. Providers prefer to have the contract signed without prior review by the company's lawyer for obvious negotiation and delay-avoidance reasons. Nevertheless, if it is sent to the company's lawyer prior to execution, providers realise that it will often be sent with the message that the contract is ready for signature by the company's business people, hence the lawyer should not delay its progress. Encouraging this message when the contract is sent to the company's lawyer is part of the groundwork done by the salespeople to minimise negotiations and hasten closing.

Providers are careful to develop one or more 'internal salesmen' or 'internal champions' as one of their standard sales techniques during their pre-negotiation groundwork with the customer. The internal champion is a vocal advocate for the acquisition of the goods or services. Usually he is the individual who is convinced the seller's products are the solution to a company need or problem and the individual who has interacted with the licensor's salesperson for some time.

By developing an internal champion who is sold on the transaction, providers hope to gain three things. First, support. A company employee in a responsible position will support contract execution by senior management, field any questions by senior management, and work to persuade senior management to sign the contract.

Secondly, pressure. The internal champion will bring pressure to bear on the company's lawyer for a quick and mild response to the contract either expressly, indirectly through a 'senior management is ready to sign the contract' message, or subtly by feeding the lawyer's apprehension about being perceived as a deal killer or obstacle if significant objections are raised. In-house counsel are more likely to feel this pressure than an outside counsel whose career is not affected by the company's politics, and even in-house counsel may feel sufficiently secure that he can review the agreement without feeling pressure to approve it quickly with little or no objection. However, sometimes that pressure is felt and it works to the provider's advantage in minimising or eliminating lawyer objections or negotiation demands. The pressure applied by the internal champion makes it expedient for the in-house counsel to apply a 'rubber stamp' approval to the contract.

Thirdly, help with negotiations. If negotiations are conducted, the internal champion is a friendly force that helps the provider at the negotiating table.

In the realm of company politics, the provider and the internal champion are now connected for better or for worse. The benefits of having an internal champion are well recognised by providers of software, computers, telecommunications equipment, databases, and related services.

6.1.6 Internal deal structuring and negotiations

Provider sales personnel are the provider's primary connection with customers and must inform the provider's management about any concessions required to close a major transaction. Because deviations from standard charges or fees and from standard contract terms are deviations from standard provider policies, the salesperson must argue for the concessions he feels are necessary and obtain management's blessing or alternative input regarding acceptable concessions. The credibility of the salesperson within their company plays a role in these internal negotiations and transaction structuring responses from management. Many salespeople feel that internal negotiations are more difficult than customer negotiations. Often the salesperson becomes an advocate for the customer in these internal discussions. After all, their commissions and bonuses will depend upon completed transactions.

6.1.7 Preparation of substantive fall-back positions on open points and early concerns

During the course of pre-negotiation groundwork by the salesperson it sometimes becomes apparent that a prospective customer for a major acquisition is determined to negotiate some points in the contract or has strong concerns about some aspects of the transaction. At this early stage the salesperson, and perhaps their supervisor, manager, and director, will confer with provider organisation staff and support groups affected by the points or concerns to discuss and plan responses. Some topics may be sufficiently sensitive to warrant preparation of immediate responses and one or more fall-back positions, and may warrant an early visit to the customer by a member of a staff or support group. For example, if the customer wants discounted 24-hour, seven-day on-site maintenance coverage by provider engineers, the regional director of the provider's engineer organisation is likely to visit the customer site prior to contract execution, and discuss their responses to the customer's request with the salesperson and others in the provider's sales organisation. Initial and fall-back positions on the pricing and details of this service will be planned in advance.

These situations can arise at any stage of the salesperson's interaction with the prospect. Providers are generally apprehensive about making concessions early in the sales cycle because they worry about having to make additional concessions of an as yet unknown nature at closing in order to obtain the business. For example, if a 'best price' is offered early in the cycle, a better price could be demanded at closing as a final condition to contract execution.

6.1.8 Inter-departmental meetings to plan negotiating strategy and tactics

Where negotiations are necessary, the supplier can usually reduce the number of open points and concerns raised during the sales cycle to a number that could be addressed at a transaction closing, or at least in one or two meetings after which the provider could reasonably hope to receive a signed contract. At this point the provider's management or sales force may call a formal meeting of staff and support groups affected by the open points or concerns to plan a negotiating strategy and one or more tactics. Any previously communicated positions and previously identified but unused fall-back positions will be reviewed. New positions will be formulated on open and likely discussion topics. These meetings can be intense when a staff or support group clashes with the sales force, but they usually generate successful strategies, tactics and positions. By the time these meetings occur, the prospective customer is almost always totally committed to doing business with the provider and is simply delayed by some final concerns or attempts to maximise concessions.

6.1.9 Preparation of contracts before negotiations commence

Sophisticated sellers prepare and deliver standard contracts for execution after the primary customer contact is sold on the transaction. Fees or charges may or may not be negotiated at this point, but other terms usually are not negotiated at this stage. Hence the preparation of the contract amounts to filling in a few blank spaces. Providers often do not wait, in other words, for a request for contracts, or give the customer much of an opportunity to think about preparing a contract. Where some industries typically negotiate a number of points before drafting or presenting a contract, software providers are ready with contracts after agreement on fees and charges, and sometimes before. This approach expedites contract signing and minimises the possibility of negotiations or 'buyer's remorse', which is a change of mind about a deal after deciding to accept it. Software provider contracts appear on customer desks before or immediately after an agreement on fees or charges.

6.2   CUSTOMER PREPARATIONS

6.2.1   In general

This section of the report addresses customer preparations for the negotiation of a major transaction. In general, customers will think about preparing for a very large transaction, but give less thought to preparations for transactions that are perceived as less than huge or very important deals. While understandable, this approach to major transactions often sets the stage for problems that could have been avoided. For example, if a software conversion or development project for a critical or very important enhancement or module of a program is projected to cost only a few thousand dollars, problems can be expected unless the project is planned well and some negotiations occur. As another example, large companies might view a software licence transaction projected to cost £100,000 as a modest transaction requiring little forethought, planning and negotiation. If the company has a well thought out, well drafted master agreement with the software and related service provider, this reaction may be appropriate. If not, planning and negotiations are highly recommended. Such a 'modest' transaction is in reality a major acquisition if the software is important to the customer, regardless of the customer's perception of its cost. Even cheap software if it does not work can cause large losses to a business.

In general, customers do not always plan enough for negotiations. They leave themselves open to avoidable problems as a result. Sales managers love un-negotiated major transactions.

This criticism does not suggest that every possible concession, or every 'ounce of blood', must be extracted at the negotiating table. More and more legal actions are threatened and take place each year as a result of poorly negotiated or drafted contracts. Like most legal cases, many of these claims are settled out of court. However, litigation is expensive and disruptive. Also, management, sales, purchasing and in-house legal personnel may be fired or have their careers negatively affected by problems in major software transactions. Trade publications report these events on a regular basis, and countless cases and terminations go unreported. Major transactions are serious business. A problem prevention orientation is highly advisable in these transactions. Suppliers recognise the wisdom of this orientation and act accordingly. Most customers need to focus on and recognise the importance of this orientation more than they do now.

6.2.2   In-house needs analysis and procurement decision

While an increasing number of customers employ outside consultants to analyse their technology needs and recommend a solution, it is probably safe to say that most customers make their own needs analysis either independently or with the help of a provider, and their own solution selection decision.

One of the common problems in an in-house analysis and selection decision process is a failure to see the big picture and prepare a master plan. For example, a customer with a data processing or management information services staff should have a master operational and growth plan that contains an acquisition procedure element, a development work procedure element, a staff training element, a maintenance service element, a disaster plan element, and so on, as well as anticipating hardware needs, setting downtime goals, deciding on distributed versus centralised capability and deciding whether to outsource service. Many customers lack a clear procedure for the acquisition of significant software, or its development, or its conversion. Such a plan should require communication between the customer's technical staff, the group that will benefit from the software or related services and senior management. Requiring senior management to sign contracts for major transactions is not enough. Senior management must be asked its expectations regarding a major transaction. In particular, senior management must communicate the results expected from the transaction in terms of business goals, business needs to be satisfied and business concerns to be solved. The master plan must call for this type of communication. While it can occur without a master plan or procedure, a written checklist containing this requirement helps to ensure that the communication will occur. If this communication does not occur, the success of a major transaction, as measured by senior management, is less likely than if the communication does occur.

Why, you may ask? One answer is because the background and mindset of a customer's technical staff typically has a technical and resource orientation. Like providers, customer personnel tend to focus on the technical capability of goods and services and of providing that capability to their employer's various departments. Senior management and the departmental users of such goods and services tend to focus on results that they will produce. Misunderstandings between these groups are common, and often leave the technical staff with a vague, incomplete or inaccurate understanding of the business goal, need or concern motivating the major transaction. Selecting the wrong solution or an inadequate solution often results. Only a minority of technical personnel, like a minority of lawyers or other professionals, can grasp, remain focused on and be driven by the overriding business purpose for a major transaction. Many negotiators tend to focus on the trees (details) rather than the wood (big picture business purpose). Of course, it may be necessary to focus on both the trees and the wood. To have the chance of creating this multiple focus in a major transaction, the business purpose for the transaction must be communicated to and understood by the involved technical personnel.

In summary, it is essential to synchronise management and technical personnel on the business needs, expectations and concerns that justify and motivate a major transaction in order to maximise its likelihood of success.

6.2.3 Consultant-aided needs analysis and procurement decision

6.2.3.1 Survey of senior management

Many outside or independent contractor consultants do a good job of helping their clients in major transactions. One of the first steps of these consultants is to meet with several members of the senior management team to survey their business goals, needs and concerns underlying a forthcoming major transaction. Another focus of their survey is to inquire about how the transaction fits within the company's short-term and long-term business plans. A third line of inquiry might be whether the contemplated transaction was recommended by the company's independent auditors, by another independent consultant's report, by a parent company, by a strategic alliance participant, or others. Any relevant business plans, reports, etc, will need to be reviewed by the consultant. Because some of the information in these documents, as well as some information conveyed verbally, is confidential and proprietary to the company, consideration should be given to requiring the consultant to sign a non-disclosure agreement.

6.2.3.2 Survey of technical personnel

Another initial step of an independent consultant in helping their client in a major transaction is to meet with the customer's senior or assigned technical personnel to survey their perceptions of their needs, goals and concerns. Preliminary thoughts of the technical personnel about the forthcoming transaction will be shared at this time. Details of the customer's current systems, equipment, facilities and staff may also be conveyed in these meetings.

6.2.3.3 Review of relevant business plans and goals, RFP preparation and evaluation

After the initial meetings, the outside consultant will review the relevant business plans, reports, and notes of their discussions with senior management and technical personnel. A plan of action will be formulated that often includes the consultant's preparation of a request for proposals ('RFP') from established providers with the types of products or services that may be needed by the customer. Often the RFP will ask the provider to propose solutions based on the factual information contained in the RFP. Further discussions with management, user departments and technical personnel normally follow. The consultant normally helps evaluate the proposals received and may help with subsequent negotiations.

6.2.4 Consensus need determination

Regardless of whether an outside consultant is employed to help with the task, it is very important for the involved parties within the customer's organisation to reach and recognise a consensus view of the need, goal or concern that should be addressed by the major transaction. This need, goal or concern may be obvious and understood by all involved parties at the outset of planning for the transaction. Almost invariably each individual involved presumes all others involved in the transaction share their view. Unfortunately, different views are the norm. Communication between technical personnel and senior management is vital to the long-term success of a major transaction. Senior management may impose a 'consensus' view of the need, goal or concern to be addressed, but technical personnel will not be certain of management's view without communication on the subject. The individuals who suffer the consequences of a different view are usually the technical personnel. Staff personnel such as an in-house lawyer who will join the negotiating team or review contracts need to understand the goal or concern motivating the major transaction, and it must be clearly explained in advance.

The immediate result of different views of a transaction may be delays in contract execution. A subsequent likely result may be delays and cost overruns in implementation. The third likely result is problems following implementation that make it clear that a mistake was made prior to contract execution. For example, if a customer needs to establish communications between recently ordered minicomputers that will be installed at remote locations and the customer's mainframe or selected microcomputers at the company's headquarters, technical personnel will tend to focus on the best software solution given the types of equipment then employed. Senior management wants the communications link, but may also want to ensure that it will work when new equipment for the headquarters' site is acquired in a year or two. The technical personnel charged with the responsibility of acquiring or developing communications software that will enable communications between remote and headquarters' computers may or may not be aware of the possibility that the headquarters' equipment will be replaced in the foreseeable future. Even if the technical personnel are aware of this possibility, or that it is probable, the future plans can easily be overlooked or forgotten by a technical evaluator charged with the responsibility of acquiring or developing software to establish the communications link as quickly as possible after the remote site computers are delivered in a few weeks or months.

If there is insufficient or no communication with senior management prior to software acquisition, three events are immediately probable. First, senior management will not express the need for the new software to work on both current and future equipment. Secondly, the technical staff will not explain to senior management that only certain types of new equipment will be compatible with the communications software and may be acquired in the future if the company's long-term need is to acquire a communications program that works now and in the future on different equipment. Thirdly, the company's staff personnel reviewing the software contract will probably not be informed of the long-term need and are unlikely to require assurances in the contract that the program acquired will work with certain types of new equipment likely to replace the current headquarters' equipment in the foreseeable future.

A possible delayed consequence of not addressing future compatibility prior to contract execution is that incompatible replacement equipment will be ordered for the headquarters' site in one or two years. When senior management is informed of the need for new communications software at that point, the reaction is likely to be negative unless the software licence fees for the current communications program were not paid in a lump sum and the licence agreement can be terminated quickly. Few senior managers like to pay twice for the same type of software in a relatively short time span. Technical personnel have been fired, demoted or received smaller than normal raises in similar situations. This is only one of countless examples of how unsynchronised views of a customer's needs, goals or concerns can create problems for the customer.

6.2.4.1 Focus on personnel

Few customers recognise the importance of key provider personnel and key customer personnel to some transactions. Provider and customer personnel are key resources in software development and conversion transactions. Customers should consider identifying key provider personnel in such projects and requiring them to remain at the customer's site until the project is completed. Providers are reluctant to make such commitments in contracts but may be persuaded in a major transaction.

In a different vein, customer personnel should be selected in advance for the key roles they will play in the transaction, for example, for the negotiating team, a project manager, etc.

6.2.4.2 Focus on necessary services

The services provided in a major transaction may be critical to the success of the transaction as a whole. If independent, third-party service providers seem likely to provide better or equivalent services at a lower cost, they should be considered in pre-negotiation planning. One important question in this regard will be whether the independent service supplier needs access to the proprietary material provided by another provider to the customer.

6.2.4.3 Line up political support

One of the mistakes commonly made by the leader of the customer's negotiating team is the failure to line up political support for their role in the forthcoming negotiations. Appointment to the role and ascertaining senior management's desired results are not enough. Senior management should be willing to stand behind the decisions, strategy and tactics of the negotiating team and should make that commitment in advance of negotiations. Providers are masters at going around obstacles in negotiations by persuading the customer's senior management to order their removal. Providers also sense a lack of senior management support or neutrality very quickly and use that situation to their advantage at the negotiating table. A united customer tends to help the customer's negotiating team.

6.2.4.4 Form negotiating team

As mentioned earlier, the best people available should be selected to form an interdisciplinary negotiating team for major transactions. A leader should be designated as the main spokesperson and liaisor with senior management. Obviously a small company engaging in a major transaction might not form a team for negotiations. Personnel in small companies tend to wear several hats, or have several areas of responsibility. In theory, one person can represent a customer as well as several in the context of negotiations whether the customer is large, small or somewhere in between. However, the best approach to negotiating a major transaction is often the interdisciplinary team approach because it involves personnel from various interested disciplines from the outset of negotiations, it permits them full knowledge and decision-making opportunities and it generally ensures that they 'buy into' the transaction. A one-man approach creates the risk that the other groups in the customer organisation will present their concerns, or argue that their needs were not met by the transaction, after negotiations are completed. Even worse is the possibility that the other groups may argue that aspects of the transaction required their prior approval which was not obtained. The single negotiator may have intentionally or inadvertently ignored the approval requirement of the other groups, but in any event the post-negotiation negative reactions of other groups may slow down contract execution, may kill the deal and may embarrass the single negotiator. Sometimes such negative post-negotiation reactions are simply based on the perception that the individual negotiator encroached on another group's 'turf' or area of responsibility. Sometimes these reactions are based on legitimate concerns that the individual negotiator overlooked or ignored and that will be difficult or impossible to address following negotiation completion.

An obvious variation of the single man approach is to have the single negotiator tell the provider(s) that deal approval is required by other groups before the contract is signed. This approach can work well in small, relatively unimportant transactions. At least two problems arise when it is employed in major transactions. First, there is usually some delay in closing the deal while the reviewing groups review and learn about the transaction. Secondly, it can be difficult to obtain changes in the contract(s) for the transaction at this stage. A small number of unimportant changes are commonly accepted at this stage, but providers tend to become disturbed by significant changes requested after negotiations have been completed with the customer's primary negotiator. With some justification providers can question the customer's good faith and seriousness of interest in the transaction under these circumstances. The provider's complaints can create pressure on the reviewing groups to retract or modify their request. Whether or not important changes are made, the reviewing groups may become irritated at the sole customer negotiator and the customer's relationship with the provider may become strained. A solo negotiator runs political risks in this approach to negotiating a major transaction whether or not those risks are perceived in advance. More than a few solo negotiators of major transactions have had their careers negatively impacted because representatives of other groups were not parties to the negotiation of the deal. Nevertheless, this approach is used with some frequency.

The best negotiating team usually includes a technical person, a legal representative and someone from a financial or controllers group. Of course, the degree of importance of the transaction affects the customer's judgment on the parties involved. A financial person may not be needed as long as budget constraints are not exceeded. Alternatively, a member of senior management may participate in the negotiations.

Sophisticated customers always involve their legal group in negotiations. Not being involved in negotiations of a major transaction from the outset is a major complaint of customer solicitors. If one is involved early in the negotiations, a customer's lawyer can help structure the deal in a logical manner, can raise important legal issues early, and can protect the customer's interests while the parties are engaged in give and take discussions. Also, the legal group will seldom object to a deal if one of its people were involved in the negotiations from the outset. Delays can be minimised if a legal person is involved with negotiations, contrary to the perception of many businesspeople. Where the legal group is not included in the negotiating team, the potential for significant delays is maximised rather than minimised.

6.2.5 Selection of acquisition structure and negotiating strategy and tactics

After the negotiating team is selected, prior plans should be reviewed and incorporated as basic elements in the structural plan for the transaction, and in the strategic and tactical plans of the team. Discussion of the other elements of the structure, strategy and tactics should then occur. A master plan should be agreed upon at this time. As with any 'game plan', adjustments may be required later. Nevertheless, a sophisticated customer will spend time and invest careful thought in a master plan for forthcoming negotiations.

Another step that may be taken by the team is practice negotiation sessions. If the basic contract(s) for the transaction are in the customer's possession prior to its negotiation, practice sessions can be helpful in finalising the customer's negotiating plans. If not, these sessions may still be helpful to some degree.

6.2.6 Obtain management support

After the master plan for the pending negotiations is completed to the negotiating team's satisfaction this plan should be reviewed in some detail with one or more members of senior management. Helpful suggestions are often the result of these meetings. In addition, they give senior management the opportunity to confirm that the plan is consistent with the company's needs, goals or concerns. Equally as important is the blessing of senior management on the plan. If the senior manager 'buys into' the plan, three benefits normally result. First, it is unlikely that a contract or result consistent with the plan will be criticised following negotiations. Secondly, delays because of senior management review of a transaction prior to contract execution become unlikely or are minimised in length. Thirdly, if the provider tries to solicit support from senior management during negotiations on a topic or position rejected by the negotiating team, the provider's attempt to go around the team is more likely to fail as long as the team is acting in accordance with the approved master plan. The substantive and political support of senior management for the negotiating team can be very important to the team's success in negotiations.

6.2.7 Select one team member as leader and interface

Often a negotiating team leader will be selected in the normal course of planning for the forthcoming negotiations. If this selection has not been made prior to commencement of negotiations, it should be an item on a planning checklist that is resolved at this stage. One spokesperson is important to the progress of negotiations. Other team members may contribute on topics in their areas of responsibility, but one leader is necessary to prevent a disorganised negotiation. Failure to agree upon a team leader sets the stage for disagreements or irritations among team members that providers can exploit. A united front is important in team negotiations. Providers are extremely perceptive of opportunities to play one team member against another at the negotiating table.

6.2.8 Know when to hire outside help

Some customers are sensitive to the need for outside consultants or lawyers in their negotiations of major transactions, but most are not. Customers usually need outside help more often than providers because providers employ sophisticated negotiators and normally approach negotiations from a superior bargaining position. Outside help can neutralise the provider's superior position and skill in negotiations, or at least minimise both, providing the consultant or solicitor is an experienced expert. If outside help is employed, it is better to involve the helper at the pre-negotiation planning stage than to rush him in at the start of negotiations. The money saved and concessions gained, through the help of outside experts, frequently exceeds the value of the service they provide.

Some companies have a large, in-house legal department with experienced solicitors who will handle the negotiations. Big companies may also have a procurement department which handles purchases and has many years of experience of negotiating contracts. Others bring in their regular solicitor who is an expert in IT contracts to amend draft agreements and provide advice on what to concede and what to accept.

Part IV
Preparing for drafting

7 Preparing the contracts

7.1 PRE-CONTRACTUAL DOCUMENTS AND CONFIDENTIALITY

7.1.1 Introduction

In the course of negotiations or discussions leading towards a contract the parties demonstrate considerable elements of trust at a time when they do not know enough about each other for trust really to exist.

There is often an assumption that until the contract is signed neither party is in any way bound to the other. This is not necessarily the case. During the course of negotiations the parties will not only exchange information which may be regarded as confidential, but will also create contractual obligations so that at the point of dispute, whilst there may not be a signed contract, there are often contractual obligations.

When parties are exchanging information they should clearly state whether they intend the information to be legally binding or not. This applies as much to exchanges of information by e-mail as it does to exchanges of information in paper form. The parties should use protective language to ensure that no contractual obligation exists, unless, of course, they wish their exchange of information to create binding obligations.

Before a contract is signed, the exchanges between the parties may be formalised in a number of ways:

- a term sheet;
- a letter of intent;
- a comfort letter;
- a Memorandum of understanding;
- heads of terms;
- heads of agreement.

The terminology used is less important than the binding or non-binding nature of the document. These pre-contractual documents will be discussed later.

7.1.2   Business secrets and confidentiality

Whether or not the parties enter into a pre-contractual 'agreement' (binding or otherwise) it is usually the case that in the course of negotiations, one party will reveal to the other information that is confidential. It is important to ensure, as early as possible, that the parties agree how to deal with business secrets and other confidential information and issues such as this are best dealt with by the use of confidentiality letters or agreements often called 'confidentiality agreements' or 'non-disclosure agreements' or 'NDAs'.

Even if the NDA is kept short and is executed in the form of a letter it is still essential that a number of key issues are addressed and these are as follows:

- *The parties.* The parties to the NDA should clearly be defined and it should be considered carefully as to whether or not a party that is a group company should be defined as a specific company rather than the group as a whole. The risk of sharing information for the benefit of an entire group is that many of the group companies may be in jurisdictions where an enforcement of the agreement may be difficult and expensive and in any event the wider that confidential information is shared, the greater the risk.

- *Consideration.* For a contract to be legally binding, it is usual for there to be some form of consideration whether in the form of monetary value or by way of performance. In mutual NDAs there are often obligations passing both ways and therefore consideration is achieved. In one-way confidentiality agreements consideration may not pass between the parties and therefore the disclosing party may wish to include some form of nominal consideration with the other party or sign it as a deed.

- *Obligations of confidence.* Even if the NDA is not binding common law may imply a duty of confidence if it is clear that the nature of the information being exchanged was obvious to the parties as confidential. It can be very risky to rely on this. It is better to have express terms of confidentiality in the agreement.

- *Term.* Some confidentiality agreements are open ended. This may be useful if the parties accept that confidentiality should last in perpetuity particularly if information will still be confidential for decades. If the parties are certain nothing that is exchanged is likely to be confidential in, say, five years then a five-year term on confidentiality and obligations only to use the information for the defined purpose may be acceptable, dependent upon the nature of the information being exchanged.

- *Subject matter.* The parties should clearly define what items are the subject of confidentiality and how information should be flagged as being confidential. In addition, the parties should define the circumstances in which confidential information is to be disclosed and used.

- *Exceptions.* The parties need to state clearly when confidential information is not to be treated as confidential. Typically this arises when the information in question is either already in the public domain or comes into the possession of the recipient via a third party or was already known to the recipient prior to disclosure.

- *Restrictions on use.* The parties should indicate how confidential information is to be protected and used and what obligations are to be placed on a disclosing party to ensure that sufficient steps are taken to maintain the proprietary value of the information and to state the information will only be used for a defined purpose. For example, an author who wishes their work to be analysed by a company with the view to publication should take responsibility for protecting their intellectual property at all times.

- *Duties of the parties.* Once confidential information has been disclosed the NDA needs to define the obligations of the disclosing party and the recipient during the period of disclosure. In addition, there needs to be a formula as to how confidential information is handled on termination of the NDA or on the confidential information ceasing to be of use to the recipient.

- *Law and disputes.* The parties need to agree on the applicable law of the NDA and on mechanisms as to how any disputes are to be dealt with.

7.2 THE USE OF HEADS OF AGREEMENT

7.2.1 Introduction

There are occasions when the parties negotiate upon a standard form of conditions of the licensor and it may be that many of those terms remain intact, complete and unchanged and only a few clauses are changed, for example, those relating to pricing, delivery dates and ownership of intellectual property rights, to name a few.

In many cases very little of the provider's standard terms and conditions are used and larger companies and corporations use the provider's terms and conditions or standard forms as a starting point only.

There are, however, occasions, particularly where the deal relates to bespoke software, where the parties start negotiations with a blank sheet of paper and create a final contract based around each other's specific requirements within the deal. There are standard terms which will always be necessary in any form of software licence but how do the parties in negotiation construct a satisfactory contract from a blank sheet of paper with or without their lawyer being present throughout the deal making? Perhaps by the use of Heads of Agreement or a Memorandum of Understanding. Whatever is used be very clear as to whether it is intended to be legally binding or not and say so in the document.

7.2.2 Contract skeleton

There are essential elements in any form of contract and the who, what, when, where, why and how process is applicable here. In other words, you need to agree on who the parties are; what the product is and the other essential elements of the deal are; when delivery is to take place and when other milestones are to be achieved; where delivery is to take place, where the software is to be located, where the territory is to be in terms of distribution; why certain obligations of the parties arise and why this particular contract is being formed; and, finally, how will certain obligations be performed, certain disputes settled and how will the contract come to an end or be terminated.

In building the contract there are certain logical places for certain specific terms to be included. Without stating the obvious, the first portion of the contract should deal with the date of the contract, the details of the parties, the reasoning for the contract being entered into and the definitions. So, first, you will have outlined the effective date of the contract, who the contract is being made between, why it is being entered into and, finally, what all the subsequent specific terms and words in the contract will mean.

In effect the next portion of the contract is the major portion, which includes the essential terms such as the nature of the program, the duration of the contract, the rights granted and excluded, the obligations of the parties, the warranties, the ownership of intellectual property rights, acceptance tests and so on.

The next major portion of the contract comprises what in the UK are known as 'boiler plate' clauses, such as severability, arbitration, governing law and jurisdiction, *force majeure*, notices and so on.

Finally, there may be schedules which give the opportunity for the parties to list detailed and specific items such as milestones, detail on the software products, list of intellectual property rights attaching to them such as trade names, trademarks, patents and so on.

7.2.3 Drafting the Heads

The Heads of Agreement or Memorandum of Understanding forms not only an *aide-memoire* during the course of negotiations but also registers in plain language the terms agreed.

Heads of Agreement are not prepared with the intention that they are the contract itself (or at least not often) but rather that they are the precursor to the full form contract which the parties' lawyers will finalise.

As to whether the Heads of Agreement are in themselves contractually binding will depend upon the nature of the wording of the Heads of Agreement, but it is the writer's opinion that Heads of Agreement should be 'subject to formal contract' and certainly signed with the wording 'Subject to board approval' or 'Subject to final contract'. In this way whilst the terms negotiated and agreed by the negotiating teams are reduced to written form, neither party is bound by the Heads of Agreement but will only be bound at the point that the final agreement is signed, dated and exchanged. Sometimes a few of the terms will be legally binding, eg, an exclusivity period for negotiations and a confidentiality clause and some choice of law/boilerplate standard clauses. If so state in the specific clause that that clause is legally binding (but not the rest of the document).

When producing the Heads of Agreement, keep the language simple and plain but cover the essential points. It is often difficult in the computer industry to avoid jargon but, where jargon is used, it may be worthwhile defining it (particularly where the customer is not experienced but the licensor is) and even if both parties understand the jargon remember that the purpose of Heads of Agreement is to record the negotiated deal in case of a breakdown and where a breakdown occurs it may be a lay person who will have to decide the precise interpretation of jargon.

Keep the clauses short and clear. Heads of Agreement are precisely that – they are bullet points or headings and are not intended to be lengthy clauses – that is something for the final agreement.

Try to use consistent numbering or phrasing so that whoever prepares the final agreement can logically follow through and interpret the particular bullet points and their subheadings.

Be sure that words are correctly spelt. A typing error can have a dramatic effect. For example, 'the Licensee is *not* entitled to more than one free copy' means something entirely different from 'the Licensee is *now* entitled to more than one free copy'.

Try to ensure no work is done until the Heads of Agreement are followed up with a signed contract. It is dangerous to operate on the basis of Heads of Agreement only.

7.2.4 Three golden rules

During the course of negotiations, although the parties may agree on points, certain assumptions may have been made, and the licensor and the licensee may have an entirely different view of what has been agreed.

The first golden rule applicable to drafting contractual documents, whether Heads of Agreement or not, is:

- *Those who think they have agreed generally have not*

Where the negotiating teams have gained mutual respect and believe that they are working towards the same common goal the second golden rule applies:

- *Those who think that they get on well will generally fall out*

Finally, whether negotiations take a matter of hours, a matter of days or a matter of months and nothing has been reduced to final contract form but the parties are already dealing with each other as if there were contracts, the third golden rule applies:

- *An oral agreement is not worth the paper it is written on*

The following is a list of do's and don'ts for the initial stages of negotiation. Act reasonably and in a friendly manner as the object of negotiations is to reach agreement and not to win an argument.

When a written statement has been submitted by your opposite number (OPPO), do:

(a) enquire about each significant point asking why it is made unless it is obvious;

(b) appear ignorant, even if this is not true, in order that a particular statement that you do not agree with can be explained at length;

(c) note points with which you disagree and reserve your position;

(d) make certain each point has been fully understood even if this means going over the ground twice – this applies particularly if the languages are not the same;

(e) test out the strength of OPPO's view of each point of significance so that at a later time one can assess how far a particular point is a sticking point or is negotiable;

(f) be aware of the interrelationship between different contract points and the possible counter-arguments which will be developed if success is achieved on any particular one;

(g) correct your OPPO if he is proceeding on a false belief as to a factual position for which you are responsible.

Do not:

(a) speculate on OPPO's reasons or put words into their mouth;

(b) show the depth of your knowledge by answering questions put to your OPPO by another member of your team;

(c) agree significant points immediately, even if agreement will be reached in the end;

(d) snatch at what appears to be a favourable bargain or interpretation of OPPO's views;

(e) be drawn into lengthy arguments on any individual point for which it may be difficult to withdraw;

(f) betray feelings by showing anger, surprise or delight at OPPO's remarks;

(g) improve OPPO's judgment unless it is advantageous.

When you have submitted a written proposal do:

(a)   limit answers to questions to the minimum necessary;

(b)   test out the strength of OPPO's suggestions by seeing if he will withdraw them without requiring any corresponding concessions.

Do not:

(a)   elaborate at length on motives;

(b)   concede anything or be drawn into trade-off negotiations before all points have been discussed.

When no written statement has been submitted by either side do:

(a)   identify all the points to be discussed;

(b)   cover each point in sufficient depth for both sides to be aware of each other's position;

(c)   keep the discussion explanatory;

(d)   correct your OPPO if he is proceeding on a false belief as to a factual position for which you are responsible;

(e)   be aware of the interrelationship between different contract points and the possible counter arguments which will be developed if success is achieved on any particular one.

Do not:

(a)   let the discussions ramble on without any defined order;

(b)   concentrate the discussion on one point to the exclusion of all others;

(c)   be drawn into definite commitments either in the form of making a firm concession or taking up a position from which it may be difficult later to withdraw.

In the course of initial negotiations it may be necessary to reveal confidential information to your OPPO, which you will necessarily need to protect should the deal not proceed, and I suggest either a letter of confidentiality is entered into or if the circumstances dictate a more comprehensive non-disclosure agreement is signed.

8 Checklist of the contents of a typical software licence agreement

8.1 OVERVIEW

It is a truism in the computer and software industries that everything is negotiable if the deal is big enough to warrant the discounts or risks required to obtain the business. This maxim has limits, for example, sophisticated providers will avoid unprofitable transactions and pay heed to legal limitations on their ability to make price and non-price concessions. Nevertheless, because many points may be negotiated in a major software licence transaction, this section of the book briefly comments on various types of provisions commonly found in several types of licence agreements for a major software transaction. Some standard contracts employed in such transactions are contained in the Appendix to this book. These agreements may be referenced for examples of provisions that capture many of the types of terms noted below. It should be remembered, however, that contract terms appropriate in one major software transaction may not be appropriate in another.

It is perhaps an obvious piece of advice, but one that is often overlooked, that it is extremely useful for software contracts to be given a title or heading so that as a matter of good practice and administration, it is easy upon picking up a contract to understand what its content is likely to be about. In other words, the agreement should be described as what it is, for example, a software licence agreement or a distribution agreement or a development agreement and so on.

8.1.1 Parties

It is worthwhile considering whether the parties to the contract are the correct contracting parties.

From the provider's point of view, the provider should be sure that it is using the correct supplying or trading company as the contracting party and, furthermore, that that contracting party is capable of giving all of the warranties and guarantees that may be set out later in the agreement. For UK companies look at websites and also Companies House for correct company names.

From the customer's point of view, it is essential that the customer is sure that the customer's contracting entity is that which the customer actually requires to be party to the contract. The customer may need to make sure that its company is described as including its subsidiaries and associated companies, all of whom may wish to have the benefit of the licensed software.

Many providers 'ring fence' their intellectual property rights by placing ownership of software and other assets into non-trading holding companies which may be situated offshore or in other jurisdictions separate from the jurisdiction in which the trading or supplying-provider company is actually based. If ownership of intellectual property rights and other assets are vested in such a manner, then the customer needs to be sure that the provider company with whom it is contracting is capable of making the guarantees and warranties in the agreement and is also in a position to control source code if it is placed in escrow. If the contracting provider's company is not the owner of the software then the customer may need to ask for some further assurances from the provider that the true owner of the software can provide the necessary escrow arrangements and performance warranties which only the true owner can give.

In the case of small software developers, often the developer company is no more than the corporate embodiment of one or two essential programmers and the customer may want to contract not only with the developer company, but also with its director/shareholder programmers in order to obtain the maximum guarantees and warranties as to performance, quality and the like of the services being provided.

8.1.2 Recitals (Background Clauses)

Some software contracts recite or state at the outset the reasons as to why the contract is being entered into and often describe the background or knowledge of the parties concerned. For example, 'the licensor is experienced in the provision of software solutions for the higher educational sector'.

Such a recital may well be an accurate description of the expertise of the licensor but it may also, in the case of litigation, be used by the customer as an argument (in the event of a failure of the software to perform) that the licensor was representing an expertise which it did not in fact have.

In some cases, where standard software contracts are used to apply to non-standard situations, the incorporation of standard recitals may be highly inappropriate and therefore whilst recitals at the outset of the contract may be of use, their precise wording should be carefully considered by both parties.

In other cases where the parties have had earlier agreements between them recitals can be extremely useful in setting out the background.

8.1.3 Definitions

Definitions are very important in many major software transactions. Why? There are several answers. First, technical terminology is not always consistently used by provider and customer technical personnel, much less their business or staff personnel. One reason for such inconsistency is that all technical personnel do not have the same level of knowledge, experience and understanding. A definition of key technical terms helps to reduce the chances of a misunderstanding among personnel. Usually, a capital letter is used throughout the contract where a defined term has been used even though that word would not normally be capitalised in English, eg, Software with capital S means the term is defined in the definitions.

Secondly, software and related service providers are not totally consistent in their use of non- technical terms in their standard form agreements. Software is not always called software. A customer using software from four different sources could encounter four different generally descriptive names for the providers' products, for example, programs, program products, tools, conversion tools, software tools, software programs, source code, utility programs, spreadsheets, operating systems, productivity aids, courseware, microcode, executable programs, etc. The likelihood of confusion among customers increases as providers wax eloquent in their use of vague names for their various services, especially where some services are bundled and some are not, but their names are virtually identical. Clear definitions would help almost every provider's standard form agreements: vague definitions, few definitions, or no definitions are more common.

Thirdly, providers and customers alike tend to forget or overlook the potential audiences for their contracts. Judges and arbitrators may understand clear definitions of key technical or business words common in the type of transaction reflected by the parties' agreement, but they are not likely to understand such words except with clear definitions.

This analysis does not suggest that every term capable of being misunderstood or that might be foreign to a judge or jury must be defined. Rather, it suggests that key words call for definitions.

Definitions can be inserted in a contract in several ways. The introduction to the contract and statement of the parties' desires may contain defined terms. The first section of the agreement may define additional terms. Sometimes definitions are located in an appendix to the agreement. The other major approach to definitions is to define terms the first time they are used in an agreement. These approaches can be combined in an agreement.

8.1.4 Payment(s)

8.1.4.1 Amount(s)

The amount(s) paid in a software licence agreement are the business heart of the contract. From a businessperson's standpoint, payment(s) should be clearly stated even if nothing else in the contract is clear.

The amount(s) payable can be couched in various forms. For example, some software licence agreements require payment of a one-time, lump-sum licence fee. Others require annual or monthly licence fee payments. In development projects, payments may hinge on satisfaction of milestone requirements during the project. Some portion of a licence fee may be conditional upon acceptance. Countless payment schemes are used in different situations and the scheme employed helps to dictate the amount(s) payable at one or more points in time.

The location of the payment(s) provision in a software licence agreement also varies. It may be contained in the licence grant, in an attached schedule, or in a separate provision. Alternatively, the amount(s) due may be stated in a provider's standard price or fee schedule or list and incorporated in the agreement by reference. Generally speaking, it is preferable from a clarity standpoint to specify the amounts due somewhere in a software licence agreement. There are exceptions to this principle, however, such as the amount due for a microcomputer software program distributed under a shrink-wrap licence agreement. Here a price tag may be affixed to the container for disks bearing the software.

8.1.4.2 Due date(s)

The due date(s) for payment will vary according to the payment scheme adopted in the software licence agreement or necessitated by the type of transaction. For example, internet ordered software is usually paid for in advance of receipt via credit card.

The due date(s) for payment are frequently negotiated in a major software transaction. Much time may be devoted to the timing for payments in discussions between the software provider and customer. This attention is especially common in software development and conversion transactions, but is also fairly common in other types of transactions involving a software licence, such as distribution arrangements. The timing of payment and mechanisms to ensure payment are very important in international distribution arrangements. The larger the international transaction, the more likely it is that letters of credit will be employed to ensure payment by a point in time.

8.1.4.3 Increases and caps

Software users paying an annual or other periodic payment may sign agreements allowing the provider to increase licence fees, maintenance fees, etc over the life of the contract. Sophisticated users will attempt to negotiate a 'cap' or limit on such increases in any given year or other period during the agreement's term. In a major transaction many providers will agree to a reasonable ceiling on their increases per period. For software as a service arrangements monthly fees throughout are the norm.

8.1.4.4   Cure period for late payments

A cure period for late payments is a contract provision that allows a payment to slip past its due date without creating a breach of contract, provided the payment is made during the specified extension or 'cure' period. The provider is sometimes required to notify the customer of the provider's failure to receive a timely payment before the cure period is triggered. A cure period for late payments is worded differently from an extension of invoice payment time from 30 to 45 or 60 days which moves the due date for payment backward. The cure period does not move the provider's originally requested due date backwards, although that can be the practical effect, rather the cure period is a grace period intended to allow occasional, limited flexibility in the customer's, distributor's, etc payment performance, and a mechanism for inadvertent payment oversights to be corrected.

8.1.4.5   Interest on late payment

Customers who are slow to pay their invoices are a problem for software providers as they are in any business. Some software providers will attempt to discourage late payments by including an interest charge on outstanding overdue balances in their standard software licence agreements that call for multiple periodic payments. Even without this the Late Payment of Commercial Debts (Interest) Act 1998 allows interest and a collection charge to be charged. If the rate of interest is much higher than the UK statutory rate however (which is bank base rate plus 8%) then the clause is void so it is often better simply just to rely on the statutory provisions. In certain jurisdictions excessive amounts of interest charged may be viewed as unreasonable, usury or a 'penalty' thus invalidating the provision.

8.1.4.6   Reductions in charges or fees

Software providers infrequently, but occasionally, reduce their standard licence fee for a product and convey the savings to customers. Competitive pressures sometimes force such reductions. They also occur on occasion when older products are being phased out in favour of newer, improved products although these reductions may be offset by increases in standard maintenance charges for the older products.

In the context of software development or conversion transactions, reductions in specified charges may appear as contingencies built into the parties' agreement that are triggered by failure to complete the project, or a portion of the work, by a specified date or within a specified period after an event. Obviously a customer must negotiate for such a plan prior to contract execution. Such reductions appear more often in contracts with government departments than in a commercial customer context. Here the reductions may be accomplished by the department filing a claim against a performance bond required of the provider, even if no specific sum was identified as the proper reduction in project cost for failure to satisfy a milestone or meet a completion date.

8.1.4.7 Bonus

In the same context of software development or conversion transactions, and occasionally in the context of a facilities management, maintenance, service bureau or distribution agreements, the customer will agree to pay the service provider a bonus for some performance in excess or advance of that required by the parties' agreement. Service providers must negotiate for such a plan prior to contract execution, but the door may be opened in negotiations by a customer who desires a reduction in charges upon a failure to meet a deadline or satisfy milestone criteria after several attempts. One natural response to such a customer is to request bonuses at least as numerous and significant as the requested reductions.

8.1.4.8 Retention against acceptance

In development and conversion transactions, in major software acquisitions, in turnkey equipment and software acquisitions, and some other software-related arrangements it is usually prudent for the party making the payment(s) to attempt to negotiate a 25% or greater retention from the agreed upon fees or charges until acceptance occurs. While providers of software or related services do not like to concede such a partial withholding of agreed upon payment(s), such concessions can be reasonable and obtainable through negotiations. To make such a request reasonable the criteria for acceptance must be clear and mutually acceptable. Many customers feel that a reserve for acceptance mechanism in their agreement keeps providers motivated to fix problems and to work hard to prevent them from happening, for example, delivery delays, acceptance test failures, etc.

8.1.5 Licence grant

The licence grant in a software licence agreement is one of its most important provisions. Even in software as a service agreement the user is licensed to use the product and the licensing is just as important as in a classical software licence. The grant provision defines the rights of the customer-licensee with respect to the software licensed and usually contains the restrictions or limitations imposed by the licensor on the licensee's rights. As a general rule, rights not granted expressly or by implication in the grant clause are not conveyed by the licence agreement. Of course, rights are sometimes conveyed and restrictions are fairly often located in other sections of a licence agreement. Also, additional rights may be conveyed verbally after contract execution, implied through the parties' course of dealing with one another, or added to a contract in an addendum. The following discussion explores the rights and restrictions commonly found in the grant clauses of software licence agreements for major software transactions.

Note that the licence grant contains a mixture of business considerations addressed in more or less legal sounding terminology.

8.1.5.1   Exclusive or non-exclusive

A key point of any licence grant is whether it is exclusive or non-exclusive. 'Exclusive' means only that the licensee is allowed to use the software in that territory or as otherwise set out. The word 'sole' on the other hand means 'only' and is not as restrictive as it means the licensor may compete with the licensee. Use these words carefully. When a copyright owner grants an exclusive licence to all of their copyright rights, they give exclusive rights for the duration of the grant and within the confines of the grant's limitations. Exclusive licences are more likely to be granted by developers to publishers or publishers to distributors than they are to be conveyed from publishers to software users. By definition, only one user could have an exclusive licence grant for a particular protected right without the publisher breaching a contract by giving a second user the same right. Publishers would go bankrupt if they could grant only one licence.

A non-exclusive licence is the opposite of an exclusive licence in that it means 'one of (potentially) many'. The licensor of software under a non-exclusive licence has discretion to license hundreds or thousands of copies, or only one copy. Non-exclusive copyright licences do not convey ownership of any right and nor do exclusive copyright licences. Non-exclusive licences are frequently granted to commercial software users.

8.1.5.2   To use; make or reproduce; distribute by sale, lease, rental, loan, gift, or licence; publicly display; publicly perform

A second key point of any licence grant is the rights conveyed to the licensee. The variety of the possible rights conveyed illustrates the breadth of the legal concept of a software licence and the various uses of a software licence agreement. For example, a software user-licensee obtains possession of a copy of software and the right to use the copy either expressly or by implication in a software licence grant. The user may also receive the right to reproduce the copy received for backup or archive purposes. In contrast, a software conversion or reproduction house normally receives only the right to reproduce copies of a program for a publisher or distributor. A distributor normally receives the right to distribute copies of a program by sale, lease or licence; and may receive the right to reproduce copies, directly or through a subcontractor, or the right publicly to display the operation of the program in the course of marketing efforts, for example, to display the operation of a microcomputer program at trade shows, in training classes, etc and to allow dealers or retailers to display its operation to potential customers. If the program is a game or entertainment program, the distributor and its dealers may receive the right publicly to perform the game in the course of marketing efforts.

Of course, if a program is sold to a user or distributor, that party can treat the copy purchased as a book may be treated, assuming copyright protection. For example, the purchaser could resell the copy, rent or lease it to another, modify the program as necessary to make it operate on their computer, etc. However, this discussion focuses on licensed software and presumes a valid and enforceable software licence agreement. Such agreements may prohibit user-licensee modifications, reproductions, transfers, etc or may prohibit a distributor from modifying and using the program while allowing its distribution.

In general, a licensee of software protected by copyright law will infringe the owner's copyright if the licensee's actions exceed the scope of its licence grant. The licensor need not expressly retain rights not granted, in other words, in order to prohibit unlicensed actions. Copyright licence grants will be interpreted as prohibiting actions not otherwise expressly allowed.

The decision in the case of *Laurence Wrenn & Integrated Multi-Media Solutions Ltd v Stephen Landamore* [2007] EWHC 1833 (Ch) demonstrates that where computer software is commissioned it is essential to clarify in the contract rights of ownership and licence terms.

In the case in question, where the commissioning company and its sole director, Mr Wrenn, commissioned Mr Landamore to develop certain software programs there was no initial contract and whilst there did not appear to be any dispute over the fact that ownership of the programs remained with the programmer, Mr Landamore, when the parties fell out with each other and tried to confirm their legal rights and obligations by subsequent contract the issues of ownership and right became more confused.

Ultimately the UK High Court held that although the software programs were commissioned by Mr Wrenn and his company there was no need to imply an assignment of copyright in order for Mr Wrenn and his company to commercialise the software and therefore an exclusive licence was a satisfactory solution.

In addition, the Court held that for Mr Wrenn and his company to make use of the software, it was necessary to have access to the source code even though ownership remained with Mr Landamore.

With hindsight, the parties would have been better to have reduced their respective understandings to contract at the earliest possible stage. The complexity of code in programs means that an assignment of outright ownership is unlikely to work and the parties need to carefully construct licensing and source code access arrangements.

8.1.5.3 Territory, host(s) and site(s)

Often a licence grant specifies a limitation on the licensee's actions regarding the licensed software in the nature of a territorial, system or location statement. For example, a distributor might have the territory within which it may distribute copies of software specified in the licence grant. A user might be told by the licence grant that it may use the licensed copy on a single computer, a single network or at a single site.

Of course, there are variations on this theme. A user-licensee may be informed by the licence grant provision of a software licence agreement that it may use the software at any company-owned location, or that the use allowed is limited to use in connection with information from one company location. The latter right is designed to prohibit processing information from remote locations. Licence agreements with a government department may allow use by any government department. Even if such agreements are intended to be limited to a specific department or user within a department, DEFCONS (which are incorporated into such agreements) may override these provisions. Knowledgeable counsel is a necessity for software providers doing business with departments if they wish to retain control of their intellectual property rights in their software products.

In a similar vein, the laws of foreign countries may nullify or override attempts to provide exclusivity of territory. For example, the Treaty on the Functioning of the European Union (or Lisbon Treaty), arts 101 and 102 (formerly the Treaty of Rome, arts 81 and 82) may, subject to certain exceptions, prevent attempts to provide exclusivity which create or may create a monopoly – those rules apply in the EU. The UK has similar competition laws in the Competition Act 1998. Once again, any lawyers knowledgeable in this area can assist software providers in maintaining control over their rights and products and in avoiding unenforceable or illegal contract provisions.

8.1.5.4 Duration-limited, evergreen, perpetual, unspecified

The duration of the licence grant is usually stated in the grant clause and varies with the type of software and situation in question. Software is often licensed on a perpetual basis, although paying monthly fees whilst the software is hosted on the cloud is more common nowadays.

Some licence agreements are of limited duration but renewable under an 'evergreen' clause that continues the life of the licence until it is terminated by the licensor or licensee. Once again the licence grant in these agreements may have a specified duration or may track the life of the licence agreement.

8.1.5.5   Relationship of licence term to term of contract

The duration of the licence grant does not always coincide with the duration of the software licence agreement. For example, the licence agreement may be signed by the parties and the software may be delivered subsequently with its licence term commencing upon its acceptance. The term of such an agreement may commence upon contract execution rather than acceptance of the program. The same contract may serve as the licence agreement for a second program acquired months or years after contract execution. The second program could be brought under the terms and conditions of the agreement via a letter or schedule signed by the parties. The two programs would then be licensed under the same licence agreement, but the duration of their individual licences may be inconsistent with each other and with the duration of the licence agreement. The licence for either of the programs may be terminable without terminating the licence agreement. Sometimes the licences of all programs used or distributed under one licence agreement will be terminated but the parties will continue the life of the agreement expecting it to be given new application to another program licensed in the future.

Software is commonly licensed under an agreement whose licence grant expires contemporaneously with the life of the agreement, and program licences can be structured to have a contemporaneous term. Where equipment is leased and several programs are licensed at the same time, the user may negotiate to make the lease term and licence terms contemporaneous so that the software can be replaced when the equipment is replaced.

8.1.5.6   Number of copies licensed

Licence grant provisions in software user licence agreements normally specify the number of copies of each program licensed. In distribution agreements a quantity of each program distributed may be stated as a quota, or the distributor may be required to maintain a specified minimum inventory. A site licence or company licence may give a user the right to reproduce and use at the site or throughout the company a specified quantity of copies, a maximum number of copies or an unlimited number of copies of the licensed software. It should be made clear that if the number of users is the number of concurrent users (ie, if two users, one in US and one in UK) they can share a licence as long as they don't use it at same time). Often a personalised login for named individuals that cannot be shared helps restrict the use of the individuals allowed to use the software within the licensee company.

8.1.5.7   Types of code licensed object, source, etc

It is common for software licence agreements with users to specify in their grant provisions that object code is being licensed to the user and that source code is only made available pursuant to a separable source code licence. Where source code is licensed it is common for the licence grant to identify this fact.

8.1.5.8 Transferable or non-transferable rights

Grant provisions in user licence agreements often specify that the licensed rights are non- transferable, meaning that the user may not unilaterally transfer the software to another party without the licensor's permission. Violating this limitation on the licence grant may subject the user to a claim that it has infringed the licensor's right to control the distribution of their software. Some software providers who also furnish equipment will allow a user to transfer its licence to a subsequent purchaser of the equipment provided they are notified of the transfer in advance and have the option to approve or disapprove the subsequent licensee. This approval option is normally considered important in a licence agreement calling for ongoing fee payments because the subsequent user may be a credit risk. Even if there is no ongoing fee, the licensor may want to impose or transfer charge, or recover any taxes imposed on the transfer. Also, if the new user is a known software pirate, the licensor may want a new agreement with the new user or may be reluctant to approve the transfer.

Government regulations or foreign laws may nullify or override the restriction on transfers that a non-transferable licence grant conveys.

Be careful of perpetual licences which restrict assignment in the EU and UK such as in the *UsedSoft GmbH v Oracle International Corp* case. The Court of Justice of the European Union judgment in case C/128/11 of 3 July 2012 held that such a clause could be anti-competitive and void under EU competition law – see also Chapter 1 above).

8.1.5.9 Payment type: one-time fee, fixed periodic royalty, royalty free or other

As discussed earlier, the payment schemes evident in software licence agreements vary considerably. Where the licence is granted on a royalty-free basis or one lump-sum payment, this fact may be conveyed in the licence grant provision. Where multiple or periodic payments are required in user, distributor, development or other agreements involving software, the payment terms are often stated in a separate provision or in an attached schedule. As noted in **8.1.4.1**, price tags or mail order catalogues may convey the cost of mass-marketed software.

8.1.5.10 Software defined to include documentation, updates and enhancements

Some software licence grants will encompass not only the initially delivered program, but also its updates, enhancements and user documentation. These items may be addressed separately in other provisions, but the customer should ensure their receipt and the licensed rights to deal with updates and enhancements in the same manner that they are authorised to deal with the originally delivered program, be it for personal use, distribution or some other right.

Copies of user documentation are usually sold or provided at no charge as items bundled with the software. Sophisticated user-licensees will define the software to include the documentation for warranty and indemnification purposes, or require the documentation to be mentioned separately in licensor warranty and indemnification provisions. Software licensors who desire to license the use of documentation rather than sell or give away copies may include the user documentation in a definition of the licensed software.

8.1.5.11 Number of copies that can be reproduced

Licence grants sometimes specify that a user-licensee may make one or more archive copies of the licensed software. This right may be conveyed elsewhere in the licence agreement, but the important point is to ensure that the right is stated somewhere or that backup copies are unnecessary because of maintenance coverage or for some other reason. In the UK restrictions on backup may be void as a result of the Copyright (Computer Programs) Regulations[1] resulting from the EC Directive on the Legal Protection of Computer Programs.[2] The Regulations and the Directive, incorporated in an amendment to the Copyright, Design and Patents Act 1988,[3] state that a lawful acquirer, a licensee of the program, is permitted to carry out any form of copying which is necessary for the program to be used and in order to make a security backup without having to obtain express consent. There is even a stated right that error correction will be permitted but this is only for the purpose of enabling the program to run correctly. It will not affect the requirement for maintenance and support contracts to be entered into.

Even if maintenance coverage seems to make a backup copy unnecessary, a disaster might leave a user-licensee unable to recover a copy of software from a non-operative computer so that it could be removed to a hot site. Hot sites are discussed further in **8.1.5.13** below. Hence, backup copies are important in most situations.

1   S1 1992/3233.
2   91/250 [1991] OJ L122/42 now consolidated into Directive 2009/24.
3   Copyright, Designs and Patents Act 1988, s 50A.

8.1.5.12 Modifications or maintenance by licence allowed and rights regarding modified version

If the user-licensee desires to perform maintenance on licensed software, the grant clause should express the right to modify the program to make corrections and fix defects. The same principle applies if the user-licensee desires to improve the licensed program. Generally, the right to make changes in a program protected by copyright law is an exclusive right of the copyright owner. However, the previously mentioned Copyright (Computer Programs) Regulations[1] allow maintenance to the extent of error correction.

In addition it is worth mentioning at this point that, under English law, reverse engineering or decompilation remains an infringement of copyright but the

Regulation mentioned above, as a result of the EC Directive on the Legal Protection of Computer Programs,[2] now allows a lawful licensee to analyse the underlying code, copy and translate the program and investigate the functioning of the program in order to evaluate and understand its ideas and principles without the need to obtain consent of the copyright holder, but only for the purpose of achieving inter-operability of an independently created program with the licensed software subject to a number of conditions. This is an implied right which may not be excluded by licensing arrangements within the EU. Where a clause prohibiting decompilation is included it is automatically void. Instead, it is essential in order to render the clause valid to state any such restriction is subject to the limited decompilation rights under the above legislation or 'save in so far as the law allows'. The court would not rewrite a clause to comply with the law. Instead, it would hold the entire restriction on decompilation is void. Therefore draft and amend such clauses with care. In addition, if the user-licensee desires to own modifications or improvements they make in the licensor's program, that ownership should be specified in the licence agreement. Some agreements contain standard provisions making all modifications or improvements the property of the licensor. Licensors often wish to incorporate valuable user modifications in their standard product. Where the licensor's programmers will make the modifications or improvements under a service contract, their ownership should be negotiated if the user-licensee pays for the work. Even if the user-licensee has no desire to own or market the changes they paid for, their ownership may be used as a bargaining chip in negotiations. For example, their use and distribution by the licensor could justify price concessions or royalties.

1   SI 1992/3233.
2   91/250 [1991] OJ L122/42 now consolidated into Directive 2009/24.

8.1.5.13   Use of copy at a hot-site or cold-site allowed

If the user-licensee has a hot-site or cold-site arrangement, live and backup server arrangements or a mirrored server arrangement, or believes they may make such arrangements in the future, then they need flexibility in their licence grant to transfer the original copy or a backup copy of the licensed software. Some provider standard forms allow movement of the licensed copy or a backup to another location in the event of a disaster, but most do not. Hence the point often requires negotiation.

8.1.5.14   Use, reproduction, and modification of source code and technical information received from escrow agent

Unless a separate agreement or an addendum to the licence agreement allows the use, reproduction and modification of source code and technical information received by a user-licensee from a source-code agent, the licence grant needs to address the user's right to so deal with these items. The typical user licence grant covering executable code will not allow the use of source code. The user who insists on a source code escrow arrangement needs to ensure that they have the rights to deal with the source code as necessary upon its receipt from the escrow agent.

8.1.5.15 Grant subject to other terms of contract

The typical well-drafted licence grant in a software licence agreement will include the concept that the grant is made subject to the other terms of the software licence agreement. All of the desired qualifications on a licence grant may not fit well into one or even a few paragraphs. Some of them may be most conveniently expressed elsewhere in the agreement. Also, the licensor may intend to allow the grant to continue only so long as all conditions are complied with. For all of these reasons, and others, it is prudent for a software licensor to so draft its licence grant provisions.

8.1.6 Delivery

Delivery is an important element in many major software transactions although in these days of downloads it is more an issue of who downloads the software and when or if the licensor will attend at the premises to help or be responsible for a large new installation, installing software as it goes about its work. As a general rule, the licensor will not specify in the licence agreement a firm delivery date or deadline, and the licensee must negotiate for clarification and written commitments on this point if it is important to him. The same is true regarding computer acquisitions.

8.1.7 Site and host preparation

Standard licensor form agreements sometimes require the licensee to prepare the site and host computer for software installation, perhaps according to the licensor's specifications. This site preparation requirement is more common with respect to computers.

The site and host are important in this context for several reasons. First, computers and software operating on them can be affected by the environment. Prudent users will require the provider in a major transaction to inspect and approve the site prior to computer installation.

Secondly, software must be compatible with its host computer environment in order to operate on the computer. Prudent users will take steps to ensure that compatibility before expending large sums in major software transactions.

8.1.8 Installation

Some software providers install licensed software without cost, some demand an installation charge and some tell users they must install the program themselves. If the licensor installs a program, it is common for their installers to run diagnostic tests upon installation in order to confirm proper loading and operation of the program. After these tests are passed, the licensor gives or sends the user an invoice for the software. If the user wants the opportunity to confirm the functionality of the program before an invoice issues, they must negotiate for an acceptance test.

8.1.9   Acceptance tests

The acceptance test is another key element of a software licence agreement in a major software transaction. As indicated above, software providers often use installation tests as the acceptance standard. If the user-licensee desires another arrangement, they must negotiate for it. Whatever type of subjective or objective acceptance test is negotiated, customers should be careful to also negotiate the consequences of an acceptance test failure and to include these consequences in the parties' contract.

It is important for both parties to communicate clearly to each other, agree upon and then express in the contract precisely what the parties intend the software and system to do. If the supplier warrants that its product will perform in accordance with its own documentation, then this is substantially in favour of the supplier because it is hardly likely to warrant that its own product will not perform in line with documentation which it, the supplier, has already prepared. On the other hand, customers are all too often willing to rely upon the supplier to provide performance criteria and performance specifications. In many cases the definition of the performance and functionality of the software is no more than a schedule of hardware and software descriptions and technical serial numbers. In other words, there is still nothing in the contract that really explains what solution and interpretation the software is intended to perform or give effect to.

In the case of *Anglo Group plc v Winther Browne & CO Ltd*,[1] the court held that customers have a responsibility to communicate adequately to their suppliers their particular needs for the product that is being supplied to them. In this case, the dispute centred on a system which was subsequently found to have bugs in it. The judge ruled that not only was there a responsibility on the customer to choose the most suitable system for its own business needs, but there was also a duty on the customer to co-operate with the supplier and accept reasonable solutions to any problems that might arise.

The effect of this court decision is that suppliers should prepare adequate specifications of their requirements and needs and ensure that these are integrated into the contract documents as well as into the actual acceptance procedures for the work product.

The *Anglo Group* case does not, however, absolve the supplier from its obligations to deliver software of satisfactory quality or services of satisfactory quality. In the case of *South West Water Services Ltd v International Computers*

Ltd,[2] the court held that South West Water was entitled to terminate a software integration contract because of persistent failure by International Computers Ltd to meet the customer's specification.

In the *South West Water* case the customer had agreed a specification with the supplier, but the supplier had vastly underestimated the amount of work necessary to meet that specification and, in addition, the supplier had misrepresented its ability to comply with the contract terms.

1   (2000) 144 Sol Jo LB 197.
2   [1999] BLR 420.

8.1.9.1   Offsite benchmark test

One step a software user can take in requiring satisfaction of an acceptance test prior to (initial) payment is to negotiate an offsite benchmark test of the software. In fact, this test can be required before the parties' agreement is signed, and this test is most often employed by government agencies. In this test, an offsite host computer such as the provider's must operate the desired program under some normal operating conditions, for example, an 'actual-work' processing requirement. If the test is satisfied according to the subjective or objective criteria established by the parties, then the user will sign the agreement or accept delivery, as the case may be.

8.1.9.2   Onsite ready for use

A declaration that a program is 'ready for use' by a software provider is nothing more than a statement that the provider's installation tests have been satisfactorily completed. No user acceptance test is involved where the customer pays for software declared ready for use by the software provider unless a user test requirement is negotiated.

8.1.9.3   Onsite objective criteria

One form of user acceptance tests for software licensed in a major acquisition is an onsite test requiring the operation of the desired program under identified work conditions and the satisfaction of agreed upon objective criteria for user acceptance. If the software passes the test, the user will sign an agreement or accept delivery if an agreement is already signed.

Generally speaking, objective standard acceptance tests are more reasonable and even-handed than subjective evaluation acceptance tests. The only difficulties with objective standard tests are things like user difficulty in deciding on standards, provider and user difficulty in reaching agreement on objective standards, difficulty in drafting the standards clearly, difficulty in interpreting the standards, the degree to which subjective evaluation of the satisfaction of objective standards creeps into the test, etc.

8.1.9.4 Onsite subjective standard

The major alternative to an objective acceptance test is a subjective standard for acceptance, although some tests contain mixtures of objective and subjective elements. Customers, especially as an opening position in negotiations, fairly often demand a totally subjective acceptance test for the program in question. The same is true in computer acquisitions. Then the burden is on the software provider to negotiate for an objective test or to refuse an acceptance test altogether. Much time can be spent on the negotiation of acceptance tests, but the time spent can be worthwhile. At a minimum, an acceptance test can help a user-licensee ensure that they are acquiring a product that will produce the desired business result, and furnish such an indicator before the product is paid for.

Software providers in major transactions increasingly respond to acceptance test demands with an offer of a trial usage period. This is a reasonable counteroffer, but it also gives the provider a slight advantage over their position in an acceptance test. The provider knows from experience that after a program has been installed for 30, 60 or 90 days it is unlikely that the customer will order it removed. Even if the program does not generate the desired business result, it usually generates sufficient business and/or technical improvements that the customer will conclude it is worthwhile keeping.

Whichever tests or standards are adopted, it is important to involve those with technical expertise in defining the criteria for the acceptance tests. Furthermore, it must be remembered that, unless the licence says otherwise, any use of the software may be deemed to be acceptance of such software.

8.1.10 Term of the agreement

Many of the most important details about the term of a software licence agreement are discussed below. From a business standpoint it is obviously important to know and possibly negotiate the duration of a transaction over which periodic revenue may be received, and to know and possibly negotiate when the parties' obligations are satisfied. This section and the next section on termination set the stage for such determinations and negotiations.

8.1.10.1 Commencement before software is delivered

As indicated earlier, the term of a software licence agreement may commence upon its execution, upon the delivery or installation of a product licensed under an agreement or upon some other event. The term of a licence agreement in a major software transaction need not coincide with the term of the licence grant for software licensed under the agreement. In fact, software licence agreements often serve as the parties' basic agreements for several programs licensed at different points in the agreements' lives.

It is important to recognise that the term of a software licence agreement and the term of a licence grant for a particular program acquired pursuant to the agreement are separate but related topics in contract negotiations. These topics are related chiefly because the term of a licence grant normally expires when the agreement expires, unless an event or clause that allows continued life for the licence grant, for example, a clause allowing continued use for a short period, or transferring the licence grant to another agreement. These topics are also rated because the licensee may want all licence fee payment obligations to start or stop at the same point regardless of how long the software has been licensed for or installed, for example, to stop when leased equipment hosting the software is replaced. It makes no sense to continue paying application program licence fees after the only computer that can host the software is replaced with an incompatible machine.

Licensees are well advised to co-ordinate the life of their software grant and the life of their agreement in a manner that makes sense in the transaction in question.

8.1.10.2 Limited term expires unless parties renew

One approach to an agreement's life is to give it a fixed, limited term after which it expires unless an agreement between the parties renews it. This approach can be favoured in agreements with foreign distributors and representatives as a means of avoiding termination penalties imposed in some foreign countries. This approach will not nullify such penalties in every country, but it will in some. In some jurisdictions, particularly the Middle East, the duty to compensate a distributor will arise even on a failure to renew or extend a fixed-term agreement.

8.1.10.3 Evergreen clause term automatically renews indefinitely

Under an evergreen clause arrangement, the initial term will be fixed, but will automatically renew, or extend on an annual basis until one of the parties terminates the agreement. Many software providers prefer this approach regarding major agreements with users. Both parties are normally given only a narrow window of opportunity to terminate such an agreement each renewal period. This window can easily close unnoticed. If the term of the software licence grant also renews under a separate evergreen clause with a narrow window for termination, or under the agreement's evergreen clause, users must be observant and plan ahead or they can be locked into licence fees for another period after deciding a program is no longer required. Of course, such clauses also allow the provider to administer thousands of user licence agreements at a lower cost than if all users could terminate at will after an initial licence period.

8.1.10.4   Perpetual term

A perpetual term gives 'forever' life to a contract, and it is much more common in shrink-wrap licence agreements than in signed licensed agreements. A perpetual term raises the question of whether the licence agreement is really a sale agreement.

In the case of *Harbinger UK Ltd v GE Information Services Ltd*[1] the Court of Appeal had to consider the effect of a support and maintenance obligation provided in perpetuity. The licensor in this case had granted a distribution agreement together with support and maintenance obligations which were expressed to be 'in perpetuity'.

The licensor terminated the distribution agreement and delivered that its obligations to support and maintain were also thereby extinguished. The court, however, held that the obligation to support and maintain should exist for so long as the distributor was also obliged to support and maintain the software for its own customers.

1   [2000] 1 All ER (Comm) 166.

8.1.10.5   Unspecified term until agreement is terminated

An unspecified contract duration gives the agreement an indefinite term and means the agreement's life will end only when the agreement is terminated by one of the parties. Such an arrangement is more often the result of sloppy legal drafting, or non-legal contract drafting, than it is the result of intelligent planning.

8.1.10.6   Grace period

A grace period extends all or part of a contract's life for a fixed or identifiable period. Such provisions are more common in distributor licence agreements than in user licence agreements. Grace periods allow distributors the ability to clear out their remaining inventory and/or the inventory held by dealers, and prevent breach of contract and copyright infringement claims for unauthorised post-termination distribution.

8.1.11   Termination or expiration and result

Sometimes a distinction is drawn between a termination and a cancellation. A termination can mean an imposed end of the contract's life that is allowed by its terms. A cancellation is an imposed ending that is not allowed by contract terms and that may or may not be allowed by law. An expiration always means a natural death, that is, an end of the contract specified by its terms. For our purposes it is sufficient to use 'termination' to mean either an allowed or an unanticipated ending to a contract's life imposed by one of the parties. Note that parties to a contract may agree to end its life for unplanned or unanticipated reasons. Contract termination does not always result from one party imposing an end or from a planned expiration.

8.1.11.1 Termination upon breach

One of the most common types of termination results from a breach of contract obligations by one party. The breach is often a non-performance of a required obligation, but it may be an inadequate performance as well. If the breach is material, contract law may well allow termination. On the other hand, in some foreign countries any minor breach may allow termination.

Litigation is common after a termination for a breach of contract. The defendant usually counterclaims as well as defending against the claimant's claims. If the claimant is not faultless in the parties' business dealings, both parties may end up partial winners and partial losers.

8.1.11.2 Termination without cause

Some contracts allow one or all of the parties to terminate 'at will' or without a breach of contract by another party. This right may be exercisable at any time without prior notice, only with prior notice of a specified period, or only at specified points with or without notice. This is the type of termination that most often gives rise to penalties when foreign distributors or sales representatives are terminated.

8.1.11.3 Expiration at end of term

As indicated earlier, the expiration of an agreement at the end of its initial term is a natural death for a contract in the sense that it is preordained by the agreement's terms. If the agreement contains an option to renew that is not exercised, the expiration is still anticipated and planned for in the agreement. In contrast, if the agreement automatically renews subject to termination, then the end of the contract results from a termination, not its expiration.

8.1.11.4 Expiration upon lapse of intellectual property rights

A variation on the theme of a natural expiration can be found in some technology licences where the technology is protected by an intellectual property law. In this variation, the contract may call for its expiration upon the end of the protected life of the intellectual property. For example, a patent licence may specify the end of the patent's life as the end of the licence agreement, and copyright licences may terminate at the end of the period of copyright.

8.1.11.5 Consequences

From a business standpoint and from the standpoint of protecting intellectual property rights in software, the consequences of the termination or expiration of a licence agreement should be specified in the agreement and negotiated if necessary. User-licensees should be required to return licensed software or erase it. Certificates of destruction help preserve trade secret protection and may be helpful in litigation over software piracy by an ex-licensee. Distributor-licensees should be required to stop distribution upon or at some point after termination or expiration of a software licence agreement. Sometimes distributors are allowed to return an inventory for a refund or credit against final payments from a publisher, and some are allowed a 'remaindering' or 'sell-off' period for 90 days after termination.

8.1.12 Service and updates maintenance

Some software providers include maintenance terms in their licence agreement which call for copies of updates containing several defect corrections as they are made generally available to customers. Others cover maintenance in a separate agreement, or in a rider or appendix to a licence agreement.

User-licensees should pay particular attention to the interplay of maintenance and warranty provisions, especially regarding their coverage and commencement, so that they are not surprised by maintenance charges for service, or by a lack of coverage at a time when the warranty was expected to provide no-charge, complete protection.

Detailed aspects of a service level agreement or support and maintenance agreements are not the subject of this work, but suffice to say that the value of the licensed software is often dependent upon the value or level of service, support and maintenance offered by and enforceable under a service level or maintenance agreement.

It is essential to define clearly what is or is not included in standard charges; whether the provider is giving full training or merely 'training the trainers'; whether the customer is obligated or not to take up new releases; and whether what may appear to be generous maintenance terms by the provider may just be a means of reducing original 'fit for purpose' warranties in the software licence.

8.1.13 Enhancements

Enhancements are usually regarded as major improvements in software functionality. Some software providers charge for enhancements, some do not, and some will charge only for especially significant enhancement. Whatever the case may be, user-licensees need to ensure that enhancements are addressed in their software licence agreements, and to attempt to negotiate any unsatisfactory arrangement for enhancements.

8.1.14 Escrow

A source code escrow is deposit of source code with a party with the intention to have the code released to a user of executable code, or a joint venture partner, etc, upon one or more events such as a failure to provide timely maintenance service. In the context of user licence agreements, source code escrows address two fundamental concerns: that a provider will not furnish satisfactory maintenance service; or that a provider will liquidate or fall into bankruptcy. In either event, the user will need a copy of the provider's source code in order to have a chance of successfully maintaining the licensed program. Technical information regarding the program will also be required.

User-licensees should consider requiring a licensor of executable code to either furnish a copy of source code, or establish a source code escrow for the user's benefit whenever the software in question is critical or very important to the user's business and when there is no similar substitute for the program readily available in the marketplace. The substitute should be compatible with the user's equipment and likely to be available in the foreseeable future. A program at the end of its lifecycle may not be available in the marketplace for long.

Many licensors have established an escrow to service all of their customers requesting one. User-licensees should ensure that established escrows meet their needs, as they should with an escrow created in response to their request. The escrow should call for the deposit of source code, technical information and user documentation for the originally supplied program. User verification or independent verification of the materials supplied should be a feature of the escrow assuming the software in question is important or critical to the user's business. Source code deposits of updates and enhancements should be required and verified before deposit. The triggering events for release of the deposited materials should be identified. The user's rights regarding the licensed materials should be specified, including the right to prepare and utilise altered code and modified versions of the program. Responsibility for payment for the escrow should be assigned. A mutually acceptable independent escrow agent should be utilised. Conflict of interest problems may arise if the user's or provider's bank, insurance company or solicitor serve as the escrow agent. These are not all of the issues that should be addressed, but they serve as illustrations of the important issues in source code escrow arrangements. Source code escrows are a type of technology escrow arrangement utilised in various technology-based industries. Ideally, the source code escrow arrangement will be negotiated simultaneously with other contract terms, and made a part of the parties' licence agreement.

8.1.15 Training

Training seldom receives as much attention as it deserves. Adequate user training can have a significant impact on the success of a software licence transaction. The amount and cost of training should be identified in the parties' agreement. Training charges are one of the most easily negotiated charges in a software licence arrangement. User-licensees usually prefer onsite, as opposed to the provider's site, training sessions. The location of the training sessions should be negotiated and specified in the parties' contract.

8.1.16 Consulting and development services

Major software licence transactions often involve a small amount of provider consulting and/or development services. Minor customising work on pre-written programs may be adequately covered in the parties' agreement. In contrast, significant consulting or development work necessitates a separate agreement or at least an appendix to the licence agreement. Writing interface code and menus or shells may or may not require major effort, but they justify a separate agreement or appendix or both so that all of the important issues they raise can be addressed.

Consulting and development services are often major software transactions. New software development projects are rarely completed without problems of some sort. Hence, they deserve negotiation and a carefully drafted contract. System selection consulting, and system analysis or design projects by independent consultants, may focus on important or critical programs, or cost enough, to justify a separate, negotiated agreement or appendix.

While it is beyond the scope of this book to discuss the issues idiosyncratic to these transactions, detailed specifications are very important to successful major development projects. Customers are well advised to apportion payment for these projects among milestones requiring well-identified deliverables. A portion of the project payment should be reserved for system acceptance.

8.1.17 Warranties in general

As a general rule suppliers will seek to warrant their goods and services to the minimum and it is usual for the customer to have to negotiate in extended express warranties to cover their particular requirements and needs.

The more mass market, high volume, low value the software the more usual it is for the software to be warranted on an 'as is – as available' basis or WYSIWYG (What you see is what you get).

The more complex the solution delivery is the more likely it is that the warranties will be broken down into warranties for hardware, software, third party products, professional consultancy and programming and the like.

There has already been much discussion as to whether or not software is 'goods' for the purposes of implied warranties under the Sale of Goods Act 1979 in the UK and on the whole, the more mass market the software, the more it is likely to be seen as 'goods'. The more the software is delivered on an integration and commission basis the more likely it is that the software will be treated as 'services', thereby weakening the degree of implied warranties. For consumer contracts under the Consumer Rights Act 2015 there are now specific implied warranties for digital downloads, but these are not implied into business to business contracts.

In general, the more that a customer negotiates extended warranties into a contract the more the supplier will seek to limit the impact of those warranties under the Limitation of Liability Clauses (which will be discussed later).

On an increasing basis now, where warranties are divided up between hardware, software, third party products, consultancy and the like, the more it becomes important to balance each express warranty against each express limitation of liability clause and, indeed, each insurable aspect of the risk associated therewith. In other words, when negotiating and drafting software contracts in the area of warranties, it is essential to consider at the same time those other clauses that impact upon warranties such as limitations of liability, indemnity and insurance.

Set out hereafter are a series of the types of express warranty that might well be included in a computer contract.

8.1.18   Limited warranty

Limited warranties are standard provisions in software licence agreements. Some warranties address only the media for the software and indicate the software is provided without any warranty. Some warranties submit that the software will satisfy licensor specifications. Others focus on defects in material and workmanship. In a major software licence transaction, as in a major computer acquisition, a user is best served by a warranty that the acquired product will furnish the user's desired business results. Software providers are reluctant to provide such warranties, but they can be negotiated in some deals. Reasonable qualifications can be added to such warranties to protect software providers against events beyond their control causing a violation of such a warranty.

8.1.19   Ongoing performance obligations

Ongoing performance obligations are most often found in agreements with government agencies even though they can be helpful to commercial user-licensees. These provisions require software to meet specified performance standards over the life of the licence agreement or for a long period, in contrast to the short duration of most limited warranty provisions.

If time has been spent in defining a detailed specification and functionality for the software solution, then by incorporating such specification and functionality description into the contract, the customer particularly will set a standard against which performance warranties can be matched. Ongoing performance warranties can apply equally to hardware as to software and usually for software a warranty that it will 'comply with supplier specification or manual' will be of value provided that such specification or manual is satisfactorily incorporated into the contract.

In the case of ongoing service performance the customer should require that the supplier warrants compliance with service description but this in turn places an obligation upon the customer to ensure that the service description is accurate in terms of what is required.

If the solution being provided by the supplier relates to a total integration package where software, hardware and consultancy is being provided for the customer, then the customer may wish to negotiate a general ongoing performance warranty for the total solution ('the System').

An example of such a warranty might be:

The supplier warrants that [upon installation] [for a period of [X] months from the Acceptance Date] the System will provide the functionality and performances specified in the Schedule.

8.1.20 Virus and error warranty

In so far as viruses, bugs and latent defect errors are not already covered under any undertaking and warranties of the provider or are not specifically items included in any specification to which the provider is obligated to deliver matching software, it may be wise for customers to require specific undertakings or warranties to be given by providers.

No provider will usually guarantee that software is error or bug free, but, equally, customers will not want to acquire software solutions that are flawed. It may also be reasonable for a customer to accept that the provider does not warrant that the software will be free from minor interruptions or errors.

Many providers will provide limited warranties for the software after delivery or acceptance but will expect subsequent errors or defects to be cured under ongoing maintenance and support arrangements. From the provider's point of view, unusual defects which are outside of acceptance tests or specifications, or which indeed were never contemplated by either of the parties at the time the transaction was entered into, would be unusual error corrections provided under the maintenance agreement, but as additional expense to the customer and not within the standard maintenance fee.

An example of such a warranty might be:

(i) The provider shall ensure that it and its employees, consultants, agents and sub-contractors take all reasonable precautions to ensure that no known viruses for which detection and antidote software is generally available are coded or introduced into the buyer's software when the provider is supplying any hardware or software or any services under this Agreement.

(ii) In the event that the provider identifies a computer virus on the buyer's system it shall immediately notify the buyer.

(iii) The provider undertakes to remove, at its own expense, any virus whose presence on the buyer's system should have been prevented by the provider had it properly discharged its duties pursuant to clause (i) above and, where necessary, pay for the cost of reconfiguring the System and installing virus-free software at no cost to the buyer.

(iv) If a virus is identified on the buyer's system, notwithstanding the use by the provider of reasonable precautions as defined under clause (i) above, all subsequent remedial work undertaken by the provider shall be paid for by the customer on a time and materials basis.

8.1.21 Euros warranty

Where the licensee is in a country in the EU but not in the euro zone but might enter the euro zone in due course a warranty along the following lines might be wanted.

The following warranty is a suggestion only:

The Supplier warrants that the system will:

(a) Recognise and manage directly all single and multiple currency changes necessitated by the implementation of the Euro in part or all of the EU, such functionality to be available for use by the customer regardless of whether or not, or when, the country joins the euro; and

(b) Correctly implement all conversion, rounding, triangulation and other technical requirements for all stages of implementation of the Euro as laid down by EU law.

8.1.22 Representations, warranties and indemnification regarding intellectual property rights

User-licensees and distributor-licensees alike hope to enjoy the benefits of their licensed rights peacefully. Neither would enjoy having the exercise of those rights enjoined by a third-party action against the licensor. Nor would they enjoy being named in a damages suit against the licensor for copyright infringement or trade secret misappropriation.

For such reasons, sophisticated licensees require representations and warranties regarding the ownership or right to license the software in question, and indemnification regarding a damages award against them as a result of exercising their licensed rights. Many software licensors provide part, but not all, of these assurances. For example, trade secret rights are sometimes omitted from standard intellectual property representations, warranties and indemnification provisions. While these omissions address a legal topic rather than a business topic, they can give rise to business disruption. Hence they are worthy topics for negotiation by business as well as legal personnel in a customer organisation.

8.1.23 Limitation of liability and remedy

The limitation of liability and remedy provision is an important legal protection in many contracts across many industries. Typically this provision attempts to safeguard the provider of goods and services against certain types of legal liability. Providers typically limit liability by providing only a limited warranty and then excluding all other warranties, in the alternative, no warranty at all may be provided and all warranties may be excluded. An example of provisions that reflect this plan in a US provider's standard software licence agreement is set out below. For an English law agreement however, the Unfair Contract Terms Act 1977 has the effect that 'carve outs' for death and personal injury liability would be needed (in a clause excluding liability) otherwise the clause would be void (as stated below).

The Customer is responsible for selecting equipment, software, and services suitable for the Customer's needs. No prior statement or promise by the Licensor relating to the services or Products provided hereunder shall be deemed an express warranty or part of the basis of this Agreement.

The Software, Documentation and all services provided hereunder are provided 'AS IS' with no warranty whatsoever. The Licensor does not warrant that the functions contained in the Software will meet the Customer's needs, or that the operation of the Software will be uninterrupted or error free, or that defects in the Software will be corrected.

THERE ARE NO WARRANTIES, EXPRESS OR IMPLIED, BY OPERATION OF LAW OR OTHERWISE, OF THE PRODUCTS OR SERVICES FURNISHED HEREUNDER. THE LICENSOR DISCLAIMS ANY IMPLIED WARRANTY OF MERCHANTABILITY OR FITNESS FOR A PARTICULAR PURPOSE. THE ENTIRE RISK AS TO THE QUALITY AND PERFORMANCE OF THE SOFTWARE IS WITH YOU. SHOULD THE SOFTWARE PROVE DEFECTIVE, YOU ASSUME THE ENTIRE COST OF ALL NECESSARY SERVICING, REPAIR, OR CORRECTION.

The Customer assumes responsibility for the supervision, management and control of the Equipment and modifications and revisions thereto including, but not limited to: (1) assuring proper configuration of the Equipment for Software installation, audit controls and operating methods; (2) implementing sufficient procedures and checkpoints to satisfy its requirements for security and accuracy for input as well as restart and recovery in the event of malfunction; (3) accomplishing the productive utilisation of the Equipment in the use of the Software in processing of the Customer's work.

Where the agreement contains a limited warranty or some other provisions that provide remedies addressing various types of problems the provider may attempt to exclude all types of remedies and damages other than out-of-pocket expense reimbursement damages. An example of provisions that reflect this plan in a US provider's standard software licence agreement is set forth below.

— The licensor's entire liability and customer's sole and exclusive remedy for any and all liability or claims in connection with or arising out of this agreement or the existence, non-delivery, furnishing, functioning, or the customer's use of products or services provided under this agreement, for any cause whatsoever, and regardless of the form or nature of the liability or claim, whether in contract or in tort, including, without limitation, claims of negligence or strict liability, is set forth in paragraph 2.

— If the licensor fails, after repeated attempts, to perform any of its obligations or to provide the remedies set out in this agreement, the licensor's liability shall be the customer's actual, direct damages such as would be provable in a court of law, but not to exceed the software licence fee stated herein which the customer has paid for the specific item that caused the damage. Notwithstanding the provisions of any applicable statute, the remedies available to the customer in this agreement are exclusive remedies, and all other remedies, statutory or otherwise, with respect to the matter hereof, are hereby expressly waived by the customer.

— In no event shall the licensor be liable for: (1) any incidental, indirect, special or consequential damages whatsoever, including, but not limited to, damages for business interruption, loss of business information, loss of software use, loss of goodwill or loss of revenue or profit, even if the licensor has been advised, knew, or should have known of the possibility of such damages; or (2) damages caused by the customer's failure to perform its obligations and responsibilities under this agreement; or (3) claims, demands, or actions against the customer by any other party.

In the UK and within the EU as a result of the UK's Unfair Contract Terms Act 1977 and the EC's legislation on unfair terms in consumer contracts,[1] first any ambiguity in a clause which attempts to limit liability with a customer, the end-user, will be interpreted against the person imposing it (the licensor) and, secondly, any attempt to exclude liability for death or personal injury arising out of the negligence of the person imposing such clause (the licensor) will be invalid. Therefore, the clauses which are outlined above might find some lack of favour within the UK and thus an example of a more appropriate attempt to limit liability is set forth below:

— Nothing in this clause shall limit or exclude the liability of either party to the other for death or personal injury caused by negligence nor for fraud.

— Except as expressly stated in this clause and elsewhere in this Licence Agreement, any liability of the Licensor for breach of this Agreement will not exceed in the aggregate of damages, costs, fees and expenses capable of being awarded to the customer the contract price paid or due to be paid by the customer under this Agreement in the 12 months prior to a claim.

> — Except as provided above, in no event will the Licensor be liable to the customer for special, indirect or consequential damages including, but not limited to, loss of profits or arising from loss of data or unfitness for user purposes.

Since the case of *St Albans City and District Council v International Computers Ltd*[2] it has become clear that where a customer suffers loss as a result of faulty software and no terms and conditions vary the implied terms of satisfactory quality or fitness for purpose (if they are implied into a goods contract0 or the common law implied terms which were not replaced by the Sale of Goods Act 1979 , then any attempt by the supplier to limit its liability for such loss below what is deemed to be a reasonable figure (perhaps such a figure being linked to the suppliers' insurance cover for such losses) will be void as an unfair contract term if it is unreasonable.

Alternative limitation of liability clauses could be the following.

- *100% approach.* Except as provided above in the case of personal injury, death, and damage to tangible property, Supplier's maximum liability to Customer for any cause whatsoever (whether in the form of the additional cost of remedial services or otherwise) will be for direct costs and damages only, and will be limited to the price paid to Supplier for the product or the annual charge for the service that is the subject of Customer's claim, OR

- *125% approach.* Except as provided above in the case of personal injury, death, and damage to tangible property, Supplier's maximum liability to Customer for any cause whatsoever (whether in the form of the additional cost of remedial services or otherwise) will be for direct costs and damages only, and will be limited to a sum equivalent to the price paid to Supplier for the products or services that are the subject of Customer's claim plus damages limited to twenty-five per cent of the same amount for any additional costs directly, reasonably and necessarily incurred by Customer in obtaining alternative products and/or services, OR

- *Approach reflecting insurance cover.* Except as provided above in the case of personal injury, death, and damage to tangible property, Supplier's maximum liability to Customer for any cause whatsoever (whether in the form of the additional cost of remedial services or otherwise) will be for direct costs and damages only, and will be limited to the greater of (a) [amount linked to value of insurance cover e.g. one million pounds] or (b) a sum equivalent to the price paid to Supplier for the products or services that are the subject of Customer's claim, plus damages limited to twenty-five per cent of the same amount for any additional costs directly, reasonably and necessarily incurred by Customer in obtaining alternative products and/or services, OR

- *Actual Insurance Recovery approach.* Except as provided above in the case of personal injury, death, and damage to tangible property, Supplier's maximum liability to Customer for any cause whatsoever (whether in the form of the additional cost of remedial services or otherwise) will be for direct costs and damages only, and will be limited to either (a) where the event is covered by Supplier's insurance policies, the amount which Supplier actually recovers from its insurers under those policies, to a maximum of one million pounds or (b) in all other cases, a sum equivalent to the price paid to Supplier for the products or services that are the subject of Customer's claim, plus damages limited to twenty-five per cent of the same amount for any additional costs directly, reasonably and necessarily incurred by Customer in obtaining alternative products and/or services, AND

- *Maximum liability*. Except as provided above in the case of personal injury, death, and damage to tangible property, Supplier's maximum liability to Customer for any cause whatsoever (whether in the form of the additional cost of remedial services or otherwise) will be for direct costs and damages only, and will be limited to a sum equivalent to the price paid to Supplier for the products or services that are the subject of Customer's claim plus damages limited to twenty-five per cent of the same amount for any additional costs directly, reasonably and necessarily incurred by Customer in obtaining alternative products and/or services.

However in the 2001 UK case of *Watford Electronics Ltd v Sanderson CFL Ltd*[3] it was held that provisions in a contract for the supply of computer software that both excluded the supplier liability for indirect loss, as well as limiting the damages recoverable to the amount paid by the customer under the contract, satisfied the reasonableness test under the Unfair Contract Terms Act 1977, s 11. On appeal the court decided that the contract had been negotiated between experienced businessmen of equal bargaining power and skill and, as such, the supplier limitation clause was reasonable. There have been plenty of cases since along similar lines.

1   In the UK the latest EU law in that field was reflected in the Consumer Rights Act 2015.
2   [1996] 4 All ER 481.
3   [2001] EWCA Civ 317, [2001] 1 All ER (Comm) 696.

8.1.24   Limitation on recoverable damages

A limitation on recoverable damages provision states a maximum compensatory damage award limitation. In cases where a user-licensee wins a judgment of liability against a provider on a tort claim of misrepresentation, this clause will not limit the court's ability to award damages that exceed the contract's limitation. In cases where a user-licensee wins a judgment of liability against a provider on a breach of contract claim, this clause will limit the court's ability to award damages that exceed the contract's limitation absent unusual circumstances, for example, a determination that the contract is invalid, or that the provision is drafted in such a way that it does not apply to the breach in question.

Limitations on recoverable damages are reasonable provisions from a provider's standpoint. Several lawsuits resulting in large damage awards for breaches of contract can quickly drain the corporate treasury of small companies and dent the earnings of mid-sized and large companies. Bankruptcy is sometimes caused by large damage awards. Small companies can seldom afford to set aside large sums as contingent reserves for possible damage awards. Limitations on recoverable damages run to the heart of any corporation, its treasury.

On the other hand, customers can argue that the best way to avoid large compensatory damage awards in breach of contract claims is for the provider to perform as required by the contract. Simply do not breach the contract and you need not worry about large damage awards.

Providers can counter that the question of whether or not a contract is breached can be a matter of interpretation, especially where common law requires reasonable and not perfect performance, as a general rule.

The debate can go on and on, and much time can be wasted. One course of action can be for the customer to explore what insurance may be available to buyers of software systems (for example, loss of business insurance). It may be cheaper to purchase such insurance rather than to attempt high limits of liability from the provider. The essential point for our purposes is that prudent providers will insert such provisions, and sophisticated customers at least sometimes attempt to raise the limitation, or to delete the clause altogether. By inserting this provision in its standard form agreement the provider puts the customer in the position of one who must argue for its removal or change, a disadvantageous position. If the customer drafts a tailor-made agreement for the transaction or requires use of a standard customer form agreement, then the provider is normally in the position of having to argue for the addition of such a provision, which is a non-favoured position.

An example of a provision that limits recoverable damages in a provider's standard software licence agreement is quoted below.

> XYZ's liability for actual damages from any cause whatsoever will be limited to the greater of (1) £100,000 or (2) the one-time charge paid for, or any charges which would be due for 12 months' use of, the individual Program that caused the damages or is the subject matter of, or is directly related to, the cause of action. Such charges shall be those in effect when the cause of action arose and shall include any upgrade, initial or process charges paid to XYZ. This limitation will apply, except as otherwise stated in this Section, regardless of the form of action, whether in contract or in tort, including negligence.

Again the clause shown above might well be acceptable within the US but within the UK and the EU would be subject to the same limitations as previously discussed (see section 8.1.22) in that it may be impossible to limit liability where the claim is for damages for personal injury or death resulting from negligence.

8.1.25 Nature and scope of consequential damages exclusion

Software providers like to exclude the possibility of consequential damages arising from a breach of contract claim except in areas not permitted by law such as death or personal injury caused by negligence and for fraud. Consequential damages can be simply defined as damages that arise from the consequences of a breach of contract on the claimant's business other than any actual, identifiable out-of-pocket expenses or losses that compensatory damage awards reimburse. Consequential damages can be very large monetary awards and cover such items as lost profits or the loss of goodwill.

Sophisticated customers may accept an all encompassing consequential damages exclusion by a provider, or they may argue that the provision must be reciprocal, that is, it must be written so as to benefit both parties equally. Another possible reaction of a sophisticated customer is to argue that a provider should not be able to exclude its exposure to either actual or consequential damages suffered by the customer as a result of suits by third parties based on a claim of intellectual property infringement or misappropriation. The customer's rights to deal with software as allowed in its licence agreement stem from the licensor's ownership or right to license intellectual property rights in the software. If the licensor does not have the ability to grant the licensed rights and the customer is enjoined or must pay damages as a result, the customer's lost profits resulting from the injunction order to stop use of the software, as well as the customer's out-of-pocket damages, should be recoverable from the provider according to this argument. This argument is based on the concept that licensees should not bear losses arising from fundamental defects in the very thing the customers paid for, whether or not they are out-of-pocket losses. While providers may argue that no transaction can be made risk free, the customer has a reasonable point in this context.

An example of a provision that excludes consequential damages in a provider's standard software licence agreement is quoted below.

> In no event will XYZ be liable for any damages arising from performance or non-performance of the Program during the Program testing period or for any damages caused by your failure to perform your responsibilities. In addition, XYZ will not be liable for any lost profits, lost savings, incidental damages, lost data or other economic consequential damages, even if XYZ has been advised of the possibility of such damages. Furthermore, XYZ will not be liable for any damages claimed by you based on any third-party claim.

Several cases, including *British Sugar plc v NEI Power Projects Ltd*[1] and *Hotel Services Ltd v Hilton International Hotels*[2], have highlighted the fact that an attempt to exclude all loss apart from direct loss by using catch-all words such as 'indirect loss or other consequential damages' may have the opposite effect. Care should be taken to draft such an exclusion clause so as to include or exclude specific types of anticipated damage. Where it is desired to exclude liability for a loss which flows directly from a breach then it may be better to use a catch-all phrase such as 'all other direct losses'. If it is necessary to keep the use of the word 'consequential', care should be taken when listing specified damages and then adding the words 'or other indirect or consequential losses', as this may be interpreted to allow the courts to include a loss which might otherwise have been excluded.

1   (1997) 87 BLR 42.
2   [2000] BLR 235.

8.1.26   Liquidated damages

A liquidated damages clause is often used in contracts as a means of ensuring that the parties know up-front what the consequences will be of a breach of the agreement and are thus a contractually agreed pre-estimate of damages that would otherwise be awarded by a court of law.

Liquidated damages can be applied to contractual breaches such as delay in the performance of an obligation, failure of timely supply, breach of agreed service levels or breach of time critical delivery.

Liquidated damages are often referred to by the parties as 'penalties' but this is precisely what they should not be! A court will uphold a liquidated damages clause if satisfied that the parties have taken steps to genuinely estimate the anticipated loss following a breach. Whilst courts generally do not interfere in the commercial arrangements between parties to a contract they will refuse to enforce a liquidated damages clause because it is a 'penalty' or an instance of 'usury' if the pre-determined sum is considered to be an unreasonable estimate of the probable loss or it has been used by one party as a means of pressure or oppression on the other.

The leading UK cases on liquidated damages are generally in relation to construction or engineering contracts but whilst the 2005 case of *Alfred McAlpine Capital Projects Ltd v Tilebox Ltd*[1] confirms that a court will be slow to interfere with an arm's-length negotiated liquidated damages clause, the older case of *Dunlop Neumatic Tyre Co. Ltd v New Garage and Motor Co. Ltd*[2] sets down the guidelines as to the distinction between liquidated damages and penalty clauses namely that:

1.   Clause titles are irrelevant and a liquidated damages clause labelled as 'a penalty clause' may still be enforceable as the court will look beyond the clauses title and interpret its substance.

2.   The essence of a liquidated damages clause is that it should be a genuine pre-estimate of damage.

3.   The essence of a penalty clause is that it operates by way of a threat.

4.   It is a matter of construction as to whether or not the clause in question creates liquidated damages or a penalty and the courts will interpret

the clause as a result of all the facts surrounding the negotiations at the time the contract was entered into.

In negotiating and drafting the parties should take into account the guidelines above so that the clause is enforceable and thus worth all the time spent on negotiation and in order to do this it is suggested that:

1.   The liquidated damages should be based on genuine pre-estimates of loss.

2.   Where it is difficult to pre-estimate loss then the parties should document the methodology for the mechanism they use in the clause for estimating damages or service credits.

3.   Wherever possible the liquidated damages should be expressed in precise terms based on documented examples of failure or breach and not on generic formulas.

4.   If the parties intend liquidated damages to be the exhaustive remedy then this should be clearly stated as otherwise the aggrieved party can seek unliquidated damages whether or not there is a liquidated damages clause in the contract.

5.   Liquidated damages may well be more enforceable if the amount of the damages is calculated on a scale linked to the seriousness of the breach in question.

In addition to the above points it should be remembered that a liquidated damages clause needs to be negotiated and drafted in parallel with all complementary clauses relating to warranties, limitations of liability, intellectual property infringement, indemnities and insurance.

Make it clear in any clause that the sum is a reasonable pre-estimate of loss, avoid using the word penalty, the clause may provide for service credits and state if the clause is the only remedy ('sole remedy') for a failure to meet a particular contractual requirement such as percentage uptime guaranteed or delivery by a certain date or if the liquidated damages are 'without prejudice to other rights'.

1   [2005] EWHC 2H1 (TCC).
2   [1915] AC 79.

8.1.27   Most favoured customer

In the US, and now in the UK, some institutions, government agencies and authorities are seeking to include a 'most favoured customer' clause. This is an undertaking by the provider that it has offered no better terms to any other third party at the time of the contract with the customer, and/or that if it offers better terms to any other third party in the future it will offer the same terms to the customer. The UK's Competition and Markets Authority regularly examines such clauses and sometimes they can be anti-competitive (eg, Amazon UK was required to remove its most favoured customer clause) so do take competition law advice as regards the UK's Competition Act 1998 before imposing them.

Most providers seek to avoid such a clause or at least agree that it only applies to charges such as training, call-out fees and incidentals. Examples of such clauses are as follows:

> The Licensor represents that the charges, fees, costs, other payments and discounts set forth in this Agreement are no less favourable to the Licensee than the most favourable terms offered or received to or by any other customer of the Licensor as of the time this Agreement is signed by the Licensee.
>
> If, during the term, the Licensor signs any contract for similar software that contains payment terms, discounts, charges, fees or costs that are more favourable to another customer, then these more favourable provisions will immediately be extended to the Licensee.

8.1.28 Change control

Unless the delivery is of a simple software product the chances are that in the course of commissioning and acceptance and, indeed, if not before that date, the parties will make changes to their deliverables and/or requirements.

It is important to consider putting into the contract a clause which sets out the formula by which such changes can be mutually agreed. An example of such a change control clause is as follows:

> 1. Any change or variation to the scope of work or nature of services or products to be supplied pursuant to this Agreement will be referred to as a 'Change' and will be subject to a Change Notice in accordance with the following Change Procedure. Both parties agree that it is in their best interests to implement Changes as quickly and as efficiently as possible.
>
> 2. If either party considers that a Change is necessary, or that a Change is in effect being forced upon it by the other party, it shall serve a Change Notice on the other party. A Change Notice can be in any form but must provide reasonable details of the Change and, if possible, the party's estimate of the effect (if any) of the Change on the contract price or rates, its impact on delivery dates or supply times, and any other effect which it is considered the Change will have.
>
> 3. The other party will respond in writing by return if possible, but in any event within seven calendar days of receipt of the Change Notice, indicating whether or not it accepts the proposed Change, and giving its own estimate of the effects which the Change will have, including any costs expected to arise in connection with evaluating the proposed Change.
>
> 4. Each party shall respond to all further correspondence by return if possible, but in any event within seven days of receipt of previous correspondence, until agreement on the proposed Change is reached and recorded in an Agreed Contract Amendment signed by both parties.

5. Neither party shall be under any obligation to accept any Change that is not subject to an Agreed Contract Amendment [which just states the position under the law of contract].

8.1.29 Availability of licensee's computer system to licensor for maintenance, training, and development purposes

A standard clause in the provider's licence agreement forms requires the licensee to make its host computer available to the provider from time to time for purposes of training the licensee's employees in the licensed program's operation, in order to perform software development work or software diagnostic tests, or so that the provider may repair or enhance the software. The timing of such availability is usually vague in a provider's standard form agreement and should be clarified. Customers can be disrupted, and providers can be taken advantage of, if a reasonable plan cannot be agreed upon and captured in contract language.

8.1.30 Recovery of lawyers' fees by prevailing party

In the UK the prevailing party in civil litigation can recover some of its lawyers' fees (usually about two thirds), but in the US and many European courts this is not the case. Hence, many standard form agreements contain provisions allowing the recovery of reasonable lawyers' fees. Relatively few laws allow their recovery so the concept seems reasonable provided the provision is sufficiently qualified. For example, it might be made reciprocal or come into play only after the last appeal of the other party's loss is either denied or lost.

8.1.31 Statute of limitations

The UK's Limitation Act 1980 allows breach of contract claims only for a six year period. The length of time varies with the type of legal claim. Parties to a contract may agree to shorten the period allowed by law in many commercial contexts. Thus it is common to see a one or two year window for litigation specified in standard form licence agreements. Generally such limitations will be enforced against breach of contract claims filed after the specified period has elapsed.

8.1.32 Risk of loss or damage during transit

It is not within the scope of this book to explain terms like 'CIF' and 'FOB' under Incoterms 2020. The point here is that the risk of loss or damage during transit may become important in a software licence agreement. Remember that where reference to terms such as 'CIF' and 'FOB' are used it is worthwhile linking such terms to their specific definition within *ICC INCOTERMS*. For example, where software is shipped to a foreign distributor, the risk of loss or damage to inventory shipped from a UK publisher is as important as it is in agreements for other exported products of the same value. As terms such as FOB mean the goods must be sent on a ship – free on board – and most software is downloaded online it is rare Incoterms are used. However, with shipment of large computer systems internationally they may be applicable.

8.1.33   Indemnities

There is often confusion as to the role of an indemnity clause as opposed to a warranty clause.

Broadly speaking, an indemnity clause, more often than not, requires the indemnifying party to compensate the aggrieved party for losses that it has directly suffered as a result of the indemnifying party's breach, usually where the loss has been generated through a third party claim. In English law there is no duty to mitigate loss with indemnities and much more can be claimed than from a mere breach of warranty.

Usually indemnities are not subject to the cap on liability in the contract but always make it clear if they are or are not so there is no confusion.

Under English law, the courts often take a wider view of what will be recoverable under an indemnity claim as opposed to a warranty claim and in particular will not restrict the loss to direct damages. The almost 'blank cheque' nature of the liability of the indemnifying party results from the fact that the beneficiary of the indemnity clause is as stated above because that party is under no obligation to mitigate its loss.

Although indemnity clauses are usually in relation to losses arising through breach of IPR or confidentiality there is no reason why indemnity clauses cannot also be used for other areas where the beneficiary suffers loss including loss or misappropriation of information and personal data, wilful or malicious conduct or fraud, damage to tangible property and breach of relevant laws and regulations. Indeed, no clause may validly exclude liability for fraud under English law in any event.

Given all of the above comments, the negotiating and drafting of an indemnity clause requires considerable attention. The areas in respect of which an indemnity claim can be made need to be carefully considered by both parties and particular attention needs to be given to the mechanism by which the indemnifying party can take control of any claim in respect of which the beneficiary is entitled to subsequently claim.

A supplier always avoids a buyer's contract clause which requires an indemnity for any breach of contract including poor performance of the product.

It is common for a supplier, however, to provide a full indemnity against IPR infringement of the product, breach of confidentiality and breach of UK GDPR and other data protection obligations.

Since an indemnity clause is another contractual mechanism whereby the indemnifying party will have to pay damages or perhaps be forced by specific injunction to perform services over and above those which it anticipated, there is no reason why there should not be a limitation on the damages under an indemnity clause just as there are limitations of liability under warranty clauses.

An example of a warranty and indemnity clause is as follows.

Owner warrants that it has the right to enter into and perform its obligations under this Agreement and will indemnify and hold harmless CUSTOMER against any loss or expense (including reasonable lawyer's fees and expenses) as a result of any claim that the normal use or possession of PRODUCT and associated documentation infringes the intellectual property rights of any third party, provided that the claim does not arise as a result of the use of PRODUCT and associated documentation otherwise than in accordance with the terms of this Agreement or the PRODUCT Licence Agreement and subject to the following conditions:

CUSTOMER must promptly notify Owner in writing of any allegation of infringement.

CUSTOMER must make no admission without Owner's consent.

CUSTOMER must, at Owner's request, allow Owner to conduct and/or settle all negotiations and litigation and must give Owner all reasonable assistance at Owner's expense. The cost incurred or recovered in such negotiations and litigation will be for Owner's account.

Owner will have the right to change all or part of PRODUCT and associated documentation or to grant or obtain licences for the use of all or part of the PRODUCT in order to avoid litigation.

Failure of CUSTOMER to notify Owner under this clause shall not relieve Owner of its obligations hereunder except to the extent that Owner is prejudiced by such failure. CUSTOMER may participate in its own defence at its own expense.

8.1.34 Force majeure

A *force majeure* provision is intended to recognise that circumstances beyond reasonable control like the 2020-21 Covid 19 (coronavirus) pandemic, fire, floods, possibly strikes, acts of God may disrupt performance, and to allow a grace period for performance where this causes a delay, for example, a flood. In many industries this concept is stretched to include man-made events for example, labour disputes. Some software providers further stretch the concept to cover events within their control, for example, an exhausted inventory of software.

Another aspect of *force majeure* provisions is how long they shield non-performance from becoming a breach of contract. A fixed period may be specified, for example, up to six months, or the period may be indefinite.

An example of a *force majeure* provision in a provider's standard software licence agreement is quoted below.

> The Licensor is not responsible for failure to fulfil its obligations hereunder due to labour disputes, fire, flood, government rules or regulations, temporary shortages of parts or Software, unavailability of Software, or any other similar or dissimilar causes beyond the Licensor's reasonable control that directly or indirectly delay or prevent the Licensor's timely performance hereunder. Dates or times by which the Licensor is required to render performance under this Agreement shall be postponed automatically to the extent that the Licensor is delayed or prevented from meeting them by such causes.

The customer may wish to specifically exclude certain events from the *force majeure* clause, such as default of the provider's sub-contractor, or lock-outs.

8.1.35 Assignment of contract rights and obligations

Software providers like to have the flexibility of transferring their rights and obligations to purchasers of their companies and other parties without the customer's consent. Some standard provider agreements specify this right and some are silent, reasoning that silence on this topic will be interpreted by a court as allowing assignment.

Conversely, most software providers do not want the customer assigning software licence agreements without express permission. Providers need to retain control over their software trade secrets in order to preserve their status as trade secrets. Also, the assignee may be a poor credit risk or an unsavoury character. Thus, many standard software provider agreements prohibit assignment of the licence agreement as a whole and all software licences except with the express, written permission of the provider except where the assignee is an associate of the licensee or the assignment is a result of reconstruction or amalgamation.

Some customers may want to negotiate a specific right to assign licences to companies within their corporate group or to assign licences to the purchaser of the entire business of the licensee.

8.1.36 Notice provisions

A notice provision addresses all of the notices that are required by the agreement. Some notice provisions specify the names of individuals in the parties' organisations, their addresses and the allowable types of mail or couriers. Others refer to the address of the parties in the introductory paragraph of the agreement. Still others are silent as to addresses or individual addressees. Another factor sometimes addressed in these provisions is the effective date of the notice, for example, the date of depositing a letter in the mail, the date of its receipt, etc. Customers need to ensure that an acceptable and practical arrangement is stated in these provisions, or, if not, to negotiate changes. For large customer companies it may be desirable to have notices addressed to both (a) the project manager and (b) the company secretary in order to deal with staff turnover. Job titles are safer than individual names.

Most agreements prohibit modifications except those agreed upon in writing and signed by the parties. Separately, it is normal for the parties to agree that they may change their addresses for notices upon a verbal or written notice which the other party will not sign. Few agreements reconcile these differences and expressly carve an exception in the first clause which recognises that notice address changes may be unilateral.

8.1.37 Entire agreement and variations

Following discussions and negotiations where the terms are reduced to written form it is important that the parties to the final contract know what has been finally agreed and where the parameters of that contract exist. During negotiations many representations and statements may have been made by the parties, either verbally or in writing, and the party receiving such representations may or may not have placed reliance upon them in ultimately agreeing to deal.

For this reason the final agreement should include a clause which confirms that the agreement being signed is the complete agreement and that any prior representations are not relied upon.

An example of such a clause is set out below.

This Agreement supersedes all prior agreement arrangements and undertakings between the parties and constitutes the entire agreement between the parties relating to the subject matter hereof. No addition to, or modification of, any provision of this Agreement should be binding upon the parties unless made by a written instrument signed by a duly authorised representative of each of the parties.

Beware of automatically using this form of clause without considering whether prior agreements should be overridden. In a case in which the writer of an earlier edition was involved a substantial contract ended up in arbitration and one of the mistakes that had been made by the licensor was that in the course of negotiations the licensor's standard agreement had been continually amended and that when the final agreement was signed two years after the commencement of negotiations it was, in fact, the eighth version of the licensor's original standard contract. Every contract that had been entered into contained an entire agreement clause thereby nullifying each prior agreement in succession so that when the final agreement was signed (being substantially different from the original and biased more in favour of the licensee than prior versions), the entire agreement did away with certain terms which the licensor subsequently claimed always had been intended to have been included by the parties. The licensee was entirely happy with the final version since it matched precisely the licensee's needs and it was the licensor (whose negotiating team had changed on several occasions during the two-year period) that found themselves receiving substantially less royalties than they were likely to receive during the term of the contract as against those which they had anticipated receiving under the terms of the original standard form. The lesson to be learnt from this is that you should be sure that where an entire agreement clause is used, if there are terms from earlier agreements that you do not wish to nullify these should be brought in to the final agreement or you do not use an entire agreement at all.

The same problems can occur where, in a software licence deal, there are collateral agreements which are fundamental to the main software licence agreement, such as maintenance and support agreements and escrow agreements, because, although each are separate agreements, they all interrelate and may all have been entered into at different times and dates and consequently entire agreement clauses must be carefully thought through.

Following the decision in *Watford Electronics Ltd v Sanderson CFL Ltd1* an entire agreement clause cannot be used as an exclusion clause.

The Sanderson standard terms and conditions contained an entire agreement clause, that stated 'no statement or representation made by either party have been relied upon by the other in agreeing to enter into the contracts', and a limitation clause, that stated 'neither the company nor the customer shall be liable to the other for any claims for indirect or consequential losses whether arising from negligence or otherwise'. The bespoke system supplied did not perform satisfactorily and Watford sued for damages.

On appeal the Court of Appeal held that the limitation clause could be split into two – the first part covering 'indirect or consequential losses' and the second part covering the cap on liability. Each of these could be read and applied separately and were reasonable in the circumstances.

The effect of the entire agreement clause was to acknowledge non-reliance of representations made before the contract. The court stated that there were two good reasons to allow these clauses in a commercial contract: The first that the parties, who were of equal bargaining power, were entitled to some commercial certainty and the second that it was reasonable to assume that the price paid reflected the commercial risks taken by both parties.

The acknowledgement of non-reliance did not purport to prevent a party from proving a representation was made but did prevent them from relying on it. The court stated that the fact that the acknowledgement did not achieve its purpose did not make it an exclusion clause.

Therefore the first part of the limitation clause (the limit of losses) has to be looked at in connection with the entire agreement clause, on the basis that the whole agreement was to be incorporated into the document which they signed and that no one should rely on anything else. There was no reason why the parties should have intended to include the liability of any negligent pre-contract misrepresentation.

A case of 28 May 2002 between BCT Software Solutions Ltd, a software support and maintenance provider and Arnold Laver & Co Ltd, a timber company licensing the said software, highlighted some important issues and potential hazards of incorporating a document into a contract by reference. The dispute arose after Arnold Laver terminated their contract for BCT's ongoing support and maintenance of their Great Plains financial software package. BCT claimed that by terminating the support and maintenance agreement, Arnold Laver had also terminated their right to license the software from BCT, as stated in the standard Terms and Conditions referred to in the agreement. Arnold Laver argued that during negotiation of the agreements and subsequent provision and billing of the two services, it was understood that the software licence and the support and maintenance were separate services and as such were not dependent on each other.

The case relied on the extent to which both parties had incorporated the BCT's standard terms and conditions. These terms and conditions had been significantly revised by BCT after the commencement of the negotiations between BCT and Arnold Laver. The old terms and conditions had stated that purchase of the software licence would comprise a one-off payment for unlimited use, with the support and maintenance services being charged separately on an annual basis according to the number of software licences supplied. The new terms and conditions indicated that the licence fee would cover both the software licence and the support and maintenance services, but charged out monthly.

This alteration created an entirely different regime, particularly regarding the way in which the use of the software was licensed. Under the old terms and conditions, the client would pay an initial sum for the licence of the software and could continue to use it regardless of whether they required the support and maintenance services. Under the new terms and conditions, the software licence only lasted as long as the customer continued to pay for the support and maintenance services. Importantly, throughout this negotiation period, the BCT salesman involved in setting up the Arnold Laver agreements claimed to be unaware of the changes in the terms and conditions and continued to refer to, and negotiate with, the old conditions in mind. This, despite being unintentionally misleading, led to Arnold Laver signing a final contract that referred to the new terms and conditions, whilst believing that the old terms and conditions still applied. Arnold Laver claimed never to have been shown a copy of the new terms and conditions and not to have had them brought to their attention.

An accounting irregularity later caused BCT to go into receivership. BCT's intellectual property and book debts were purchased by Electronic Data Processing (EDP) who had previously been in acquisition talks with BCT. As a result of the receivership, Arnold Laver terminated its agreement with

BCT, no longer requiring support and maintenance services and believing that it had the licence to continue running the Great Plains software package. EDP then demanded that under the standard terms and conditions of the agreement between BCT and Arnold Laver, Arnold Laver must terminate using the software which was to be re-claimed by EDP.

The law states clearly that when one party signs a document to accept an offer made in the document, in this case the terms of the agreement, it is taken that they accept those terms regardless of whether they read them or not. This also applies to terms incorporated by reference. Previous rulings however have highlighted the importance of the court reviewing all of the evidence to see what bargain was struck between two parties. It has also been noted that, in the case of new terms conflicting with those previously agreed – the original terms must prevail. After reviewing the case, Deputy High Court Judge Kevin Garnett QC concluded that only one payment for the software licence was required from Arnold Laver and that their continued use of the software was not conditional on payment of BCT's support and maintenance service.

This case highlights the importance of the contract negotiators being fully aware of the terms of any documents that are being incorporated into an agreement by reference. Always read the small print when you sign an agreement, whether it be a new contract or a renewal of a long-standing agreement and review all documents referred to in the agreement.

It is essential that staff are fully briefed of any changes in the working environment that may affect them. This is particularly important in a sales environment where they will have to be aware of terminology alterations and changes in negotiation tactics. Do not rely on sending staff updated documents to read or for them to install on their computers as they may not be actioned, as in the BCT case.

1   [2001] EWCA Civ 317.

8.1.38   Severability

As software providers know and customers are also aware, statutes, regulations and court decisions change from time to time during the life of a contract. Terms which may have been included in a software agreement may be valid at the time that the agreement is entered into but may at some point in the future become void, illegal, invalid or unenforceable and the effect of the invalidity of those terms is that the whole agreement fails.

Consequently, it is wise to include a severability clause in a contract to ensure that where only a portion of the contract becomes unenforceable or invalid that only that portion is extracted from the contract and the remainder of the contract continues in force as was the intention of the parties.

An example of a severability clause is shown below.

> If any of the provisions of this Agreement are judged to be illegal, invalid or unenforceable then the continuation in full force and effect of the remainder of this Agreement will not be prejudiced unless the substantive purpose of this Agreement is then frustrated in which case either party may terminate this Agreement forthwith by notice in writing to the other party.

One of the most crucial areas where this clause can be effected is where the parties unwittingly use wording in respect of pricing policy, discounts, exclusive territories, intellectual property rights and activities which in some way breach the competition laws of the parties' jurisdictions. Where parties have entered into software licence restrictions, in such licences there may be a breach of UK or EU competition law so a severability clause is useful in terms of enabling the majority of the software licence to remain in force.

8.1.39 Confidentiality

Notwithstanding that a confidentiality agreement or non-disclosure agreement may have already been entered into between the parties prior to the negotiation and drafting of the software contact itself, it is important to provide a confidentiality clause in order that the parties clearly understand what business secrets should be dealt with.

Although confidentiality clauses are regarded as 'standard' they do require more attention than is often given.

A typical confidentiality clause normally stipulates that information which the parties state or mark as confidential and pass to each other shall be treated as confidential except where the receiving party can show that the confidential information was already in the public domain or had been acquired by it from a third party or is regarded by the receiving party for one reason or another as not being confidential. It is, however, better to describe in some detail precisely what type of information should be marked or treated as confidential whilst also having general provisions as well to cover information not listed. A party receiving confidential information might well find that its ability to carry on research in a particular field is hampered by the fact that it has signed an agreement containing a confidentiality clause under which it has received from the supplier information which is similar to information which it had already developed itself, but which it cannot now use. One way of solving this is to split confidential information between that which is commercial and in respect of which the restrictions are all embracing and confidential information which is merely technical, where the restrictions may be slightly more relaxed.

Most software copyright owners want the obligations of confidence to apply without limit as to time, rather than only for a short, fixed period.

8.1.40 Remote access

In order for customers to comply with good IT security practices it may be prudent to consider what risk may be associated with the fact that many suppliers are given internet or other remote access to the customer's networks for the purposes of error correction and 'patching'.

Many software suppliers as part of their service level agreements, request and, indeed, almost automatically implement, modem links so that minor problems can be corrected without the supplier having physically to attend the customer's premises.

One of the risks here is that such remote access implementations mean that the security of the customer's network is potentially breached.

As a consequence the following clause is suggested.

Where the Supplier[1] has internet/ modem access to any part of the User's Equipment in the course of performing its obligations under this Licence the following provisions of this Clause [...][2] shall apply additionally. The Supplier:

1. will (a) only use a remote access method approved by the User (such approval not to be unreasonably withheld or delayed), (b) provide the User with the name of each individual who will have remote access to the User's Equipment and the phone number at which the individual may be reached during dial-in, (c) ensure that any computer used by its personnel to remotely access the User's Equipment will not simultaneously access the internet or any other third-party network while logged on to the User's Equipment;

2. further warrants and agrees that its personnel will not remotely access the User's Equipment from a networked computer unless the network is protected from all third-party networks by a firewall that is maintained by a 7x24 administrative staff. Said firewall must be certified by the International Computer Security Association (or an equivalent certification as determined by the User) if the connection to the User's network is an ongoing connection such as frame relay or TI line;

3. will restrict remote access by the Supplier to only the User's test and/or training systems and nothing in this Clause shall entitle the Supplier to have access to the User's live production copy of the Software unless the parties have expressly agreed in writing that such access is to take place and the User has given written confirmation of the date on which such access was implemented. The Supplier shall report in writing when such access takes places detailing all activities and actions taken during such access;

4. will comply at all times with UK GDPR and the Data Protection Act 2018 as amended in relation to any processing of personal data as a data processor on behalf of the User and will indemnify the User for any liability that the User incurs as a result of a breach of this warranty.

---

1   Change terms like 'supplier' or 'user' to reflect the actual terms used in the contract, for example, 'licensor' or 'licensee'.
2   Insert correct clause number as appropriate to the contract in question.

8.1.41 Data protection

UK GDPR and the Data Protection Act 2018 as amended since Brexit (and in the EU the equivalent legislation known as GDPR) both impose a requirement upon the controller of personal data to comply with certain data protection principles and other obligations. Amongst those principles are the obligations for a data controller to protect the integrity of personal data both in its processing and in its transfer. The draft Data Protection and Digital Information (No. 2) Bill 2023 is likely to make some changes to this area once in force so readers should watch this area of law closely for future changes.

Where a company outsources its technology or utilises third parties to support its business offsite (in the case of disaster recovery or website hosting) it is necessary for the data controller to impose risk controls on those third parties and to have written contracts.

Where a consultant, or an integration company or an Internet Service Provider or a web development company, might have access to the systems and thereby the personal data in the control of a customer, the customer might wish to include the following clause in its contracts:

> The Supplier warrants that it is compliant with UK GDPR and the Data Protection Act 2018 as amended and all other relevant data protection law and will indemnify the Customer from and against all costs, claims, liabilities and demands arising out of any breach by the supplier of its obligations to keep data secure and to adhere to such legislation.

Other examples of processors representations and warranties are as follows.

> Representation
>
> The Supplier and its subsidiaries have, in all material respects, processed the data in accordance with all applicable laws and regulations. Without limiting the foregoing, the data have been collected and further processed, in all material respects, in accordance with all notice and consent requirements of such laws and regulations and have been processed only for the purposes for which such data were collected or to which the data subject subsequently consented. The terms 'processing', 'process', and 'processed' shall mean any operation or set of operations which is performed upon data, whether or not by automatic means, such as collection, recording, organisation, storage, adaptation or alteration, retrieval, consultation, use, disclosure by transmission, dissemination or otherwise making available, alignment or combination, blocking, erasure or destruction.
>
> Warranty
>
> The Controller warrants that it has obtained all necessary consents from individuals whose personal data Controller supplies to the Processor, and the Controller and the Processor warrant to each other that they are respectively compliant with UK data protection legislation.

If the recipient of the data is not a company within the UK, then the supplying customer will need to be even more cautious about the supplier having access to personal data because of the obligations laid down relating to data export which places restrictions upon the transfer of personal data outside the UK. Examples of data export and data processing agreements are provided as Precedents to this book. There are rights to export to territories with adequate data protection rules like the EEA and also where the data subject has consented and where the recipient signs the UK's International Data Transfer Agreement (IDTA) (again which is included as one of the precedents to this book) and some other such rights to export data such as having binding corporate rules approved.

8.1.42 Governing law and jurisdiction

Due to the increase in international trade, a supplier is likely to sell throughout the world and it therefore becomes important for the agreement to indicate what law applies to the interpretation of the contract and what legal jurisdiction will apply to the settlement of disputes.

Where the parties are based in the UK there will be an assumption that English law will apply and, in the absence of any agreement to the contrary, this is likely to be the case since the contract will have been entered into in the UK and English law is the law most applicable (UK law should never be stated in a choice of law clause as it does not exist – Scotland has a different legal system). Where, however, one party only is based in the UK and the other party is in another jurisdiction then the choice of law becomes a point for negotiation.

The seller will naturally wish to use the law which they understand and which is most applicable to the location of their business, but the customer will have the same requirements.

Within the US there is quite a variation between certain states as to applicable laws. The state law in California is substantially different from that in Louisiana, but, then, in the UK there are differences between English and Scots law as mentioned above.

US companies generally insist upon the law of their state applying to the contract and for a particular US state to be the jurisdiction for litigation. When a UK customer is faced with this imposition, on occasions, they may give way, but this can be unwise without first understanding the precise implications of the US state law to future disputes.

If there is a deadlock then, on occasions, the parties may choose neutral ground and opt for a third-party law and jurisdiction.

In an agreement entered into between a US licensor and a Turkish licensee the language of the contract was English, the applicable law was the Swiss Code of Obligation but the jurisdiction was Zurich Canton, Switzerland. This was a balance between the needs of the two parties in that the Americans were happy with English language and Swiss law because many aspects of Swiss commercial law are similar to US law and, from the Turkish point of view, English language was acceptable and since Turkish law is based on German law and the Swiss Code of Obligation, in turn, is similar to German law, there were substantial comparisons.

Several institutions now operate arbitration facilities within the UK and there are, of course, international arbitration bodies, such as the International Chamber of Commerce and the American Arbitration Association, who have substantial experience in the field of dispute settlement.

In choosing the method of arbitration and the body to act as arbitrators it is necessary to have some understanding of the particular rules and requirements of each method. For example, arbitration provided by an expert appointed through the British Computer Society may be a relatively informal procedure, whereas arbitration under the UK Arbitration Acts which have specific procedures may be slightly more complex and, at the other end of the scale, arbitration through the International Chamber of Commerce Court of Arbitration or under UNCITRAL Rules may be extremely expensive although highly appropriate in the more substantial deals.

Apart from litigation and arbitration many companies are now insisting that all disputes are referred to Alternative Dispute Resolution (ADR) before the parties get to court. ADR is a voluntary mediation service which has gained considerable popularity in Canada and the US, where the ADR procedure and mediator's decision is often agreed upon to be binding on the parties.

In the software industry, as well as many other sectors, ADR offers an attractive method of resolving disputes because the parties want a quick, cost-effective and conciliatory procedure which ADR can provide, more so than litigation or arbitration proceedings. In the UK one of the leading ADR service providers, the Centre for Effective Dispute Resolution (CEDR) suggests that ADR has several advantages of which the following are examples:

- *Speed.* ADR proceedings can be set up as quickly as the parties require and the actual 'hearing' may only take a day or two.

- *Confidentiality.* Unwanted publicity is avoided as proceedings are confidential and held in private.

- *Cost.* The costs and expenses usually associated with litigation or arbitration are substantially reduced by use of ADR.

- *Control.* As ADR is voluntary and the parties agree upon the process, they have more control than in other dispute procedures.

- *Business relations.* ADR is not intended to be adversarial. ADR is intended to assist the parties to reach a negotiated compromise which helps to preserve relationships.

The Arbitration Act 1996 has introduced power for a court to 'stay' proceedings until matters have first gone to ADR or arbitration, if that is what the parties had contractually agreed. In other words, if the contracts contain an ADR clause then if only one party proceeds straight to litigation in court, the court has the right to refer the dispute to ADR before hearing the case further.

An example of an escalating ADR clause is as follows:

The following procedures will be adhered to in all disputes arising under this Agreement:

1. Each party recognises that the other party's business relies upon the protection of its intellectual property rights and other proprietary information and trade secrets (IPR) and that, in the event of a breach or threatened breach of IPR, the other party will be caused irreparable damage and such other party will therefore be entitled to injunctive or other equitable relief in order to prevent a breach or threatened breach of IPR.

2. With respect to all other disputes which are not IPR-related pursuant to (1) and its special rules the following procedures in (2) to (6) shall apply. Where there is a dispute, the aggrieved party shall notify the other party in writing of the nature of the dispute with as much detail as possible about the deficient performance of the other party. A representative from senior management ('representatives') of each of the parties shall meet in person or communicate by telephone within five business days of the date of the written notification in order to reach an agreement about the nature of the deficiency and the corrective action to be taken by the respective parties. The representatives shall produce a report about the nature of the dispute in detail to their respective boards and, if no agreement is reached on corrective action, the chief executives of each party shall meet, in person or by telephone, to facilitate an agreement within five business days of a written notice by one to the other. If the dispute cannot be resolved at board level within a further five business days, or if the agreed upon completion dates in any written plan of corrective action are exceeded, either party may seek its legal remedies as provided below.

3. If the parties cannot resolve a dispute in accordance with the procedure in (2) above, then they shall, with the assistance of the Centre for Effective Dispute Resolution in London, seek to resolve the dispute or difference amicably by using an Alternative Dispute Resolution (ADR) procedure acceptable to both parties before pursuing any other remedies available to them.

4. If either party fails or refuses to agree to or participate in the ADR procedure or, if in any event dispute or difference is not resolved to the satisfaction of both parties within 90 days after it has arisen, the matter shall be sealed in accordance with the procedure below.

5. The parties shall irrevocably submit to the exclusive jurisdiction of the English Courts for the purposes of hearing and determining any dispute arising out of this Agreement, if the parties cannot resolve such dispute by the procedure set out above.

6. This Agreement and all matters arising from it and any dispute resolutions referred to above shall be governed by and construed in accordance with English law, notwithstanding the conflict of law provisions and other mandatory legal provisions.

8.1.43 Third party rights

Before the Contracts (Rights of Third Parties) Act 1999 (the Act) it was the case that a person who was not a party to a contract (a third party) could not enforce any right under the contract. Similarly, a contract could not impose any obligations or liabilities on a third party. Some software licensees want the Act to apply so the licence can be to many companies within their group who can enforce the provisions directly and some software contract even have a page and a half of clauses solely dealing with this point.

However the Act attempts to draw a balance between the freedom of the parties to vary a contract and the interests of the third party. The Act means that a contractual clause benefiting a third party (eg the promisee's subsidiary company or sub-contractor or employee) will be straightforwardly enforceable by that third party if:

• the contract expressly provides that they may; or

• where a term in the contract purports to confer a benefit on them (unless on a proper construction of the contract it appears that the parties did not intend the term to be enforceable by the third party).

It is therefore prudent to include a clause to the effect of excluding the provisions of the Act. By doing so it ensures that any rights of third parties are not deemed to be enforceable by them. This is particularly the case where the parties are companies and may have subsidiaries or conversely parent companies.

An example of such a clause might be:

> The parties recognise that this Agreement is intended to benefit and shall so benefit (insert name of third party) for the purposes of the Contracts (Rights of Third Parties) Act 1999 and, subject to that, the parties confirm their intent not to confer any rights on any other third parties by virtue of this Agreement.

8.1.44 Rights of audit

It is increasingly common for technology contracts to include audit rights to protect both the supplier and the customer.

Suppliers may need to audit that customers are complying in all respects with the licence terms in respect of numbers of copies of software, notices displayed on back-up copies, access rights to network usage and so on. Customers will require an audit of the supplier in respect of hosted services, for example, where the customer needs to ensure the service provider is complying with data security regulations.

Audit rights are not necessary for every software licence or data transfer agreement and in many cases audit clauses can require considerable negotiation. From a point of inconvenience as well as the practical issue of confidentiality some suppliers will resist customer audits or insist that independent third parties carry out the audit under strict terms of confidentiality.

Audit rights can apply in a number of situations including:

- ensuring compliance with contractual requirements;
- ensuring that services are being supplied by the agreed level of personnel;
- checking the technical and organisational measures for security in place;
- ensuring that business continuity and disaster recovery measures are being met;
- establishing compliance with the parties' respective obligations under relevant legislation including data protection, financial services for authority requirements and health and safety;
- checking that specific issues in respect of the licence usage of software are complied with;
- establishing that agreed insurance coverage is in place.

Where audit rights are required there will, as has already been indicated, be a need to manage such rights including:

- limiting the frequency of audits within a particular period;
- requiring advance notice for an audit;
- implementing confidentiality in non-disclosure procedures;
- limiting the scope of an audit;
- requiring the use of independent third parties;
- ensuring audits do not disrupt business;
- ensuring auditors comply with onsite legal and regulatory requirements;
- agreeing who pays the cost of audit.

A High Court decision provides useful guidance on what information or materials are likely to be disclosable under an audit right clause and what may be reasonably withheld. In the case of *Transport for Greater Manchester v Thales Transport & Security Ltd*, the court granted specific performance in respect of the majority of the documents that the TGM had requested Thales to provide under a clause which committed TGM to request documents 'relating to ... the carrying out of any of the supplier obligations' or in order to 'audit' any of that information.

Although the case related to the construction industry it is valuable as it addresses what might reasonably be disclosable under an audit clause and in this instance indicated that the term 'audit' described a process of checking and verifying and was not limited to financial audit. As a consequence the following documents were found to be within the scope of the rights under the audit clause – namely board meeting minutes, reports produced by external advisors, internal reviews of the contract and issues arising from it, sensitive commercial information and documents that review the obligations sometime after problems had occurred.

Specific performance was refused in respect of certain documents where the categories of documents were too imprecise or the documents were covered by legal privilege or where the documents were being used as a 'fishing expedition'.

This case highlights that when drafting or negotiating an audits right clause care needs to be taken on too wide a clause for the recipient or too generic a clause from the party relying upon it. The more that legal privilege can be applied to documents the less disclosure there will be and overall as normal, precision needs to be taken in the use of language.

9 Necessary licence provisions

9.1 KEY LICENCE PROVISIONS FROM THE PROVIDER'S VIEWPOINT

9.1.1 Introduction

Vendors and licensors in English-speaking countries are somewhat more consistent and predictable than their customers in terms of their feelings toward contract clauses. This is not to say that all vendors and licensors recognise the same contract terms as 'absolutely necessary', or even that all or nearly all recognise the importance of contracts. Also, some key provisions in some UK and US contracts might be illegal and unenforceable in other countries. The point here is that, when compared with customers as a whole, most software providers who have survived or will survive their first decade in the industry are attuned to the importance of contracts and three fundamentally necessary categories of contract provisions. These categories are discussed below and examples of key terms from the licensor's viewpoint are included in the discussion.

9.1.2 What will I provide, when and for how long?

Answers to this question are key terms that should always be found in a contract for a major software transaction. A lack of clarity or full information on this topic simply sets the stage for confusion, unhappy customers, disputes and possible litigation. All goods and services provided should be identified to some reasonable level of detail, and specified in the quantity or for the duration or project agreed upon.

There should be no difficulty in identifying off-the-shelf software or other products. Smart custom-software developers-licensors also recognise the importance of detailed specifications for their projects. Most major projects are carried out on a fixed price or 'not to exceed' basis rather than on an unlimited time and expenses basis. In this context specifications are a two-edged sword, but also a two-sided benefit. They state requirements which the developer-licensor must satisfy, define products which the customer desires and expects and state the standard by which a failure or possible breach of contract may be measured. In addition, specifications define the limits of responsibility, or the maximum obligation, beyond which the developer-licensor can require additional compensation. Since the specifications for most customising projects and most custom-made software development projects are altered, supplemented or redefined by the customer, the developer-licensor can reasonably utilise the specifications ('specs') and desired changes as the basis for add-on revenue requirements.

If no specifications are developed, the developer-licensor opens the door to a situation where it can be taken advantage of by a customer who changes its mind about the definition of the deliverable and thereby requires additional work without increasing the project's fixed price or ceiling. From the developer's standpoint, specifications and a mechanism that allows increased billings for changes in specs are prudent and even essential elements of a large development project. From the customer's standpoint, specifications and a mechanism that allows mutually agreed upon changes in the specs for a major software development or customising project are equally essential because the clear definition of deliverables which specifications state are the heart of the project, and because the change mechanism gives the customer flexibility.

The 'when?' issue directs us to delivery commitments. The standard, printed form contracts of many software providers, like those of many of their equipment provider cousins, do not stipulate a timeframe for delivery and installation. The question of 'When must I deliver the software?' is intentionally not raised in these agreements. The burden is on the customer to require delivery and installation dates or timeframes, or a project completion schedule with this information. Usually the provider benefits slightly from an unspecified delivery and installation deadline. The lack of such a requirement in the parties' agreement gives the provider flexibility and may help the provider avoid a breach of contract for a delayed delivery or installation, whether it was unavoidable or subject to the provider's control.

Recommendation: in a major deal the customer should insist upon clear delivery and installation deadlines in the parties' agreement(s).

Of course, such deadlines may be conditional on such factors as the suitability of the environment for the delivered software, access to the customer's equipment, the availability of the customer's personnel to test the delivered product, or other reasonable conditions. Also, the delivery deadlines can take the form of specified dates, specified events, a specified number of days after an event, or some other form.

Obviously where the service is a software as a service (SaaS) provision via the cloud with monthly fees paid, the duration will be as long as the fees are paid and licence-right to use, in place, although in those contracts there will still be issues about how much notice must be given to terminate.

9.1.3 What will I receive, when and for how long?

This question boils down to: 'When and how will I be paid?' The answers are always necessary in a contract for a major software transaction. Most business people understand this point very well, hence it will not be examined closely. If a licensor's standard form contract is clear about nothing else, the answers to this question are usually very clearly stated.

A related topic that sometimes triggers discussion is the question of whether a cure period for correction of failures to perform in accordance with the contract should apply to late payment requirements. This topic can be important to all sides of a major transaction and it has some potential to become a 'deal breaker'. The cure period commences at some point after a deadline is missed and it delays a breach of contract until the period expires. The problem-solving compromise in some negotiations over whether to apply the cure period to late payments is to allow the cure period but to agree upon interest for late payments. A variation is to allow a reduced cure period to apply to late payments and a longer cure period to apply to other breaches of the parties' contract. Of course, some vendors and licensors require interest on late payments and refuse to allow any cure period. However, few providers are ready to terminate a customer immediately after a payment's due date. As a practical matter most customers will receive the benefit of a short grace period on payments, at least during their first transaction with a provider.

9.1.4 What business and legal risks do I face that I should minimise or neutralise?

This third category of fundamentally important contract terms, from the licensor's viewpoint, contains provisions that are common in contracts for various transactions in many industries.

Liability safeguards: most licensors who are or will be survivors in their markets recognise early in their history that there are three basic, conventional, ways to safeguard against liability: to incorporate, to buy insurance, and through protective contract provisions. Incorporating and contract language usually cost less than insurance such as a general liability policy, a product liability policy, or an errors and omissions policy. Incorporation is a common first step for a new software provider. Smart entrepreneurs usually develop standard, protective contracts within the first few years of their business life. Failure to insure may result in a court decision that an exclusion of liability is unreasonable, if appropriate insurance was available at a reasonable price.

Risks: business people tend to worry about revenue, cash flow, return on investment, and market share and other business worries, but the greatest risks anticipated are usually litigation and disputes that would (a) raid the company's accounts, or (b) throw it into bankruptcy, or (c) generate so much bad publicity that the business would be hurt badly or wither and die. These risks are generally perceived as risks which the provider should always strive to minimise or eliminate.

Protective contract terms: the standard protective clauses found in most UK and US vendor contracts, as well as in those of UK and US software licensors, include: (a) an exclusion of consequential damages; (b) a limited warranty with a specified exclusive remedy (such as the repair or replacement of a defective unit) and an alternate exclusive remedy of the refund of money paid or part of the money paid; (c) an exclusion of other express warranties; (d) a disclaimer of all implied warranties; and (e) a limitation on recoverable damages to some specified amount, to part of the sum paid, or to the entire payment for the item(s) giving rise to the dispute or litigation. Examples of these provisions were provided in Chapter 8. While these provisions can be overdone, in most software agreements some variation of these provisions is reasonable and makes good business sense. Of course, other types of liability limitations or exclusions are sometimes demanded by software providers. The reasonableness and importance of each of these provisions must be analysed on a case-by-case basis.

9.1.5   Other provisions

Depending on the nature of the software transaction other contract provisions may assume the status of a key clause. Source code licences are usually sensitive transactions for the software provider claiming trade secret law protection for some or all of a product's source code. A provider may reasonably insist on protective clauses in source code licence agreements that supplement or toughen those normally found in executable code licence agreements. For example, disclosure of the source to non-employees may be absolutely prohibited, only those licensee employees with a need to access the source in the course of their assigned duties may be allowed to use a copy, and use of the source may be specifically limited to the agreed upon purpose for which the licensee intends to employ the code. Also, sign-out and sign-in logs for all copies of source may be required, together with an audit provision. Removal of source from the building in which it is housed may be prohibited. These provisions or some variation of them are generally considered to be reasonable and essential in the context of a source code licence agreement where the source is a valuable asset of the licensor and it has not previously fallen into the public domain.

One argument for not providing an escrow source code is that the code for well-known products will normally have a commercial value and will be an asset realisable by a liquidator. The purchaser is likely to be a third-party maintainer wanting to do business in maintaining the well-known product.

9.2   KEY LICENCE PROVISIONS FROM THE CUSTOMER'S VIEWPOINT

9.2.1   Introduction

The provisions, topics and considerations surrounding major software transactions can be categorised in several ways. For example, customers often divide issues for negotiation into 'financial', 'technical', 'legal' and 'other business needs' categories, and then negotiate the categories in some selected sequence. In addition, customers often search for and attempt to identify for negotiation purposes the 'key' provisions. However, customers are not as consistent as providers in their identification of key contract terms.

The 'key' software licence provisions from the customer's viewpoint will vary to some degree, but not completely, from one major software transaction to another. Customers tend to see two general groupings of key terms, but thereafter the number and nature of key terms will vary from customer to customer and deal to deal. The major variables that affect the classification of a contract provision as a key clause in your licence agreement are listed in section 9.2.3. Of course, reasonable people may disagree about the importance of any contract clause or topic. The variables listed in the second half of this chapter explain some of the reasons for such disagreements.

9.2.2 Key questions

Regardless of whether the customer and supplier employ one contract or several agreements to capture a transaction, regardless of whether the customer is an end-user or a middleman and regardless of whether software or some software-related service is provided, the customer can ascertain a number of key contract terms by asking the questions listed in **7.2.2.1** and **7.2.2.2**.

9.2.2.1 *What do I receive, when and for how long?*

Answers to this question are terms that are always necessary in a contract for a major software transaction. Some of these answers could be conveyed by implication. For example, if you purchase equipment, purchase and transfer of title language imply that you can keep the equipment forever if you wish, assuming you pay for it in full and on time. None the less, the acquiring party should always know what is being acquired, when it will be delivered and installed, and how long it may be used, distributed, modified, displayed, and so on, before it must be returned, destroyed or discarded, if ever. Some examples of answers to this question follow.

The goods and/or services you will receive should be identified in clear detail. Vaguely identified deliverables often create problems for customers. Some examples of deliverables that should be specified clearly and in detail in your contract include:

- equipment, by manufacturer or private label; by model, quantity, characteristics, specifications, and serial number (as soon as the serial number is available);

- off-the-shelf software by name, characteristics, specifications, and quantity of copies;

- custom-made and tailored systems ('CMATS');

- mutually acceptable functional and technical specifications for the CMATS;

- mutually acceptable design and acceptance criteria for the CMATS;

- a detailed, mutually acceptable implementation plan for the CMATS;

- an incremental payment plan, or other mutually acceptable payment arrangement, for the CMATS; and

- custom-made database designs, report designs, screen designs, screen and data nomenclature and definitions, interfaces and access protocols, all according to clear, detailed specifications and a detailed implementation plan thereof, both of which are created, reduced to writing, and agreed upon before work begins, as should be the case with the CMATS deliverables.

What you receive in terms of ownership of the deliverables, or in rights to use, reproduce, distribute, modify, display, relocate or transfer the deliverables, should be clearly and precisely stated in complete detail. Surprises on these topics after a contract is signed may be hazardous to your career, not just to your organisation. Some examples of these contract provisions are listed below:

- title to equipment (when does it pass to you or is it never acquired?);

- title to the copy of software operating on the equipment, or your rights under your software agreement's licence grant provision and the limitations on those rights, which are often scattered in several contract provisions; and

- ownership of the intellectual property rights in custom-made software, or your rights to use, reproduce, distribute, modify, display, relocate or transfer this software to other equipment, to different sites, to different users, and so on.

9.2.2.2 *What do I pay, when and for how long?*

Answers to this question should always be essential contract provisions from a customer's viewpoint. Common sense demands this information in addition to business and legal requirements. It is rare for a customer to have a good business reason to be indifferent about the price, when it must be paid, or when payments must commence, their frequency, and their duration. All required and contingent payments should be clearly specified in the parties' agreement. The timing of all payments should be clearly set out, for example, due dates and any cure period for late payments. Conditions on the payments must be identified, for example, passage of acceptance tests. Some examples of these payments follow:

- equipment prices, instalment payments or lease charges and any buy-out option price for leased equipment;

- software licence fees or purchase prices, listed separately unless there is some advantage to the customer to accept a bundled cost, for example, operating system software bundled with the equipment purchase price (insisting on an unbundled cost is likely to produce a higher total cost);

- maintenance charges, unbundled so that you can control them through negotiated discounts and a ceiling or cap on periodic increases; and

- other service charges such as vendor programming, design, or analysis service charges, separately specified.

9.2.3 Other provisions

In addition to the foregoing, a few other contract terms are likely to be perceived as essential in most major software transactions. Almost any contract term can become critical to the customer's success under circumstances that elevate its importance. The following variables identify some of these circumstances and some of the contract provisions they make necessary.

9.2.3.1 *The nature of the transaction*

The nature of the transaction can play a major part in your deciding whether a contract term is essential. For example, in an off-the-shelf software licence agreement, the licence-grant clause is absolutely necessary. However, in a facility management deal, customer personnel may not be the authorised user of any software, and hence the customer may not need a licence grant. Similarly, a customer might feel that a data processing service provider need not warrant its internally used software against defects, but a software licensor is often required to provide such a warranty.

9.2.3.2 *Needs, goals and concerns and your sense of urgency*

The customer's needs, goals and concerns, and the urgency of its specific needs, are all primary factors determining which contract provisions are essential in a software or related service transaction. For example, if the customer has an urgent need, there may be no time for negotiations and the customer may be willing to sign any licensor document as stands. In this situation, getting the product is the absolute need, not the contract terms. Of course, this thinking can be dangerous and unpleasant surprises sometimes result from ignoring or treating lightly the content of contracts, for example, if you find out your licence grant does not let you do what you need to do with the licensed software after you have signed the agreement.

If you have a critical need to avoid downtime, then the ability to move software to a disaster recovery location may be a necessity, or you may decide you must have onsite spare parts and three-shift, onsite maintenance service, or you may decide you must self maintain your licensed software and/or equipment. In the latter event, access to source code is an absolute necessity, and either sending your employees to the vendor's maintenance personnel training courses or hiring vendor maintenance engineers probably becomes a necessity as well.

Are you concerned about the financial strength of your licensor and the possibility of its bankruptcy? In this case, obtaining source code or a source code escrow may be perceived as absolutely necessary.

Does your 'enterprise view' require the acquisition of software that will support your data designs and data flow in your internal databases? If so, then it may be absolutely necessary to develop some interface software when some new off-the-shelf software is acquired from a new supplier. By extension, contract provisions addressing this interface development project become absolutely necessary.

Are you concerned about whether a new system will be compatible with your existing systems? If so, a benchmark test, or an acceptance test, a trial use period, and/or a compatibility requirement and warranty might be considered essential.

9.2.3.3 Budget

Is your budget for the acquisition or alliance more than adequate, inadequate or barely adequate? This variable could make instalment payment terms, or deferred payment language, critical to the success of the deal.

9.2.3.4 Policies

Your organisation's policies sometimes dictate the importance of contract terms. For example, your law department may have a policy of requiring your country's law as the law which governs the contract.

Your organisation's policies may require you to develop and use standard contracts in lieu of the supplier's standard contracts. In this situation more than a few contract terms are necessities. Standard contracts contain numerous business decisions and limitations on risks. At least some of the provisions that capture these concepts will typically be considered absolutely necessary and 'sacred cows' that are unchangeable.

In addition, your organisation may have a policy that requires tailor-made, detailed and thorough acceptance tests for each major acquisition. Contract provisions that capture and require the application of such acceptance criteria then become necessities.

Does your organisation have a policy requiring ongoing standards of performance, or performance bonds? If so, then these provisions become extremely important.

Your organisation may require a ceiling on maintenance service charge increases. This 'cap' provision then becomes a necessity.

Do you require the flexibility to terminate ongoing payments for some or all of the software you license if your budget is reduced? If so, contract terms giving you this flexibility are vital.

Suppose you are about to acquire a new switch and you need onsite spare parts for this telecommunications system. Further, suppose that you want to buy used parts from other sources because they are significantly cheaper than new parts from the vendor. Now assume that the vendor insists upon inspecting and testing these parts to ensure that they do not short circuit the new system covered by the vendor's standard maintenance policy. If the vendor charges a very small fee for this inspection and testing, then you may not object. However, you may have a firm policy against payment of expensive inspection, testing and 'certification' charges for the vendor's approval and coverage of these spare parts under its standard maintenance policy. Avoiding expensive certification charges may be important to a customer, and a refusal to pay them has killed more than one multi-million-pound acquisition.

Many other examples could be cited, but these few should illustrate the importance of organisation policies in ascertaining the key contract terms in your deals.

9.2.3.5 Culture

The environment in which you function can dictate the necessity of some contract terms as well as your attitude toward suppliers. Your organisation's style of doing business may require you to be aggressive and demanding with suppliers, or even handed, or easy going and friendly. If your organisation's culture requires aggressive negotiations in a major deal, a 'most-favoured customer' provision may be an absolute necessity in your contract.

If your organisation is fast-moving, decisive and willing to take risks, you may not hesitate to make unqualified commitments to a supplier. On the other hand, if your organisation is slow-moving and careful, or is highly political in nature, then contract provisions giving you flexibility to make changes after the contract is signed, and/or numerous protective provisions, may be practical necessities or politically prudent.

9.2.3.6 History

Your organisation's history in dealing with a particular supplier may dictate the necessity of some contract terms, for example: warranties and representations against shut-down, slow-down, or use limitation devices in software; or a clause requiring responses to maintenance problems within a specified period. Of course, provisions like these are appropriate in contracts for major acquisitions absent a negative history with a supplier, but they become more important after a bad experience.

9.2.3.7 *The individual*

The position of the individual within the organisation and their risk-taking orientation are major factors in determining the absolutely necessary terms of a particular deal. To illustrate, in many companies junior and middle management personnel tend to focus on their individual concerns or the interests of their unit, department, section or group. The best interests of the organisation as a whole may not be their primary consideration. The paradigm examples are (a) the lawyer who focuses only on protecting the organisation against risk, and (b) the techie who focuses only on the technical evaluation of the licensed software. Such a focus is not necessarily 'wrong', but it helps to dictate the contract provisions that these individuals will deem absolutely necessary. Of course, some techies and some lawyers see the big picture as well as the trees and are business oriented. Hence, in some transactions the needs of the organisation will be understood and well served by these individuals.

The risk-taking orientation of the individual may help to dictate vendor selection as well as the number and variety of protective provisions that are deemed 'absolutely necessary'. Examples of such protective contract provisions include liability limitations, source-code escrows, credits for downtime, flexibility in termination, or other forms like bid bond or performance bond requirements.

9.2.4 Clarity and precision

From the customer's viewpoint, clarity and precision in contract language are as necessary as the key terms we have reviewed. Vagueness and ambiguity almost always favour the licensor, whether or not the licensee recognises the ways in which vague provisions can be harmful. For example, some customers insist upon vague, subjective acceptance language in the parties' contract, reasoning that it gives them control and discretion regarding acceptance of the items delivered. Perhaps these customers also feel they have insufficient time to identify and negotiate objective acceptance criteria. One difficulty with this reasoning is that a subjective acceptance mechanism invites disagreement over whether the supplier's product or service should be, or should have been, accepted. Except for some major, glaring deficiency in the product or service supplied, the supplier can claim that its product or service should be accepted as easily as the customer can claim it should not be accepted. Of course, such disagreements sometimes lead to a strained relationship, a loss of future business for the supplier, a loss of a valuable supplier to the customer or a law suit. Such disagreements are needless and many can be avoided through the use of objective acceptance criteria. In general, vagueness and ambiguity in the parties' agreement should be tolerated by the licensee only if it helps the licensee in some significant manner.

Part V
Negotiating tactics and techniques

10 Creative problem solving

10.1 INTRODUCTION – REDUCE THE ISSUE TO ECONOMICS

Inevitably situations will arise in which no fallback position and no tactic or other negotiating tool will generate a mutually acceptable resolution of an issue. One fairly well recognised 'last-resort' approach to this situation is for the provider(s) to reverse their positions and claim to be willing to make the concessions demanded for a price. This approach is usually employed only if the provider is seriously interested in obtaining the business in question and the price is usually high. The foundation for this approach to problem solving is the reasonable belief that industry-standard, customary, reasonable or modest risks should be assumed at standard price or discount levels, but that greater risks or extraordinary performance requirements should be assumed only if greater rewards are available, or at least possible, under reasonable criteria. If the provider's standard risk assumption level is reasonable, this 'greater reward for greater risk' suggestion is also reasonable. Of course, the price may be reasonable or not, and affordable or not, however reasonable this approach to the problem may be. Solutions that are less well known are suggested in the following pages of this chapter.

10.2 REDEFINING THE PROBLEM

Of all of the creative problem solving techniques known to man, the one that may be best known is the technique of redefining the problem. Some real-life situations will illustrate this technique.

CASE STUDY

Assume you are about to open negotiations for a custom-made computer program that your organisation believes will solve a major operational problem, for example, slow customer billings. Furthermore, assume that this project will be extremely expensive. You know the preferred developer's opening, fixed price quote will far exceed your budget. Tough negotiations are expected because of the degree to which you will have to ask the developer to cut its price in order for you to obtain Board approval of the contract. Regardless of whether or not you are successful, your boss, the Managing Director of your organisation, has told you that he wants

---

to recoup the development project expense by obtaining ownership of all rights in the new program and distributing it, for a fee, to other organisations like yours. Consequently, he advised you that it is 'absolutely necessary' for you to obtain ownership of the program from the independent contractor-author.

At the pre-planned time during the first face-to-face negotiating session with the developer, you explain that you will need to obtain all rights to the software, its design documents and technical and operator documentation, and its specifications, all of which will be prepared solely by the developer and approved by you prior to their acceptance. The developer responds by pointing out that it is going to own the rights to these items under current copyright law, subject to appropriate contract provisions to the contrary. The developer adds that you did not make this demand in your request for proposals, hence it is a major surprise. Furthermore, your requirement for ownership entails an asset purchase from the developer, not the anticipated non-exclusive software user licence for the developed program in executable code form. If the developer were willing to sell the asset, it would sell only the new application code and not its proprietary driver or 'engine' code in the program that has been and in the future will be built into other custom-made applications for other customers. The price of the application code sale would be at least five times the price of a paid-up licence fee for the executable code version of the program. In addition, the developer questions your ability to maintain and market the program. You have no internal or external software sales staff at the moment.

You respond that you would be willing to contract with the developer for maintenance and enhancement support, but you cannot afford the sale price. In fact, you cannot afford the quoted executable code licence fee.

After a break requested by the developer, you are told that the developer does not want to sell its rights to the program to you. You explain that you must acquire all rights to the program. Together, you and the developer explore whether additional budget monies are available from other budget categories or from anticipated future budgets that would allow you to pay for a standard licence, if not a more expensive asset purchase. You find a way to structure the payments for the standard non-exclusive licence to use the executable code, but no additional funds to apply toward the asset purchase price.

The developer repeats its refusal to sell the rights to the program and points out that you could not afford to buy the rights even if the developer were willing to sell them. You try every tactic you can think of and employ all of your pre-planned fallback positions, but to no avail.

You change strategies following a break which you request, but the developer argues that it makes no sense from a business standpoint to change its position. The developer plans to distribute the new program as a new standard product and nothing you have said convinces the developer to change its position. You are deadlocked on this ownership issue. You must have the program, and own it. Everyone in your organisation who is involved with this transaction feels strongly that this developer should write the program. What can you do?

Possible solutions: creative problem solving rides to the rescue. Try redefining the problem. The Managing Director really wants revenue from distribution of the program. Why not negotiate for a royalty from the developer on other customer licences based on the argument that you are paying for the development project and hence are entitled to a return on your 'investment'. You will have to explain the reasonableness of this alternative plan to the Managing Director, but the idea is worth exploring and it could solve your problem. Ownership becomes a much less important issue in this approach and might be easily agreed upon if a satisfactory royalty arrangement, with or without minimum payments, can be negotiated. In fact, you might even waive your demand for ownership under these circumstances.

10.3 OTHER TECHNIQUES

Numerous other creative problem solving techniques can be applied in different situations arising during the negotiation of a major transaction. The following non-exhaustive list may give you some ideas that you could employ to help you move closer to a signed contract. Note in passing that some of these ideas should be helpful during the planning stage prior to negotiations. Some of them suggest good habits to develop when planning any action in any field. Using imagination you should be able to find other contexts in which some of the following suggestions could be helpful.

10.3.1 Recognise opportunities

During the course of the negotiations of most major transactions, the other party's negotiator or a negotiating team member will say something that opens the door to a possible benefit. If you recognise this opportunity, and if you feel it is worth pursuing, you may be able to obtain this benefit simply by discussing it. An important part of creative problem solving is recognising and taking advantage of opportunities that the other side gives you. You need to listen carefully and digest what you hear in order to use this technique.

10.3.2 Borrow ideas

Ideas that helped you or someone you know resolve a problem may be helpful in negotiating a contract. These ideas may have been used in the same type of deal or in an entirely different context. Take a moment to ask yourself what impasse-solving solutions you have seen or heard of others using, as well as what ideas you have used successfully in the past, and consider their application to difficult-to-resolve issues in your current negotiation.

10.3.3 Look at the forest, not just the trees

Try to step back from the details of the topic you are attempting to negotiate and view the big picture, for example, senior management's goals and expectations for the deal, the overall consequences of the transaction for your organisation, and other events which are contingent upon closing the deal. Is the other side's position reasonable when considered as a part of the whole transaction? Is your need in this topic area absolutely necessary because of its importance to the big picture of the entire transaction? Perhaps explaining this view will help you solve the problem at hand.

10.3.4 Look for patterns

Looking for patterns can be a very helpful habit in negotiations. Patterns of behaviour by the other side's negotiating team may tip off undisclosed information. Often neither party discloses its bottom line on important issues. If the other side repeats a concept several times in a manner you believe might be sincere, then the observed pattern of this return to the same position or concept may mean that it lies close to the other side's bottom line.

Often these patterns of behaviour are discernible only if you read body language. For example, if the provider's other team members often cover their mouths while the provider team's lead negotiator makes a new proposal, and you have observed this pattern of behaviour in the past whenever a proposal was one or two levels away from the provider's bottom line on the issue then in question, you could logically infer that the provider may be willing to give you more than the current proposal offers.

10.3.5 Don't ignore the obvious

Sometimes the solution to your problem is obvious and apparent, but for some reason it is overlooked or ignored as options are explored or points are expressed at the negotiating table. Try stepping back mentally and asking yourself if there is an obvious solution available. Once in a while the surprising answer might be 'yes'.

10.3.6 Look at the difficulty differently

This suggestion can take various forms. It could amount to redefining the problem as has been suggested before. Alternatively it could suggest looking at the other side's reasoning for not accepting your proposal in a different way in order to ascertain flaws. Are there any inconsistencies between the other side's position on the issue at hand and its position on other issues? Can required performance be assured in another manner besides delivery of one initially specified item? Can you assure yourself that acceptable services will be provided in some other manner, for example, through credits against billings if the services are not acceptable?

10.3.7 Ask: What if?

What if you accepted the other side's position? What would the consequences be? Are they acceptable? What if you altered your position slightly? Could you accept the consequences? What if you halted negotiations and sought another supplier or walked away from this prospective provider? Would this provider return with a more acceptable proposal? (Often, but not always, the answer is 'yes'.) Do you have sufficient time to use this technique, or will you get into trouble if you do?

10.3.8 What rules can you break?

Breaking rules can be politically dangerous and the results can be positive or negative. In the case study presented in section 10.2 the proposed solution required the customer's negotiator to violate explicit, direct orders from the Managing Director. Obviously the negotiator should seek the Managing Director's approval for the altered plan, but a solution that broke the rules was essential to a successful closing.

10.3.9 Combine or link ideas

Sometimes each party will have rejected some proposals of the other that are considered important. Perhaps if you combine one of your important proposals with one of the other side's important proposals both sides can benefit. This approach is not 'horse trading' one concession for another. Rather, it involves a linkage of ideas that were previously raised as separate topics. The combination may be acceptable to both parties because of the mutually beneficial result created by or perceived in the combination.

10.3.10 Change names

Technical, legal, and even business terminology is not always consistently used by all people. Moreover, some people have a negative reaction to some names or labels. You may be able to defuse negative emotion or eliminate misunderstandings simply by suggesting a different name for the item in question and consistently using that new name.

10.3.11 Imagine how someone else would solve the problem

Sitting back and trying to picture how another person might resolve your problem, someone like your boss, might help you find a way to close the issue at hand.

10.3.12 Notice the positive

Some people, perhaps most, tend to reject new ideas proposed by another person, either because of a 'not-invented-here' negative bias, or because one aspect of the idea seems flawed, so the entire idea is rejected. A diplomatic and sometimes helpful approach to a new problem solving proposal from the other side is to notice and comment on the positive aspects of the other side's idea, if you can find any, before you comment on the negative aspects. This simple technique encourages the other party to fix the negative aspects of its proposal and the use of the revised idea to solve your problem, provided the negative aspects of the proposal are capable of being fixed.

10.3.13 Expect resistance and sell

Whenever you propose a new problem solving idea you should expect resistance from the other side of the negotiating table. If you anticipate and plan for this resistance by developing persuasive arguments supporting your proposal, you may avoid a 'knee-jerk' negative reaction. The one limitation on this technique is to recognise when the other side has bought your proposal and immediately to stop selling. The danger in continuing to sell your idea is that you will say something the other side had not thought of that will trigger a rejection.

This technique of supporting your proposals with persuasive arguments will complement praise for the positive aspects of the other party's proposals before you give negative feedback. By using these two simple techniques in combination, you can expedite problem solving and deal closings more than you might expect.

11 The use of non-verbals in negotiation

11.1 INTRODUCTION

In recent years there has been a great deal of research into and use of non-verbal communication within negotiation.

In this chapter we will consider the use and threat of silence in negotiation, the value of appreciating body language and its signals in negotiating situations and also the issues relating to personal space.

All of these matters are variable depending upon culture and, to some extent, individual characteristics but, broadly speaking, there are some clear consistencies within the use of silence and the awareness of body language and personal space when negotiating at the table, or even discussing transactions in an informal 'cocktail party' environment.

11.2 SILENCE – NEGOTIATING WITH YOURSELF

Silence can be a very effective negotiating tool for customers, or for providers who feel no pressure to accept customer proposals at the negotiating table. Many of us abhor lapses in conversation and feel compelled to fill in gaps. Also, in the UK, silence is perceived as a negative reaction in the context of negotiating business transactions. If a customer's negotiator says nothing after the provider's negotiator explains their position on an issue, the provider's negotiator will be strongly tempted to start talking and soften the stance or sweeten the proposal just explained. Only the most experienced negotiators will resist this urge and let the silence continue. The typical response of immediately offering some concession in order to appease the silent party and get him talking again amounts to making a concession without a request or demand for the concession. In other words, if you respond to silence this way, you are negotiating with yourself. Oriental negotiators use silence very effectively, especially against US, UK, Canadian and Australian opponents.

11.3   BODY LANGUAGE

Many of us do not realise just how much use non-verbal communication has in discussions and negotiations with other people. We use body language unconsciously and yet, with training and observation, it is possible not only to learn the feelings of other people from their non-verbal reactions, but also to use body language as a positive means within negotiation.

Students of body language often qualify their analyses by explaining that body language is culturally dependent. One must be aware of possible differences in body signal meaning when observing someone from another culture. For example, a gesture or movement by an Italian may have a different meaning when it is made by an Englishman. On the other hand, foreign signal meanings often become assimilated into the local culture for one reason or another. Hence, people reading this book are likely to understand the body language of some foreigners even if the readers have never left their home town.

Some students of body language attempt to supplement their understanding by self-analysis and projection. The feelings you have when you are doing something with your hands, feet, legs, arms, head or eyes might be the same feelings another person has when they move in the same way. The obvious danger of projecting your feelings on someone else is that you may be wrong regardless of the identical body language being displayed. The way to overcome this potential pitfall is to question the individual displaying the signal and try to confirm the accuracy of your signal reading through their answers. Of course, your questions may be subtle, or not, depending on the delicacy of the situation.

Also, you should be aware that some sophisticated negotiators will intentionally signal attitudes and feelings that are not real in the hope of evoking the reaction they desire from you. The more experienced a negotiator is, the more careful you must be to confirm your reading of their body language.

With these introductions, three examples of body language used in the course of negotiating are set out in **11.3.1–11.3.3** below.

Understanding non-verbal communication is extremely useful in all walks of life, but particularly in negotiations, since much can be gleaned about the feelings or reactions of the other side by observing body language.

The way in which you interact with the other side in negotiations may be enhanced by synchronising your body language with that of the person that you are negotiating with, or by adopting more attentive sitting positions, or by making the seating arrangements at the negotiating table less adversarial.

For example, discussions in a round table arrangement are often more informal than those which are conducted face to face across a wide table, since there is an invisible barrier created between the parties down the centre of such a table.

Observing and adapting to body language differences, particularly when those differences arise culturally, is a distinct advantage in negotiation but is only part of the answer. As we have seen above, the non-verbals that are apparent in certain situations may not be entirely indicative of the feelings or emotions of the person displaying those verbals and therefore further questioning by the observer will clarify whether the body language observed is truly indicative of the feelings that may be underlying such body language.

11.3.1 Crossed arms

Some body language is situation dependent, not just culture dependent, and some signals can also be gender dependent. For example, crossed arms can have a different meaning in a social setting than at the negotiating table, and women and men often signal different things when they cross their arms. An American woman crossing her arms is usually signalling that she is cold; she is simply trying to increase body warmth. An American man crossing his arms at a social gathering may do so simply for comfort or because he is bored; on occasion he will be having a gas attack and indigestion.

On the other hand, a man attempting to work out the details of an important deal signals something entirely different when he crosses his arms at the negotiating table. Here crossed arms will usually mean a negative reaction of some sort to a statement by the other side, perhaps a feeling of defensiveness, or a signal that his mind is made up and closed – he is rejecting the other side's request or demand. If the man leans back in his chair, pushes away from the table, and crosses his legs as well as his arms, then he is totally uninterested in the speaker's message and is probably 'tuning out'.

A woman at the table may signal the same feelings in the same ways, but caution is required here lest you misread the woman's signals. Remember she may be cold, or she could be cold and bored if the topic is not in her area of responsibility. You should ask questions before you finish your analysis, for example, 'Does it feel chilly in this room?', or 'I'm cold, are you?', or 'Are you cold?'. The total verbal and non-verbal response should enable you to determine whether she is cold or whether her crossed arms have another meaning.

11.3.2 The hand over the mouth

In the context of discussing and negotiating major transactions, a hand over the mouth of a person on the opposite side of the negotiations is an important body language signal. The lips must be covered for this signal to have the meaning about to be ascribed. It does not matter whether the lips are covered by one finger or the entire hand, or by one hand or two, as long as they are completely covered. Then this signal, in the context under discussion, will convey a wealth of information.

It will aid our discussion to label the person flashing the hand over the mouth signal as 'A', and the observer as 'B'. Assume B is the speaker and A is listening. Remember that A and B are on opposite sides of the negotiation. When B observes A's hand over A's mouth in the context under discussion, B knows that B has credibility. B is being believed as they speak. Whatever point B is trying to make, B has succeeded, at least with A, the person flashing the signal. In addition, A conveys a feeling of inadequacy when A flashes this signal. This feeling is often accompanied by a feeling of anxiety and uneasiness, and it usually arises because of a lack of knowledge about, or experience with, the topic being addressed by B. Alternatively, this feeling could arise from uncertainty about how a problem can be resolved, or from a lack of memory about a past event under discussion. Any aspect of the topic about which A has less than adequate knowledge and experience will almost always trigger at least a momentary hand over the mouth signal unless, of course, A is trained to avoid giving this signal. In this writer's experience in our context of major transactions, B's credibility and A's feeling of inadequacy on the topic under discussion always accompany one another when this signal is flashed, even though the two are obviously not absolutely necessary partners. The same meaning for the hand over the mouth body language is apparent in many other contexts, but they remain beyond the scope of this book.

The hand over the mouth signal is usually gender, age and culture neutral, and it retains its meaning in many contexts beyond that of our focus.

Within the scope of our examination, the hand over the mouth signal can have a different meaning when it appears among the speaker's negotiating team members as the speaker makes a proposal or suggestion. The speaker's team members may be signalling that the speaker's proposal or suggestion is not their bottom line on the issue in question. Also, a hand over the mouth of one or more speaker team members while the speaker makes a proposal or suggestion can make the other side suspicious: the speaker's team can be viewed as hiding something or being devious. As a result, the other party's trust and confidence in the speaker's organisation can weaken.

11.3.3 The eyes

If you knew your opponent was telling you a lie, how much would that information help you? Obviously it could be very helpful. The eyes sometimes give away a lie. While your opponent is talking, look for their eyes to dart to the right, that is, to their right. The eyes should return from this super-fast shift after less than a second. If you see this movement, the speaker is probably telling a lie.

Several points of this explanation require clarification. First, no head movement is involved with this body-language signal. The head does not move at all. Secondly, this glance to the right is truly super fast. This is not a casual glance to the right. Nor is it a glance at the window to a speaker's right to see some birds flying by, or a glance at someone walking in a door to the speaker's right.

Thirdly, this signal is not, and does not include, a glance up, down or to the speaker's left. Those movements have other meanings. For example, a look down accompanied with the head moving down indicates strong emotion about the topic which the speaker is addressing, at least usually. Alternatively, it might simply indicate fatigue.

Fourthly, on occasion a speaker will attempt to observe the reaction to their words by an opponent sitting to their right, or attempt to signal a colleague sitting to their right to speak up in support of the statement they are making, or simply attempt to sneak a quick glance at an attractive member of the opposite gender sitting to the speaker's right. Obviously no lie is indicated by any of these glances. The lesson from these examples is that you must be alert to distractions from or communications to those sitting to the speaker's right before you attach meaning to their eye movement.

How else can you tell when a glance to the right does not mean a lie? You ask questions, subtle, direct, or in between, in an attempt to corroborate your impression. You may need some imagination to formulate a question whose answer can make you satisfied that you have detected a lie, but one or more questions can be helpful in this regard. Every lie is not accompanied by a glance to the speaker's right, and perhaps less than 10% of all lies are accompanied by such body language. Nevertheless, you may be able to use this information to your benefit. The first time you catch an opponent in a lie through recognition of this eye-shift body-language signal, you might want to take a break in order to recover from the shock and decide how you are going to respond.

11.4 PERSONAL SPACE

Some discussions occur while both sides are standing up rather than sitting at a negotiating table. In this situation, understanding personal space can be important to your success.

As a general rule women tend to stand 12–18 inches apart when they converse while standing up. Their business conversations are more intimate, from a space standpoint, than those of men in most English-speaking countries. For example, American, Canadian, English and Australian males tend to stand about 18 inches apart when discussing business while standing. In addition, men from these parts of the world normally stand about 18 inches from a woman who is not a 'significant other'. If they approach closer, they may be viewed with suspicion by the female.

If a man, call him 'A', moves closer than 18 inches to another man ('B'), or to another woman ('C'), then A may be perceived in several negative ways by an American, Englishman, Australian or Canadian, for example, as overly aggressive, possibly as having a personal agenda, as intimidating and/or as unpleasant. B or C will feel at least uncomfortable at A's encroachment on B's or C's personal space. Obviously, if A wants to sell something to B or C, then A should not encroach on their personal space.

Drill sergeants in the military have long understood that one way to intimidate a recruit is to stand nose to nose and yell. The violation of the recruit's personal space coupled with yelling succeeds in intimidating most recruits. The same result is common without yelling. Usually only those who have been warned of what to expect or those with a cultural background in which nose-to-nose exchanges are commonplace will not feel threatened or at least somewhat apprehensive by a nose-to-nose encounter.

Cultural backgrounds are important to business and social conversations in several ways, one of which is noticeable when Western business people converse with Arab or Japanese business people while standing. In some Arab cultures it is commonplace for men to stand nose to nose while discussing business. Westerners unfamiliar with this custom encounter it the first time they do business with Arabs who have not been 'Westernised'. The common result is for the Western business person to back up as the Arab moves within the Westerner's personal space. The backing up can continue until the Westerner is backed into a corner, which is a ludicrous but far too common result. The consequences are not only the uneasy, unhappy feelings of the Westerner about the invasion of their personal space and being backed into a corner, literally speaking. The Arab usually believes the Westerner is weak and inadequate or easily taken advantage of. No business, or low-quality business, may result.

In contrast, Japanese business people prefer to stand about two feet apart, largely to allow room for bowing. If a Westerner approaches within the two-foot personal space, they run the risk of offending the Japanese. The possible negative ramifications are obvious. One of the most interesting social gatherings includes Japanese and Arabs. The Japanese tend to back up even faster than the Americans.

11.5 SEATING POSITIONS

When it comes to getting around the table it is worth remembering that the seating and positioning of the parties can help or hinder negotiations.

If the table is oblong and narrow, then one party sitting close to the table will achieve a dominant but potentially aggressive position, because the other party will feel their personal space invaded and keep a position of sitting back from the table. If, of course, they also sit up to the table then the atmosphere may become very confrontational.

On the other hand, a round table tends to break down the invisible barrier which can exist down the middle of a rectangular table, although it is still possible to create such a division.

Another example of the use of positioning occurs where there is an uneven number of negotiators between one party and the other. If the numbers are equal then usually all parties will be involved in the negotiation whether the tables are oblong or round, as shown in the diagram below.

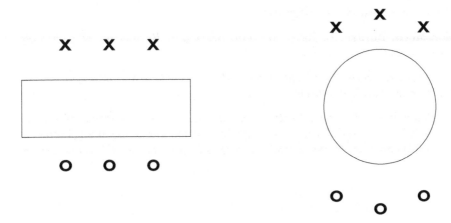

However, if the numbers are unequal one party may be at a disadvantage.

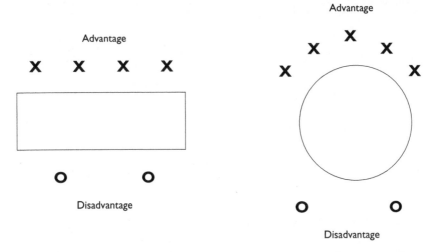

Then again the party with the smaller number can use this to its advantage by positioning the team members in order to isolate at least one of the other team's members if this is tactically sound.

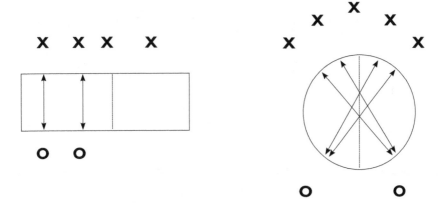

Recommended reading list

Morgan, R, Burden, D, Berry *Morgan, Berry and Burden on IT Contracts* (Sweet & Maxwell, 10th edition, 2021).

Rennie, M T, *International Computer and Internet Contracts and Law* (Sweet & Maxwell, looseleaf, 2021).

Singleton, E S, (i) *Business, the Internet and the Law* (Bloomsbury Professional 1999–2023) and (ii) *E Contracts* (Bloomsbury Professional, 2000-23), both now part of Bloomsbury Professional's *Intellectual Property and IT online service*

Index

[all references are to paragraph number]

A
Acceptance tests
  generally, 8.1.9
  offsite benchmark test, 8.1.9.1
  onsite objective criteria, 8.1.9.3
  onsite subjective standard, 8.1.9.4
  onsite ready for use, 8.1.9.2
Access software licence
  agreements
  generally, 2.11
Apache licences
  open source, 2.15.5.5
Application service provider
  licences
  generally, 2.16
Artistic Licence
  open source, 2.15.5.6
Assignment of rights
  software licence agreements, 8.1.35
Audit right clause
  software licence agreements, 8.1.44
Authentication
  e-signatures, 4.8
Availability of computer system
  software licence agreements, 8.1.29

B
Binding Corporate Rules
  new rules for processors, 4.10.8
Bonus clauses
  payment under software licence,
    8.1.4.7
Breaches of agreement
  late payment, 9.1.3
  termination clauses, 8.1.11.1
BSD licences
  open source, 2.15.5.5
Budget
  software licence agreements, 9.2.3.3

Business risks
  software licence agreements, 9.1.4
Business secrets
  pre-contract documents, 7.1.2

C
Capped payment clauses
  payment under software licence,
    8.1.4.3
Change control clauses
  software licence agreements,
    8.1.28
Clarity
  software licence agreements, 9.2.4
Click-wrap licence agreements
  generally, 2.3.3
Codes
  grant of licence, 8.1.5
  integrity of author's source code,
    2.15.3.4
  open source licences, 2.15.3.2
Cold-site arrangement clauses
  payment under software licence,
    8.1.5.13
Comfort letters
  pre-contract documents, 7.1.2
Competition law
  generally, 4.2
Computer programs
  See **Software**
Confidentiality
  pre-contract documents, 7.1.2
  software licence agreements, 8.1.39
Consequential damages
  software licence agreements, 8.1.25
Consulting services
  software licence agreements, 8.1.16
Contamination of software
  open source licences, 2.15.3.9

Index

Contents of licence agreements

acceptance tests
generally, 8.1.9
offsite benchmark test, 8.1.9.1
onsite objective criteria, 8.1.9.3
onsite subjective standard, 8.1.9.4
onsite ready for use, 8.1.9.2
assignment of rights, 8.1.35
audit right clause
disclosure of material, 8.1.44
generally, 8.1.44
availability of licensee's computer
system, 8.1.29
change control, 8.1.28
confidentiality, 8.1.39
consequential damages, 8.1.25
consulting services, 8.1.16
data protection, 8.1.41
definitions, 8.1.3
delivery, 8.1.6
development services, 8.1.16
enhancements, 8.1.13
entire agreement, 8.1.37
error warranty, 8.1.20
escrow, 8.1.14
Euros warranty, 8.1.21
force majeure, 8.1.34
governing law, 8.1.42
grant of licence
cold-site arrangement, 8.1.5.13
duration, 8.1.5.4
exclusivity, 8.1.5.1
host, 8.1.5.3
hot-site arrangement, 8.1.5.13
introduction, 8.1.5
licensed code, 8.1.5.7
maintenance, 8.1.5.12
modifications, 8.1.5.12
number of copies that can be
reproduced, 8.1.5.11
number of licensed copies, 8.1.5.6
payment type, 8.1.5.9
relationship between terms,
8.1.5.5
rights conveyed, 8.1.5.2
scope of software, 8.1.5.10
site, 8.1.5.3
source code information, 8.1.5.14
subject to other terms, 8.1.5.15
technical information, 8.1.5.14
territory, 8.1.5.3
transferability of rights, 8.1.5.8
host preparation, 8.1.7
installation, 8.1.8
intellectual property rights, 8.1.22
jurisdiction, 8.1.42
lawyer's fees, 8.1.30

Contents of licence agreements –

contd
limited warranties, 8.1.18
limitation of liability, 8.1.23
limitation on recoverable damages,
8.1.24
limitation periods, 8.1.31
liquidated damages, 8.1.26
maintenance, 8.1.12
most favoured customer, 8.1.27
necessary provisions
customer's viewpoint, from, 9.2.1–
9.2.4
provider's viewpoint, from, 9.1.1–
9.1.5
notice, 8.1.36
ongoing performance obligations,
8.1.19
overview, 8.1
parties, 8.1.1
payment
amount, 8.1.4.1
bonus, 8.1.4.7
caps, 8.1.4.3
cure period for late payments,
8.1.4.4
due date, 8.1.4.2
increases, 8.1.4.3
interest on late payment, 8.1.4.5
reductions in charges or fees, 8.1.4.6
retention against acceptance,
8.1.4.8
recitals, 8.1.2
recovery of lawyer's fees, 8.1.30
remote access, 8.1.40
risk of loss or damage during
transit, 8.1.32–8.1.33
service, 8.1.12
severability, 8.1.38
site preparation, 8.1.7
statute of limitations, 8.1.31
term of agreement
commencement before delivery of
software, 8.1.10.1
evergreen clause, 8.1.10.3
grace period, 8.1.10.6
introduction, 8.1.10
limited term, 8.1.10.2
perpetual term, 8.1.10.4
unspecified term, 8.1.10.5
termination
breach, upon, 8.1.11.1
consequences, 8.1.11.5
expiry of term, by, 8.1.11.3
introduction, 8.1.11
lapse of IPR, upon, 8.1.11.4
without cause, 8.1.11.2

Downloadable precedents

The precedents for this edition are available to download electronically from bloomsburyprofessionallaw.com/negotiatingsoftwarecontracts6thedn.

They are password-protected and the password is vxpxjqbl.

They can be downloaded individually or in totality.

If you have any problems downloading the precedents or have any questions, please contact Bloomsbury Professional customer services on 01444 416119 or by email at customerservices@bloomsburyprofessional.com.

For a Licence agreement relating to the use of this Data, please see overleaf at page 220.

Licence agreement

The Data on bloomsburyprofessionallaw.com/ negotiatingsoftwarecontracts6thedn is © Bloomsbury Professional 2023.

Bloomsbury Professional ('the Publishers') grant you a non-exclusive and non-transferable licence to use the Data from bloomsburyprofessionallaw.com/ negotiatingsoftwarecontracts6thedn.

You may download, copy or print the Data from bloomsburyprofessionallaw.com/ negotiatingsoftwarecontracts6thedn for private use or use in the ordinary course of your business but you may not make any profit from the use of the Data other than would ordinarily be made in the course of your business. You may not sell the Data under any circumstances or make or sell any copy or reproduction of it. You may not copy or print out any part of the Software for any purpose or make any modifications to the Software.

If you have any queries about the use of the Data from bloomsburyprofessionallaw.com/negotiatingsoftwarecontracts6thedn, please contact customer services at Bloomsbury Professional: customerservices@bloomsburyprofessional.com.